The *H. L. Hunley*

D0374326

ALSO BY TOM CHAFFIN

Sea of Gray: The Around-the-World Odyssey
of the Confederate Raider Shenandoah (2006)

Pathfinder: John Charles Frémont and
the Course of American Empire (2002)

Fatal Glory: Narciso López and
the First Clandestine U.S. War Against Cuba (1996)

The *H. L. Hunley*

THE SECRET HOPE OF
THE CONFEDERACY

Tom Chaffin

ℍ HILL AND WANG

A DIVISION OF FARRAR, STRAUS AND GIROUX

NEW YORK

Hill and Wang
A division of Farrar, Straus and Giroux
18 West 18th Street, New York 10011

Copyright © 2008 by Tom Chaffin
Maps copyright © 2008 by Jeffrey L. Ward
Diagram of the *H. L. Hunley* copyright © 2008 by Michael Crisafulli
All rights reserved
Distributed in Canada by D&M Publishers, Inc.
Printed in the United States of America
Published in 2008 by Hill and Wang
First paperback edition, 2010

The Library of Congress has cataloged the hardcover edition as follows:
Chaffin, Tom.
    The H. L. Hunley : the secret hope of the Confederacy / by Tom Chaffin.—
1st ed.
    p.   cm.
Includes bibliographical references and index.
ISBN: 978-0-8090-9512-4 (hardcover : alk. paper)
    1. H. L. Hunley (Submarine)   2. Submarines (Ships)—United States—History—
19th century.   3. Confederate States of America. Navy—History.   4. United
States—History—Civil War, 1861–1865—Naval operation—Submarine.
5. Charleston (S.C.)—History—Civil War, 1861–1865.   6. Charleston (S.C.)—
Antiquities.   7. Excavations (Archaeology)—South Carolina—Charleston.   I. Title.

E599.H4C53 2008
973.7'5—dc22

                                                                    2008013937

Paperback ISBN: 978-0-8090-5460-2

Designed by Jonathan D. Lippincott

www.fsgbooks.com

1   3   5   7   9   10   8   6   4   2

Once again, to Meta and Zoie

I am anxious <u>first</u> and above all for a dead silence on our part, that the enemy may be lost in uncertainty and mystery which is more dreadful than any understood evil of even the greatest magnitude. —Horace Lawson Hunley

France was a land, England was a people, but America, having about it still that quality of the idea, was harder to utter—it was the graves at Shiloh and the tired, drawn, nervous faces of its great men, and the country boys dying in the Argonne for a phrase that was empty before their bodies withered. It was a willingness of the heart. —F. Scott Fitzgerald

Contents

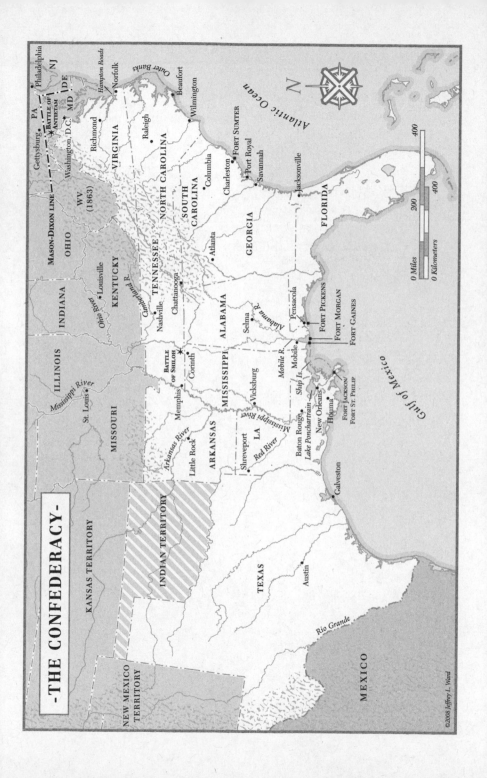

-THE CONFEDERACY-

©2008 Jeffrey L. Ward

MEXICO

Rio Grande

NEW MEXICO
TERRITORY

KANSAS TERRITORY

INDIAN TERRITORY

TEXAS

Austin

Galveston

Gulf of Mexico

Shreveport

Red River

Little Rock

ARKANSAS

Arkansas River

LA

Mississippi River

Baton Rouge
Lake Pontchartrain
New Orleans
Houma
Fort Jackson/
Fort St. Philip

Ship Is.

Mobile R.

Mobile

Fort Morgan
Fort Gaines

Pensacola

Fort Pickens

MISSISSIPPI

Vicksburg

Selma

Alabama R.

ALABAMA

Memphis

Corinth

BATTLE
OF SHILOH

St. Louis

MISSOURI

Mississippi River

ILLINOIS

INDIANA

Ohio River

KENTUCKY

Louisville

Nashville

Chattanooga

TENNESSEE

Cumberland R.

Atlanta

GEORGIA

FLORIDA

Jacksonville

Savannah

Port Royal

Charleston

Columbia

SOUTH
CAROLINA

Fort Sumter

NORTH CAROLINA

Raleigh

Wilmington

Beaufort

Outer Banks

OHIO

WV
(1863)

MASON-DIXON LINE

Gettysburg

PA

Philadelphia

NJ

DE

MD

Washington, D.C.

BATTLE OF
ANTIETAM

Richmond

VIRGINIA

Hampton Roads

Norfolk

Atlantic Ocean

N

400

200

400

0 Miles

0 Kilometers

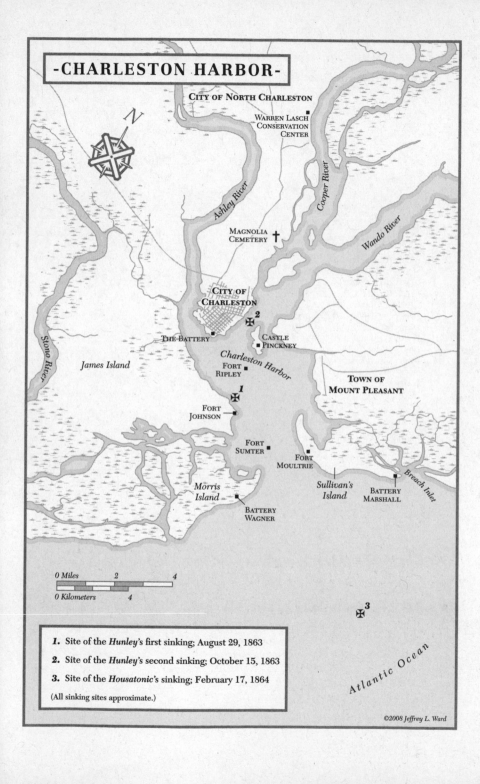

-CHARLESTON HARBOR-

CITY OF NORTH CHARLESTON

WARREN LASCH
CONSERVATION
CENTER

Ashley River

Cooper River

Wando River

MAGNOLIA
CEMETERY ✝

CITY OF
CHARLESTON

⚜ 2

THE BATTERY

CASTLE
PINCKNEY

Charleston Harbor

FORT
RIPLEY

James Island

TOWN OF
MOUNT PLEASANT

⚜ 1

Stono River

FORT
JOHNSON

FORT SUMTER

FORT
MOULTRIE

*Sullivan's
Island*

BATTERY
MARSHALL

Breach Inlet

Morris
Island

BATTERY
WAGNER

0 Miles   2   4

0 Kilometers   4

⚜ 3

Atlantic Ocean

1. Site of the *Hunley's* first sinking; August 29, 1863

2. Site of the *Hunley's* second sinking; October 15, 1863

3. Site of the *Housatonic's* sinking; February 17, 1864

(All sinking sites approximate.)

©2008 Jeffrey L. Ward

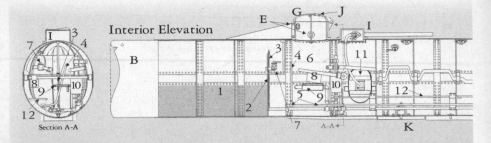

Interior Elevation

Section A-A

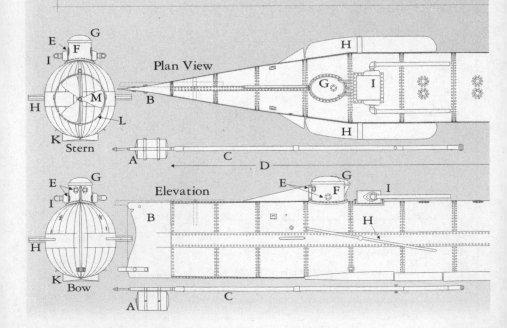

LEGEND

Exterior

A. Torpedo
B. Cast iron bow and stern caps
C. Spar
D. Main hull of about forty-two wrought iron plates
E. View ports for observation
F. Conning towers
G. Hatches
H. Diving planes
 I. Air box and snorkel pipes
 J. Deadlights to provide interior light in crew chamber
K. Keel consisting of seven iron blocks, three of them
    designed to be dropped in case of emergency
 L. Propeller shroud
M. Propeller
N. Rudder

Plan View

Stern

Elevation

Bow

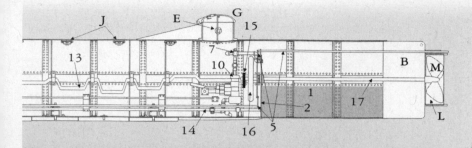

Interior
1. Ballast tanks
2. Tank bulkheads
3. Depth gauge
4. Steering lever
5. Steering linkage
6. Captain's station
7. Sea cocks for intake of water into ballast tanks
8. Dive plane lever
9. Captain's bench
10. Pumps for expulsion of water from ballast tanks
11. Bellows attached to snorkel
12. Crew bench mounted on port side of crew chamber
13. Zigzagged crankshaft turned by seven men
14. Intertank plumbing
15. Chain differential gears
16. Flywheel
17. Propeller shaft

THE HUNLEY – 1864

Hull Dimensions
Length ‚ 40 feet
Height ‚ 4 feet
Beam ‚ 3.5 feet

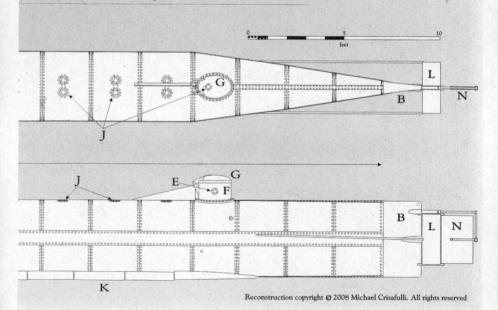

Reconstruction copyright © 2008 Michael Crisafulli. All rights reserved

Preface: Of Boats, Books, Barnacles, and Archives

ONE MORNING not long ago, while we were standing inside the temporarily drained tank in which the *H. L. Hunley* was then being excavated, Maria Jacobsen, the project's senior archaeologist, directed my attention to an aspect of the Confederate submarine boat that can be missed if one gets too focused on the details. Viewed from its stern, she noted, the craft resembles a whale—or a porpoise or a dolphin—more so than it does any vessel of war. From a vantage immediately aft of the boat's propeller, as one gazes down the craft's forty-foot hull, the appearance of this boat—with its elegant, tapered hydrodynamic shape—evokes the cetaceous more than the martial.

"Many people who come here expect it to have a cylindrical shape," she said. "But it doesn't." The craft's graceful angles bespeak a more refined aesthetic. To Jacobsen, it seemed obvious that the *Hunley*'s designers wanted their boat to look, and *move*, like an animal that swims through the sea, rather than some machine slapped together to satisfy the exigencies of military conflict. "Nothing about its design or construction seems rushed," said the Danish-born scientist. "It doesn't look at all like something built in a time of war."

Normally, the tank in which we were standing, at Clemson

University's Warren Lasch Conservation Center, in North Charleston, South Carolina, is filled with 60,800 gallons of fresh water. The water reduces the growth of fungus and algae and retards further corrosion of the wreck—a word that somehow seems ill-suited for this artifact, which, all things considered, appears to be in remarkably good condition.

The *Hunley* has rested in the Lasch Center tank since its recovery from Charleston Harbor in 2000—136 years since the evening of February 17, 1864, when, in Charleston Harbor, it became the first submarine in world history to sink an enemy vessel. Shortly thereafter—amid still-mysterious circumstances—the *Hunley* too sank to the harbor's bottom.

To be sure, the circumstances of the *Hunley*'s disappearance remain provocative seas of inquiry. But as I conducted the research for this book, it often occurred to me that another equally compelling, perhaps greater, mystery surrounds this boat. And that other mystery is the aspect of the craft to which Jacobsen alluded that day in Charleston. To wit, how did the *Hunley*'s builders, amid the rushed vagaries of war, find the time, money, and expertise to construct a craft of such grace and meticulous detail? Yes, the *Hunley* is an artifact of the American Civil War and a nationalist movement devoted to a venal objective, the perpetuation of the enslavement of African Americans. Yet this vessel also happens to be a splendid artifact of Victorian-era engineering.

But how to get to the heart of those and other mysteries of the *Hunley*?

I was convinced from the start—and my optimism was subsequently vindicated—that the research, forensic and otherwise, accomplished by the gifted international team of scientists at the Lasch Center would prove invaluable in my quest. But I was also aware that, to fully tell the *Hunley*'s story, I would need to reconnoiter the entire paper trail of this artifact of America's nineteenth-century technological sublime.

For reasons of provenance, accuracy, and richness of detail, historians prefer to work with primary-source documents. A work of narrative history thrives best when propelled by writings, visual depictions, and other documents created amid, or by people participating in or witness to, the events the author seeks to recall. While writing this book, I became doubly committed to that preference. Early in my research, I realized that the *Hunley*'s story, over the years, had become encrusted with the barnacles of accumulated lore.

For that reason, I resolved, as much as possible, to take the *Hunley*'s story back to its primary sources. In creating this narrative and in my presentation of certain events, trends, places, and people—those not central to the story—I would draw upon sound secondary sources and my own insights as a historian. But when presenting facts and details immediately pertinent to the saga of the *Hunley* and its two predecessor boats, I required those assertions to be supported by primary sources. In cases where I could find no such support, those facts and details—regardless of the frequency of their repetition in other publications—were to be unceremoniously cast overboard. In exceptional cases, when I believed a reason existed to admit into the narrative an unconfirmed fact, I would alert the reader to its questionable pedigree, or otherwise flag my own speculative gambit.

But that resolve also brought challenges. There were obstacles created by the fact that none of the principals involved in the development of the *Hunley* and its two predecessor submarine craft left behind a diary, or even a diary fragment, of the months of their association with those boats. Indeed, of the principals who animate this story, none had an on-the-scene involvement with the submarine boat project that ran the enterprise's entire New Orleans-to-Mobile-to-Charleston course. And even if one of them had maintained such an involvement, the chances are remote that he would have penned a diary.

The exigencies of war, the ever shifting locales of the boats' sponsors, and the unique need for secrecy dictated by the nature of their enterprise rendered the keeping of such diaries— or, for that matter, any other paper records—problematic. And that absence of written documents also hindered research on other fronts—including questions concerning who exactly first conceived the idea of this submarine boat project, the financing of the enterprise, and the precise roles of each of the project's principal members.

Past chroniclers have sometimes accorded Horace Hunley sole credit as the originator and even the inventor of the vessel that became the first submarine boat in world history to sink an enemy ship. It was his name, after all, that the craft carried during its moment of triumph. Even so, the *H. L. Hunley* was not that vessel's original name, and the fact that it came to bear Horace Hunley's name ultimately serves less to identify the individual who conceived the idea of building the craft or the boat's inventor than to commemorate a particular turn in the vessel's tortured history.

Based on his background and contemporary documents, it seems clear that James McClintock, among the project's three original partners, was the principal designer for all three boats. But as to who initiated the project—in their letters, in so many words—both McClintock and the project's third original partner, Baxter Watson, each laid claim to having performed that role. Curiously, alone among the boat's original three principals, only Horace Hunley, in his letters, seems to have made no allusion to the matter of who initiated the project or who designed the boats.[1]

To be sure, communications to and from some of this story's principals do exist. But they are hardly plentiful. And of those letters that do exist, few present the entire context of their composition. Rarely do we have the second-party communication that prompted, or resulted from, any given letter. Thus, those letters that do exist often raise as many questions as they answer.

Happily, however, as I dived deeper into the submarine boat's archives, I discovered—the aforementioned challenges notwithstanding—that a rich array of primary-source documents does exist for telling what I soon found to be a ceaselessly compelling story, albeit one quite different, teeming with more ironies and nuances, than the one I had expected.

Ultimately, I examined a king's ransom of documents. And for a comprehensive list of the materials that went into the writing of this book, the reader should consult this work's Bibliography. However, in this brief essay—in order to put my archival cards on the table, but also to guide future researchers—I'd like to highlight some of the richer treasures that I excavated. In the process, I also hope to convey a sense of the diverse range of primary-source materials that are available for studies of the *Hunley*.

Begin with the wealth of invaluable documents in two magisterial publications of the Federal government: the thirty-one-volume *Official Records of the Union and Confederate Navies in the War of the Rebellion* (*ORN*, 1894–1922); and the 128-volume *War of the Rebellion: A Compilation of the Official Records of the Union and Confederate Armies* (*OR*, 1880–1901). These volumes yield an astonishing array of documents, ranging from the correspondences of civilian and military leaders and reports from officers in the field to intelligence dispatches from behind-enemy-lines spies and depositions from interrogations of enemy deserters.

Given the nature of the *Hunley*'s story, it would seem logical that the navies' volumes would yield more relevant documents than those of the armies. And, indeed, I found that to be the case. But I also located many relevant documents in the armies' volumes. To an often unappreciated degree, the American Civil War's naval theater—a realm that included rivers, lakes, and estuaries as well as oceans—often straddled land and water. And on both sides of the Mason-Dixon line, that nautical theater also breached administrative boundaries, straddling the lines that otherwise separated each side's civilian and military, and army and navy spheres. Beyond that, the more particular circumstances of Horace Hunley and his fellow civilian partners' quest to build an underwater boat for the South's military inevitably cast the men as suitors—perhaps *orphans* is the better term—beseeching *both* the Confederate Army and Navy for support. Still other valuable Confederate documents relevant to the *Hunley*, but which are not included in either the *ORN* or *OR*, were located in the U.S. National Archives.

The Rev. James Peyton—a descendant of Hunley's with whom I corresponded during my research—now owns the 1821 Hunley family Bible. He kindly supplied me with photocopies of that book's family history section. And the handwritten entries darkening those pages allowed me to confirm dates for various family milestones, both during Horace's childhood years in Tennessee and after the family's move to New Orleans. For additional background on Horace's early, prewar career in New Orleans—particularly his legal career, his ownership of slaves, and his landholdings (the latter two often exaggerated)—I drew on U.S. Census materials, various other government documents, New Orleans city directories, as well as publications directed toward Louisiana's sugar planters. And for guidance in locating and describing features, often now long vanished, of the built and natural environments in and around New Orleans, Mobile, and Charleston, I read relevant local histories and consulted with historians of each of those three areas.

Soon after commencing my research, I was also delighted to learn that a diary of sorts with relevance to the *Hunley* does indeed exist—and, at that, one penned by no less a principal than Horace Hunley himself. A ledger kept by Hunley in New Orleans for several years before the Civil War, and now owned by the Louisiana State Museum, contains no allusions to submarine boats or, for that matter, to any other nautical or military topics. But its various to-do lists and random musings on matters quotidian and philosophical offer an intimate glimpse into the dreams and priorities of a talented if quixotic man.

I found no other diaries of any sort from any of the other original principals in the submarine boat project. But many of the other figures who drive this story—including General Pierre G. T. Beauregard and William Alexander—did later publish recollections of their Civil War experiences in various Southern newspapers and magazines. In particular, the British-born Alexander, who joined the partners in Mobile, became, during his twilight years, a sort of self-appointed keeper of the *Hunley* flame. In 1902–1903 he published no fewer than four articles in as many publications chronicling the story of the *Hunley* and its two predecessor boats.

These articles by Alexander and other principals—written years or even decades after the events they describe—vary greatly in both vividness of detail and credibility, and one must be guarded in accepting their contents at face value. Memories, after all, fade; and postwar memoirists, writing with an eye on posterity, often distort events or leave out self-incriminating incidents. Even so, such recollections can always be checked against other documents. And in the end, these accounts proved more enlightening than obfuscating.

In his own postwar *Personal Memoirs*, General Ulysses S. Grant remarked, "I always admired the South, as bad as I thought their cause, for the boldness with which they silenced all opposition and all croaking, by press or individuals, within their control." Young and boastful, Horace Hunley and his partners, despite their nominal commitment to discretion, never managed to keep their work a secret. Ironically, however, despite occasional lapses, the Confederacy's newspapers—to this historian's disappointment—managed to succeed where Hunley and company failed. By and large, Southern newspapers—even those of New Orleans, Mobile, and Charleston—proved to be poor sources for my research.

Ironically, however, the silence of those newspapers on submarine boats seems to have made that topic all the more intriguing for curious civilians. The conspicuous omission of coverage by the local press of a phenomenon that citizens in New Orleans, Mobile, and Charleston, in turn, were witnessing in plain view seems only to have nourished their passion, in letters and diaries, to memorialize—and speculate about—what they saw and heard. Thus, as I found my way through this project, I discovered in various repositories an abundance of relevant contemporary diaries and letters, published and unpublished.

I found many of these materials at two institutions: Charleston's South Carolina Historical Society and the University of North Carolina at Chapel Hill's Southern Historical Collection. These letters and diaries teem with myriad firsthand descriptions of the three submarine boats. In most cases, these materials were penned by citizens with no immediate connection to the submarine boat project. Even so, their accounts document various phases and events in the life spans of the three boats. They also mirror the range of public attitudes toward the partners' boats and submarine warfare in general.

Turning to particular collections, the vast Barrow Family Papers, at Tulane University in New Orleans, includes letters to and from Horace Hunley's sister, Volumnia, as well as correspondences to and from her husband—and Horace's brother-in-law and business partner—the planter Robert Ruffin

Barrow. A man of great wealth, Barrow—a former Whig, decades older than his brother-in-law Horace—ardently opposed secession; but, as a mentor to Hunley, Barrow's opinions weighed heavily on the younger man. If only for that reason, his papers—including Barrow's self-published political writings, pamphlets, broadsides, and the like, also found in this collection—make compelling reading.

The Louis J. Genella Papers, also at Tulane, and the Eustace Williams Collection, at the Mobile Public Library, both contain rich materials for *Hunley* researchers. The two collections, each similar in scope, retain materials amassed respectively by Genella and Williams, both mid-twentieth-century collectors of *Hunley* materials. Both collections include typescript copies of contemporary handwritten documents found in various archives, local newspaper clippings, and often illuminating correspondence between the two researchers and descendants of various *Hunley* principals.

Thanks to a brief infatuation in 1872 by the British Navy with the *Hunley*—or more specifically, with Horace Hunley's partner James McClintock—the National Archives of the United Kingdom, in Kew, England, hold a small but valuable collection of *Hunley*-related letters and drawings. The Royal Navy that year briefly entertained a proposal by McClintock to design a submarine for Her Majesty's fleet. The project was ultimately vetoed, but the papers and drawings associated with an interview by Royal Navy officers with McClintock make for fascinating reading.

The Historic New Orleans Collection, in New Orleans, owns the papers of Hunley's close friend Henry Leovy. For Hunley, the prosecession Leovy—a co-owner of the New Orleans *Daily Delta*—served as a countervailing influence to the antisecession Barrow. And Leovy's papers illuminate that worldview.

The Franklin Buchanan Letterbook, at the Southern Historical Collections at the University of North Carolina at Chapel
Hill, constitutes yet another essential resource. The Confederate admiral in charge of defenses at the port of Mobile,
Buchanan remained a formidable critic of the submarine boat
project and was never reticent about expressing his skepticism
in letters. And because discord tends to reveal more information than concord, I found his letters particularly illuminating.

From St. Tammany Parish, Louisiana's Clerk of Court Office, I obtained the will of Horace Lawson Hunley and copious
other documents associated with his heirs and the disburse-
ment of his properties. In contrast to Hunley, George Dixon,
the *Hunley*'s dashing final commander, died intestate. Even so,
from the Records Division of the Mobile County, Alabama,
Probate Court, I did locate the few documents filed with that
court upon his death.

Amid the sprawling Civil War collections of the National
Archives, in Washington, one document warrants particular
mention: the invaluable 105-page U.S. Navy Court of Inquiry
report on the sinking of the USS *Housatonic*. Conducted
aboard the USS *Wabash* off Charleston, mere weeks after the
Hunley's sinking of the *Housatonic*, this tribunal, meeting for
seven days, heard testimony from eighteen officers and seamen.
At that point, Union Navy personnel were still unaware of precisely which—and even what type of—Confederate craft had
destroyed the *Housatonic*. Even so, the transcribed depositions
of those witnesses are both riveting and eye-opening. And, for
those seeking to understand the *Hunley*'s fate, that Court of Inquiry Report—and, more specifically, the witness voices at the
core of that document—constitute a sort of Warren Commission Report and Zapruder film rolled into one. For better or
worse, those voices, recorded when the events they describe remained fresh in their minds, constitute the final testimony of

those qualified to bear witness to the milieu and evening of the *Hunley*'s demise.

Finally, there is the matter of the two submarine boats that preceded the *Hunley*. The first of those, the CSS *Pioneer*, was, we know, scuttled in New Orleans, then later recovered and sold for scrap metal. The second craft, the *American Diver*, sank in Mobile Harbor in winter 1863 and has not been seen since. While no definitive drawing of the *American Diver* has surfaced, fortunately a precise drawing of the *Pioneer*—a sketch that possesses a solid provenance—does exist. The drawing, in the National Archives, accompanies a January 1864 report on the craft by William Shock, a U.S. Navy engineer. Shock and another officer, who produced the drawing, were able to inspect the *Pioneer* thoroughly and record its dimensions after its recovery by Union forces in occupied New Orleans—before, that is, the vessel was sold as scrap metal.

The difficulties attendant to the documentation of those two vessels only underscore our good fortune in the case of the *Hunley*. For, unlike researchers seeking information on the *Pioneer* and the *American Diver*—or, for that matter, on such famous Civil War vessels as the *Virginia* and the *Shenandoah*—the historian following in the wake of the *Hunley* now has, and has had since its recovery in 2000, knowledge garnered from the actual boat and other physical artifacts collected around its Atlantic Ocean wreck site. Even better, today's *Hunley* researcher enjoys the expertise of the hardworking scientists at Charleston's Warren Lasch Conservation Center, who, even as this is written, continue to explore the submarine boat's wonders.

The *H. L. Hunley*

Prologue: Canal Street

FOR FRANCIS HANSON HATCH, as for so many others in New Orleans in June 1861, everything had changed and nothing had changed. The American Civil War had erupted weeks earlier, but it had been five months since Louisiana had bid adieu to, had seceded from, the Federal Union. But despite the commotion, Francis Hatch, forty-six years old, remained collector of customs for the Port of New Orleans—the same political patronage job he'd held when, months earlier, Old Glory still fluttered over the Custom House. Indeed, further testament to Hatch's versatility, for a four-week interregnum during January and February of 1861—between Louisiana's secession and the casting of its fate with the Confederacy—Customs Collector Hatch, working for an independent state of Louisiana, had even answered to bosses in the state capital of Baton Rouge.

Family connections loomed large in New Orleans politics and business. But Hatch's survival in the post was owed to other, nonnepotistic aspects of this city's life—his own political agility, of course, but also the Crescent City's appreciation for sheer talent, even among nonnatives. The Vermonter had arrived in New Orleans as a thirteen-year-old boy and soon found work as a clerk in a wholesale grocery business. By the age of twenty-one he was running the enterprise.

Through pluck, the spoils system, and an expanding circle of powerful acquaintances—including those garnered from a turn in the state legislature—Hatch, in 1857, had won his appointment, by Democratic president James Buchanan, to the coveted job of Federal customs collector. In the succeeding years he'd met the post's responsibilities to "the entire satisfaction of the mercantile community."

In New Orleans, as in other port cities, a blessed reciprocity attended the power of the customs collector's post. In return for loyally doing the bidding of his partisan overseers, the customs collector, as a de facto party manager, presided over a vast bureaucracy that awarded employment and other favors to the local party faithful. And those partisan souls, in turn—in the best spirit of quid pro quo—remained ever available to perform various party chores, whether it be delivering blocs of votes or disrupting an opponent's rally.

Only lately, rather than answering to Democratic Party superiors in Washington or Baton Rouge, Collector Hatch reported to newly installed bosses in Richmond, Virginia, the newly established capital of the Confederate States of America.[1]

The Custom House, where Hatch presided, sat—still sits—on the east side of Canal Street, near the southern end of that broad saddle of an avenue's slow rise to the low ridge that greets the Mississippi River. The massive Custom House occupied a full city block. As late as 1875—with its 334 feet of Canal Street frontage and nearly the same on Levee—the structure would rank, after the U.S. Capitol, as America's second-largest public building. But despite its decorative Egyptian-revival-styled pilasters, many regarded the white, three-storied edifice as ugly, even depressing. One critic dismissed it as "a huge sarcophagus of granite."

Even so, the imposing Custom House did offer at least one redeeming aspect—the view from its still unoccupied upper floors. In New Orleans, high levees protected the low-lying city from the surrounding rivers, lakes, and swamps that marked its edges. And those levees, in turn, generally blocked views of the Mississippi River. But from the upper floors of the Custom House—looking eastward and southward, over and beyond the Levee Street (today's Decatur Street) levee—the building offered a magnificent vista.

Above New Orleans, the Mississippi River drained a vast riparian plain that—east of the Rockies and west of the Alleghenies—fanned out over thousands of square miles. Geographically, New Orleans thus occupied an enviable position. Like the spout of a giant funnel, it served as a chief emporium for that vast valley's agricultural bounties. And, from the upper floors of the Custom House, Hatch and his colleagues could witness a scene that attested to that beneficence: they could watch as the Mississippi, in all its broad, brown glory, snaked toward the horizon and the final 107 miles of its long, 2,300-mile southbound course to the Gulf of Mexico.

Construction of the Custom House had begun in 1848, but soon stalled amid governmental infighting. Momentum picked up in 1852 under the supervision of an energetic young U.S. Army engineer, Captain Pierre G. T. Beauregard, then freshly brevetted for heroism in the Mexican-American War. But as with so many other aspects of life in this city, the South's largest, even after the talented Beauregard was put in charge, the work continued to go slowly, fretfully. By 1860, the U.S. government had sunk three million dollars into the project—which itself was steadily sinking into the loamy soil on which it rested.

Indeed, even by June 1861, the building remained unfinished; and after the war erupted, construction on it had ground to a halt. Not that such impasses were anything new for the Crescent City. After all, the broad avenue on which the Custom House sat, Canal Street—the traditional dividing line between the French Quarter and the newer "American Quarter," immediately upriver—derived its name from a never-built canal project.[2]

But such apparent torpor in no way defined New Orleans's reigning spirit that June of 1861. On Canal Street, outside Hatch's office, the summer heat—like a tippling guest who habitually calls earlier than expected, then stays longer than one wants—had already settled in for its usual sticky, extended stay. But throughout the city's tonier business precincts and residential faubourgs, amid the soft clacking of the elegant, newly installed horse carriages, a new motion stirred.

On a fundamental level, and even more so in America's popular imagination, the Civil War pitted slavery's defenders against those of free labor. More particularly, the conflict is presented as a war between the South's rural, agricultural forces and the North's urban and industrial powers. But that image, of a singularly rural agricultural South, conceals other, less often remarked-upon tensions that, throughout the war, internally roiled the Confederacy—fault lines between the South's rural, agricultural interests and those of its urban, commercial, and industrial forces. After all, the very concept of an urban Confederacy—of Confederate cities—has never squared comfortably with our collective imagination's repository of Civil War images. But the Confederacy did have cities—and like most urban realms, those cities often teemed with engineers, scientists, and technological innovators. And their interests and passions, in turn, often ran at cross-purposes to the priorities of those more familiar Civil War dramatis personae—the South's antebellum planters.

The maritime traditions of the American South likewise have eluded the region's mythologizers. Unlike New England, the Mid-Atlantic states, and those of the Pacific Coast, the coastal states of the South—uniquely among those states that front on oceans—never found, in the nation's popular imagination, a defining association with the sea and nautical enterprises. Dixie's literary equivalents—if indeed they exist—of works such as Herman Melville's *Moby-Dick* and Richard Henry Dana's *Two Years Before the Mast* never found their way into America's literary pantheon. Magnolias more than salt sprays have dominated the atmospherics of Southern literature.

Even so, the South did possess nautical traditions. During the antebellum years, New Orleans, Mobile, Savannah, and Charleston, in annual tonnage, consistently ranked among the nation's largest ports. Underscoring that point, between 1825 and 1861, following New York City's rise to tonnage supremacy after the opening of the Erie Canal, Boston and New Orleans constantly competed for second place among the nation's ports.

Beyond that, New Orleans, compared with other Southern cities of that era, coastal and hinterland, possessed yet another way to confound expectations. For—unlike, say, Richmond, Atlanta, Chattanooga, and the Confederacy's other prosaic Protestant realms—the sui generis genius of New Orleans, with its Gallic and Roman Catholic origins, could be found crystallized in one word—*gagner*. Like New Orleans, that French verb stubbornly refused to make distinctions between fortunes acquired through sweat-of-the-brow work and those won, or taken, via simple *bonne chance*.

Within the Confederacy, no city better epitomized all of those forces—urban, commercial, maritime, and devil-may-care entrepreneurial—than New Orleans. And within New Orleans, no street better personified those qualities than did a single broad avenue—Canal Street.

In June 1861, reaching deep into the Greek Revival–

becolumned hotels, banks, and shops that lined Canal and the narrower streets of the American Quarter immediately upriver, a fresh energy held dominion. To be sure, it was the same élan, the same sense of self-interested purpose, that also found its way into the warehouses and factors' offices that squatted along Levee Street's docks and wharves. For the city's mercantile community—that summer's tangle of sweat-stained, white-linen-clad lawyers, bankers, newspaper publishers and editors, merchants, clerks, shipbuilders, cotton and sugar brokers, and the like—this new war, which most expected would exhaust itself in a few months, promised a wealth of fresh opportunities for private profits from ostensibly public ventures, from everything from the manufacture of ordnance and uniforms to gunrunning and shipbuilding.

Operating in that Canal Street spirit, Customs Collector Francis Hatch's own by-the-bootstraps rise to prosperity gave him a keen eye for spotting both opportunities and the raw resourceful talent needed to convert those main chances into easy treasures. Officially, Hatch worked for the Confederacy's Treasury Department. But that month, June 1861, he had penned a discreet letter to an official in Richmond who worked for another department—the War Department. In fact, almost certainly, Hatch's interlocutor was Confederate Secretary of War Leroy Pope Walker. A civilian but acting, in this case, in a secret capacity for the Confederate military, Hatch confided that he needed one thousand dollars in cash to set in motion a "special expedition" that the two had already discussed.

Moreover, Hatch explained in his letter, he had already found just the man to carry out this scheme—and, even better, that man worked right there on Canal Street. The man was middle-aged but teemed with youthful energy. His name was Horace Lawson Hunley, a thirty-seven-year-old attorney, and he toiled in the Custom House as an assistant customs collector.

Hatch then had no way of knowing it, but his letter to Richmond would set in motion a conspiratorial chain of events involving acts of heroism as well as greed-fueled hubris that, stretching over the next three years, eventually enmeshed scores of actors. More than a few of those men, prowling dark, briny waters inside a series of cramped and mysterious cigar-shaped submarines—or submarine boats, as that age called such craft—would be dispatched toward early and watery graves.

Indeed, by the time this conspiracy reached its twisted denouement, its tentacles would even clutch Pierre Beauregard, the U.S. Army's original superintending engineer for the still unfinished New Orleans Custom House, and, by then, a highly regarded general in the Confederate Army. Moreover, the desperate arc of the submarine boats' story would eventually gather men from other cities and regions, and navigate the streets and waters of two other Confederate ports, Mobile and Charleston.

But in a very real sense, all of those roads and roadsteads—and all of the deals, dreams, and energies that propelled those men, their submarine boats, and their obsession to develop the first underwater craft to destroy an enemy ship—they all coiled back to a single mainspring of a thoroughfare, New Orleans's Canal Street. For, in a fundamental sense, from beginning to end, this would remain a Crescent City tale.[3]

PART I

NEW ORLEANS

Summer 1861–Spring 1862

1

A Man of Property,
Intelligence and Probity

THE ONE THOUSAND DOLLARS that New Orleans's customs collector Francis Hanson Hatch secretly requested from the Confederate War Department in June 1861 was needed for the "fitting out" of the *William R. King*. The schooner was built in 1849 and originally christened as *The Knight*, a private vessel. In 1853, she was purchased by the U.S. government, renamed the *William R. King*, and refitted as a lighthouse tender. In March 1861, she was seized by secessionist forces in Louisiana. And, according to Hatch's plan, the schooner—eventually refitted yet again, in July of that same year, by the Confederates—was soon to be dispatched from Louisiana to a harbor along Cuba's mangrove-choked southern coast, in the island's far western province of Pinar del Rio.

If all went as planned, the Confederate ship—soon again renamed, this time as the *Adela*—would quietly rendezvous off Pinar del Rio with a British merchantman. The *Windsor Forest* was sailing from Liverpool with a shipment of badly needed arms for the Confederacy. Hatch's various subterfuges were necessary to thwart President Lincoln's recently proclaimed blockade of New Orleans and all other Confederate ports. The naval blockade constituted the defining, constricting compo-

nent of the Union's "Anaconda" plan for eventual victory over
the Confederacy. Developed early in the war by General Winfield Scott, Anaconda—originally a mocking reference to the
snake of that name—called for a slow choking of the South
through a comprehensive naval blockade focused on its twelve
major ports but including its entire 3,500-mile coastline.

That blockade, coupled with invasions by land forces and by
gunboats down the Mississippi and the region's other major
rivers, would subdivide the South into increasingly smaller,
weaker, isolated realms. Once thus invaded and constricted, so
Anaconda's logic went, the Confederacy, denied its economic
lifeblood, would soon perish.

Union strategists eventually divided their blockading fleet
into four groups: the North Atlantic, the South Atlantic, the
East Gulf, and the West Gulf squadrons. Early in the war, these
same strategists also realized that, in order to conserve time and
resources, each squadron needed a home port inside its theater
of operation. Fortunately for the Gulf Blockading Squadron—
not until early 1862 would it be broken into East and West
squadrons—that requirement entailed no capture of a Confederate port. That happy circumstance was owed to the fact that
Fort Pickens, near Pensacola, Florida, enjoyed the distinction
of being a Federal installation that, despite its Southern location, never fell under Confederate control. Situated on Santa
Rosa Island, the pentagonal brick redoubt had been unoccupied since the Mexican-American War. In January 1861, as the
secession crisis lurched toward open confrontation, U.S. Army
forces simply reoccupied the old fort, and it remained in their
hands for the war's duration.

As Confederate strategists, meanwhile, watched the Union
blockade of their coast strengthen, they grew painfully aware of
their own navy's paltry size. To thwart the blockade, they soon
turned to private enterprise—to civilian-owned ships. Indeed,

by the war's end, civilian vessels would play substantial roles in both official and quasi-official affairs—military and commercial—of the Confederate state. Moreover, the war's early months soon yielded another realization for Confederate strategists: to pierce the Union blockade required the use of intermediate ports.

Back in the spring of 1861, a bombardment by secessionists of Fort Sumter, an island redoubt then still in Federal hands, in the harbor of Charleston, South Carolina, had opened this conflict. During those early weeks of the war, the Union's blockade of Confederate ports had been more a proclaimed policy than an active reality. But with the arrival off Charleston, on May 11, of the frigate USS *Niagara*—soon followed there and elsewhere along the Southern coast by scores of other Union war vessels—the days of easy access to Confederate docks soon ended.

Whether serving civilian or governmental customers, the South's merchants were forced to meet their European business partners at ports, usually in the Caribbean, controlled by neutral, third-party nations. There, goods, military and civilian, were transferred from oceangoing ships to smaller, swifter, shallow-draft vessels—craft capable of eluding the U.S. Navy ships athwart the various sea routes to the Confederacy's ports. As a consequence of this additional traffic—as Union and Confederate operatives suspiciously eyed each other in these various entrepôts—Nassau, Havana, and other island ports soon teemed with intrigue.[1]

It was into that shadowy theater that Horace Lawson Hunley, commanding the schooner *Adela*, sailed in the early summer of 1861. Typical of his own independence and that milieu's laissez-faire spirit, Hunley likely held no formal military rank in either the Confederate Army or Navy. The honorific of *Captain* that often prefixes his name in war correspondence, official records, and even today, on his gravestone, was likely a courtesy title recognizing his *civilian* command of the *Adela* and other Confederate ventures. Indeed, Hunley's name appears on no located Confederate—neither Army nor Navy—muster rolls.

From Francis Hanson Hatch, Hunley's senior by almost a decade, the energetic lawyer enjoyed the munificence of a dependable sponsor for ventures public and private. The customs collector had known Hunley for many years and considered him "a man of property, intelligence and probity." Indeed, back in 1860, when Hatch still toiled for the Federal government, Hunley—upon Hatch's recommendation to superiors in Washington—had temporarily filled the senior customs collector post for several months, while Hatch took a leave of absence. And even as late as June 1861, as his preparations for the trip to Cuba advanced, Hunley still occupied an office in the Canal Street Custom House as assistant customs collector.

Hatch's sailing plan called for the *Adela*, commanded by Hunley, to rendezvous off Cuba's Cape San Antonio, on the island's southwestern coast, with the British merchantman *Windsor Forest*, laden with arms for the Confederate war effort. Setting that plan into motion, the *Windsor Forest* departed Liverpool on April 27, ostensibly bound for Quebec. The *Adela*, in turn, sailed from Louisiana's Berwick Bay at dusk on June 10.[2]

But the anticipated arms transfer between the two ships never occurred. Off Key West on June 7 a passing ship alerted the *Windsor Forest*, en route to Cuba, to the presence of watchful U.S. warships to the southwest, along the British steamer's intended course. The *Windsor Forest* immediately

shifted to a northerly course and reached New York Harbor on
the twenty-third. Hunley's *Adela*, meanwhile—sailing south by
west via the Yucatán coast but delayed by strong headwinds on
her approach to Cuba—had reached Cape San Antonio by mid-
June. But, arriving woefully late and not finding the British
ship, Hunley assumed that "she had made some safe port or
been captured."

The Confederate mariners had failed to find their British
coconspirators. Ironically, however, the trip left Hunley with
bright hopes for his own blockade-running fortunes. The *Adela*
returned to Louisiana's Berwick Bay on July 1. "On our outward
voyage," he soon wrote the customs collector Hatch, "we saw
but one vessel before reaching the coast of Yucatan, & returning we saw but one till we reached the coast of Louisiana." The implications seemed inescapable: a ragged fringe of
shallow bays, bayous, and sandbars, after all, limned most of
Louisiana's coastline. "I am Confident," Hunley wrote, "that any
quantity of arms could be introduced into Louisiana over this
course, in a small light draft steamer, with very little danger."

At thirty-seven, Hunley lay two years beyond the maximum age
of conscription soon in effect for the Confederate military. In
all likelihood, he undertook the trip to Cuba driven, at least in
part, by Southern patriotism and a quest for adventure. But
equal to and perhaps stronger than those drives, he also had
pecuniary motives—whatever fee he was paid for making the
excursion—as well as a curiosity about how the Union blockade
of the Southern coast might affect his businesses.

In achieving his station in Southern society, Horace had
overcome a hardscrabble background. He relished challenges.
In the papers of his that survive, themes of business and acquis-
itive ambition—more than Confederate ideology and patriot-

ism—predominate. Clearly, Hunley cared deeply about politics, but little in any sort of ideological or activist vein. Like other urban men of his milieu, he tended to view politics, first and foremost, as a speculative arena.

Certainly, had Hunley been completely aloof from politics, he never would have won employment in that veritable temple of Democratic Party "wire-pulling," the New Orleans Custom House. And indeed the two men with whom Hunley, throughout his life, remained closest—his brother-in-law, sugar planter Robert Ruffin Barrow; and New Orleans *Daily Delta* co-owner and fellow lawyer Henry Jefferson Leovy—were each passionately involved as published polemicists, albeit on opposite sides, in that era's debates over Southern secession. By contrast, Hunley—though his letters reveal a learned erudition—seldom seemed driven by ideological concerns, and much less by any desire to present such concerns to the world at large. Indeed, while many of Hunley's letters and later actions bespoke ardent support for the Confederacy, others exhibited an indifference or even opposition to the cause of Southern nationalism. Typifying that strain in his thinking—and bearing witness to the influence of Robert Ruffin Barrow on his worldview—Hunley, in an August 1860 letter to Barrow, railed against "those horrid fellows who are willing to emperil the Union by contending for what they call the equal rights of the slave States."

At first glance, the ever-shifting range of Hunley's political views suggests a chameleonlike quality. In truth, however, to the degree that political interests drove him, those passions seem to have remained largely devoted to wagers on the outcome of electoral contests, and—even more so—to his perpetual search for new moneymaking opportunities.[3]

Horace Lawson Hunley entered this world as a son of a humble Tennessee farm family. He was born in Sumner County, near the town of Gallatin, north of Nashville, on December 29, 1823. His parents, John and Louisa Lawson Hunley, had four children. But of those only Horace and his sister Volumnia, two years his junior, lived into adulthood. In 1830 the family moved to New Orleans, where John Hunley found work as a cotton broker. The city held a sentimental allure for John. As a young man, in 1815, he had fought in General Andrew Jackson's army against British forces in the Battle of New Orleans, the War of 1812's final major engagement.

Vibrant and large with European airs, New Orleans offered the family a welcome change. But their elation proved brief. In February 1834, four years after the move, John Hunley, following a debilitating illness, died. Louisa was suddenly a widow with two children. The next few years proved difficult, but she soon remarried—this time to a wealthy planter, James R. Connor, originally from New Jersey.

Louisa Hunley's remarriage proved fortunate for her young son Horace. Growing up in modest circumstances, the boy had developed sturdy work habits. And now, with the financial and social resources of his new stepfather, he suddenly won entrée into worlds once beyond his reach. Bright and hardworking, young Horace soon gained admission to the University of Louisiana—now Tulane University—and graduated with a law degree in 1849. Indicative of the drive that would soon propel him to new adventures, by the year of his graduation he was already concluding a two-year turn, representing Orleans Parish, in the state legislature.

Upon completing his studies Hunley opened a solo law practice. He possibly began the practice, just north of New Orleans, in St. Tammany Parish. But whether or not that was the case, he soon relocated it to New Orleans. There, city directories of the 1850s list his law office at successive addresses. By 1853, his business address was listed as 80 Common Street, his home address as "on Camp," at that corridor's corner with

Melpomene—a street that took its name, prophetically for this ambitious young attorney, from the Muse of tragedy.

During those early years Hunley found additional work at the Custom House. Things were looking up—indeed, so much so that in 1859 or 1860 he purchased an eighty-acre plantation along Bayou L'Ours, in Assumption Parish, southwest of New Orleans, in the Delta sugar country. During its first year of operation under Hunley, the plantation, called Forest Place, yielded a modest but respectable fifty-six hogsheads of sugar. During that same period, Hunley also purchased land in Texas, but that acreage apparently remained unimproved and never produced income for its owner. Truth be known, whatever income Hunley, over his entire lifetime, derived from agriculture seems to have been less from growing crops and more from his role as a broker—as a buyer and seller—of crops grown by others.

In short, Hunley—by then bearded and possessed of intense dark eyes—thrived less as a man of rural Louisiana than as a man about town. And Horace's town was the city of New Orleans. And it was there, during the years before the Civil War, that he rapidly accumulated friends and acquaintances in the highest echelons of that city's business and politics.

To be sure, Hunley possessed a loner's streak and was not without a certain arrogance. Writing in 1860 from the resort town of White Sulphur Springs, Virginia—now West Virginia— he complained, "The insipidity of the place is as a dose of Castor oil to my taste." But Horace was also widely regarded as gentlemanly, kind, and solicitous. And while not wealthy, he was certainly prosperous. According to the 1850 U.S. Census, in New Orleans, by that year, eight slaves, domestic servants— ranging in age from ten to fifty-five, five of whom were women— tended to his homebound needs. A post as a corresponding clerk he accepted at the Custom House in 1857 paid an annual salary of $1,500—good money for that day. And that salary seems to have been supplemented by income from other pursuits—fees from private legal work, brokerage fees, and other commercial transactions.[4]

It was during those early years of Hunley's adulthood, during the late 1840s and the 1850s, that he befriended the two men who remained closest to him for the duration of his life: the lawyer and journalist Henry Leovy and Hunley's wealthy brother-in-law, the sugar planter Robert Ruffin Barrow.

During their shared student years at the University of Louisiana, Hunley befriended soon-to-be-fellow attorney and future New Orleans *Daily Delta* co-owner Henry Jefferson Leovy. Born in Augusta, Georgia, the son of a Jewish rice planter from South Carolina, young Henry had moved with his family to New Orleans in 1832. In 1848, during the Mexican-American War, Leovy joined a volunteer regiment, but his unit saw no military action. Afterward he studied law under a Federal judge for two years in Frankfort, Kentucky, then returned to New Orleans and enrolled for further legal studies at the University of Louisiana. And it was there that Leovy befriended Horace Hunley, three years his junior.

After completing his legal studies, Leovy joined with Robert N. Ogden—an older lawyer and one of New Orleans's most revered legal figures—to form a partnership. And it was through that firm that Leovy won his own reputation as one of the city's most skillful attorneys, representing the state's leading railroad, express, and insurance companies. Reflecting that esteem, the city of New Orleans, during the 1850s, hired Leovy to produce a codification of its accumulated municipal laws. In the latter part of that decade, Leovy jointly purchased, and took an editorial hand in, the New Orleans *Daily Delta*. His partner in the purchase was Pierre E. Bonford, a former law partner of the powerful Judah Benjamin, then a U.S. senator—and, in time, in close succession, attorney general and secretary of state for the Confederate States of America. Reflecting Leovy's and Bonford's ideological disposition, the *Daily Delta* embraced a stridently prosecession editorial outlook.[5]

Among the many differences between the two men with whom Horace Hunley was closest, Leovy's vigorous advocacy of secession contrasted starkly with the views on that same topic of Hunley's brother-in-law, the sugar planter Robert Ruffin Barrow. Among Hunley's friends accrued during his pre–Civil War days, none grew closer to him than did Barrow. But it was to be a complicated relationship.

Hunley considered Leovy his best friend, and their friendship turned on shared interests and aspirations. The two men also were roughly the same age—they were peers. Hunley's ties to Barrow, by contrast, rested not on bonds of shared generation and aspirations, but on familial ties. The Hunley-Barrow relationship was also built on deference—a deference arising from Barrow's seniority to Hunley in financial worth, age, and life experiences. Reinforcing those bonds of deference, Hunley often worked for—and borrowed money from—the older and more affluent Barrow.[6]

Barrow was born in 1798, in Halifax County, in northeastern North Carolina. Robert Ruffin's father, Bartholomew Barrow, was a planter but never obtained the level of wealth his son eventually amassed. Family tradition holds that Robert Ruffin spent his youth in North Carolina. In 1820 he accompanied his father to Louisiana. Soon afterward Bartholomew gave his son two slaves and $1,800. And from that act of paternal munificence, Robert Ruffin Barrow began building his empire.

By 1851, as an article published that year in *De Bow's Review* made clear, he was well on his way to becoming one of

Louisiana's richest sugar planters: "I would single [out] Robert R. Barrow, as one of the extraordinary men, not only of the parish, but of the state," the article asserted. "He is a man of commanding talents; and by prudence, foresight, and management, has accumulated an immense property, and bids fair to become one of the richest men in the state."

Ruggedly handsome, Barrow by 1861 was in his early sixties. Moreover, he had more than vindicated *De Bow's* earlier prediction of his future wealth. At the Civil War's outset, Barrow ranked among the South's richest men. He owned sixteen plantations in Louisiana, extensive landholdings in Texas, and, by his own estimation, "upwards of 700 slaves."

After 1859 Barrow devoted much of his time to operating a canal company he acquired that year. The enterprise was devoted to the construction of the Barataria and Lafourche Canal, an envisioned fifty-mile waterway designed to connect southwest Louisiana's sugar country to New Orleans. The company had been formed by Louisiana planters thirty years earlier, and massive state subsidies had already been sunk into it. Even so, when Barrow became sole owner of the enterprise, the canal remained far from fully operational.

Barrow had married Horace's beautiful and brainy younger sister, Volumnia, in 1850. The couple lived at "Residence," one of Barrow's plantations, in a handsome three-story mansion, approached via a moss-draped allée, near the town of Houma, in Louisiana's Terrebonne Parish. They eventually had two children—Volumnia Roberta, born in 1854, and Robert Ruffin, Jr., born in 1858. And when the couple needed a shot of the gaiety of city life—when, for instance, they attended the opera—they had their New Orleans town house, at 5 South Street.

A bachelor of long standing—he had never before married—Robert Ruffin Barrow was his wife's senior by twenty-seven years. And in time, besides serving as a mentor for his earnest young brother-in-law, Robert Barrow also became Horace Hunley's chief law client. More than that, because Horace remained a bachelor, and his and his sister's mother had died in 1857, Robert and Volumnia Barrow, along with stepfather James R. Connor, became Horace's sole family. Horace was constantly on the watch for new books to buy for Volumnia— among others, *Pilgrim's Progress*, *Don Quixote*, *The Vicar of Wakefield*, *Arabian Nights*, and Charles Dickens's *Works*. In August–September 1860, when Robert was unavailable to travel, Horace even accompanied his sister and her two children on a vacation trip to Washington.

In manners and politics, Barrow tended toward the autocratic and the idiosyncratic. The same 1851 *De Bow's Review* article that predicted his future wealth cattily described the planter as "hospitable, but unpopular with all, for what cause I am unable, or rather unwilling to say." Another writer later noted that Barrow, throughout his life, was "full of peculiar ideas." Barrow argued, for instance, that if the South should, through secession, seek the area it truly owns, it should insist on obtaining "the original Louisiana Purchase." But truth be known, many of Barrow's other ideas were, for his milieu, not so peculiar. Typical of landed aristocrats of his wealth and standing—those with the most to lose if the proposed Confederate state failed—Barrow took a fundamentally self-interested and conservative tack toward his region's and era's central political crisis, the crisis of Southern independence.[7]

Robert Ruffin Barrow shared a name with—and indeed is often, erroneously, identified as a distant cousin of—Edmund Ruffin, the Virginia planter and author who famously participated in firing the first secessionist salvo against Fort Sumter. In truth, however, the two men were not only unrelated, they were political opposites. Unlike the Virginian "fire-eater" Edmund Ruffin, the multimillionaire planter Robert Barrow, while a defender of the institution of slavery, nonetheless opposed in early 1861 what he viewed as the South's hasty and foolish embrace of disunion.

Until the demise of the Whigs in the 1850s, Barrow had been a supporter of that party. Since those days, he had found himself increasingly out of step with the two main U.S. political parties—the Democrats and the newly formed Republicans. And during the four-man presidential contest of 1860, Barrow supported the proslavery but antisecession Kentucky Democrat John Breckinridge. In a political pamphlet Barrow published in 1861, he wrote, "Even I have not yet discerned the benefits which immediate secession would bestow upon the South. When they are shown to me, I say, by all means, let us secede, but until then I shall advise moderation. I thing [sic] our rights are more secure in the Union than they would be were we a separate confederacy."

For Barrow and his ilk, attentions to "rights" tended to focus on a single issue: their Federal right, then enshrined in the U.S. Constitution, to own, buy, and sell slaves, a prerogative that Barrow saw as threatened by "the encroachments of the Abolitionists." Indeed, men like Barrow, Louisiana planters whose wealth rested on the cultivation of sugar, tended to be more conservative than others across the South. After all, the region's former Whigs, such as Barrow—unlike most secessionist Democrats—tended to support tariffs designed to protect Louisiana sugar from foreign competition.

Fueling resentments still more, Barrow and his fellow planters saw the envisioned Confederacy—a government likely to be dominated by cotton planters—as leading to a complete collapse of all remaining tariffs. "Free Trade with nations has ever been a favorite principle with the cotton States," he wrote, "and if the contemplated Southern Confederacy approves of it, the sugar planters will be ruined, as they cannot compete with the West Indies."[8]

Indeed, even after disunionists had carried the day and the Confederate States of America was a fait accompli, Barrow and many of his fellow planters, though nominally reconciled to the new political geography, would retain their misgivings about the wisdom of the South's leaving the Union.

By contrast, Horace Hunley's peers—New Orleans's ambitious lawyers, bankers, merchants, brokers, editors, publishers, clerks, and the like—tended to be Democrats with no Whiggism in their pasts. They also tended to be younger, less wealthy, scrappier, and, generally speaking, more urban and entrepreneurial than Barrow and his fellow planters. That entrepreneurial spirit, the spirit of Canal Street, found its most forceful expression in the doctrines of prosecession journalist James D. B. De Bow, who published his widely read monthly journal *De Bow's Review*. The New Orleans journalist defended the institution of slavery, but he longed to see it applied to a more diverse range of enterprises. "Our citizens," De Bow complained, "have been content with the once rich but now decaying results of *agriculture* and from ignorance of the true nature and dignity of COMMERCE and the elevating influences it is calculated to exert, have rather shunned a participation in it." Countering a famous paean of that era to cotton's supremacy in the South's economy, *De Bow's Review* took as its motto "Commerce is king."

Men like Horace Hunley, Francis Hatch, and Henry Leovy, the men of Canal Street, tended to be less directly invested in agriculture than their planter colleagues. They also tended to be readier than others to roll the dice in any large game of chance—including secession or, for that matter, any other enterprise destined to send troops marching or warships sailing. A decade earlier, after all, the filibuster Narciso López—seeking from New Orleans to invade Cuba and bring it into the United States as two or more new slave states—had received his strongest support from the city's younger, mercantile class, even as Louisiana's planters largely opposed his conspiracy. To be sure, among López's strongest supporters in New Orleans had been Laurent Sigur, a predecessor of Hunley's best friend, Henry Leovy, as an owner of the *Daily Delta*. Indeed, López had actually been Sigur's houseguest during his New Orleans stay.

The antebellum years thus found Horace Hunley suspended between two gravitational poles—caught between the attractions of the prosecession, roll-the-dice Canal Street gambler milieu epitomized by his friend Henry Leovy, and the antisecession, leave-well-enough-alone, conservative pull of his wealthy planter brother-in-law Barrow.

Not that Hunley's brother-in-law had anything against a sound or, truth be known, even a reckless wager. On the issue that loomed largest for Barrow—the preservation of his planter's wealth—a self-protective conservatism drove him. But he also possessed a wild streak that lured him toward great, often ill-considered risks. His investment in the perennially money-losing Barataria and Lafourche Canal languished comfortably inside that latter category.

Hunley, the man-about-town, often served as Barrow's eyes and ears for the latter's investments. Indeed, in 1858—as Barrow became preoccupied with his canal business—Hunley formally resumed a role he had relinquished six years earlier, managing many of his brother-in-law's investments. Land purchases took up much of his time. Introducing himself that March to a land broker in Texas, Hunley wrote, "Mr. Barrow is so overwhelmed with his business in Louisiana that he can not himself attend to the Texas land business."

Hunley also advised Barrow on speculative affairs closer to home. In a December 1860 letter, for instance, he warned Barrow away from a contemplated investment in the antisecessionist New Orleans newspaper the *True Delta*. Apparently unbeknownst to Barrow, the daily paper was already saddled with heavy debts and a large civil judgment against it. Without mention of the paper's antisecession editorial views, Hunley's letter stuck to business: "A newspaper is worse than a steam-boat to sink money, and this newspaper has swindled a large amount already."

Combining two passions, politics and money, that he and Barrow shared, Horace, early on, had followed his brother-in-law, albeit in a modest way, into the world of political wagering. And in that realm too, Hunley seems to have served Barrow as a sort of consigliere, proffering advice and often urging restraint. Typifying that role, in November 1860 Hunley penned a note to the planter concerning various high-stakes wagers on that month's four-man presidential race.

Barrow had placed individual bets on which candidates would carry which states. The surviving correspondence from that season leaves an incomplete record of which specific candidates and on which state contests Barrow had wagered. But two extant letters evoke a dismal portrait of Barrow as political prognosticator. On November 12, Hunley wrote Barrow to advise, "Later news gives Tennessee & Kentucky both to Bell by 6[,000] to 10,000 majority. I hope you have not increased your bets." Four days later, Hunley wrote again: "Kentucky they say has gone to Bell [by a] 10,000 plurality. So you lose 5000 $ by it. Your Missouri bets you lose also. Virginia will be close but will go for Breckinridge I suppose." Earlier that year, wagering with more modest stakes, Hunley himself had pocketed five dollars after New York's former U.S. senator Daniel Dickinson failed to capture that year's Democratic Party presidential nomination.

Beyond his dealings with Barrow—and despite his own steady social and financial advances—Hunley remained preoccupied with proving his worth to society, and even posterity. Tellingly, he indulged an obsession with the habits of the world's "great men." In his ledger book, he pondered the birthplaces of great men, the memory of great men, the writings of great men, the diseases great men get, and the last words of great men. One entry, haiku-like, simply asked, "Traits of character of great men—clarify." Another asked, "Inventors and discoverers. How they invented & discovered & what—?" Still another wondered, "What is the use of reading a great poem if you do not keep it in your head or at least its finest passages."

Likewise, Hunley's ledger also contained daily to-do lists— enumerations of letters to write, debts to collect, legal suits to file, and chores to perform: "Get my picture made in New York." "Get a chair for my room." "Set my books & room in order." The book also reveals Hunley's penchant for embarking upon quirky, even quixotic, indulgences. "Build in New Orleans an Octagonal brick tower—300 to 500 feet high—of hydraulic cement instead of mortar," one entry read. "Plant an avenue of the Date Palms in the Park at New Orleans & on my place," read another.

In the ledger book, Hunley often organized his days down to the hour. Conveying very much the sense of a young man in a hurry, he copied *Poor Richard's Almanac*-like aphorisms that evoked time's fleetingness: "Procrastination," read one from English poet Edward Young, "is the thief of time." "No more procrastination," read another. And still another, from Benjamin Franklin, noted, "Time is the stuff that life is made of."[9]

Hunley's voyage to Cuba had induced heady expectations of the money he hoped to make from gunrunning and other blockade-evading commerce. Perhaps, in time, if he invested those earnings shrewdly, he might even be able to approach Robert Ruffin Barrow's level of wealth. Those dreams, however, quickly receded. As more and more Union ships arrived offshore, the Federal cordoning of New Orleans and other Southern ports grew stronger. That blockade, coupled with the Confederate government's decision to embargo cotton exports, Hunley soon realized, was even damaging his own businesses.

Early in the war, Confederate officials indulged great expectations about the powers of "King Cotton" to force diplomatic recognition by Great Britain and France of their nascent nation. Their thinking, however, proved naive. Among other overlooked factors, a bountiful Southern harvest in 1860 had produced a cotton surplus that, a year later, still filled warehouses in Great Britain and France. In the end, the Confederacy's embargo of its own major export damaged the South's cotton planters more than their European customers.

As profits from his export-related businesses waned, the ever nimble Horace Hunley began looking for fresh opportunities. His next venture, rather than attempting to elude and bypass the Federal blockade, would be built around his dreams of confronting and destroying the ships that enforced the cordon.

2

The Inventive Faculty of the Country

IN MAY 1861, the editors of *Scientific American*, like most of their countrymen, had assumed that the war that had erupted weeks earlier at Fort Sumter with their brethren to the south would last no more than ninety days. Given that prospect, the magazine's editors—in the best spirit of Victorian scientific optimism—found it impossible to suppress a downright giddiness about what they viewed as the conflict's likely yield of new military technologies. "The inventive faculty of the country," the magazine crowed, "roused to extraordinary activity by the intense mental excitement pervading the community, will now be directed to an unusual extent to improvements in implements of war and in all mechanism[s] connected with naval and military operations."

In the end, the American Civil War, like most, perhaps more than most, major conflicts, produced myriad technological advances. Inventions came on both the military and home fronts—from weaponry to medicine, from transportation to communications. Among the anticipated wartime improvements celebrated by *Scientific American* were the continued development of rifled cannon and metal-plated ships. But those, the magazine promised, "are only two of an innumerable

multitude of details connected with naval and military mechanism[s]." The magazine also predicted improvements in "the
shot, the wad, the cartridge, the lock, the gun carriage, the cartridge box, the tent and tent equipage, the cooking apparatus,
preserved meats and other provisions, and, in short, everything
related to the operations, the armaments and the supplies of
navies and armies."

Conspicuous by their absence on the magazine's list of welcome technologies were two—the submarine boat and the torpedo—that had been in the works long before the Civil War.
For coverage of those two developments, *Scientific American*'s
readers needed only to turn to another article, briefer and less
sanguine in tone, in that same issue. The notice recited advances in underwater warfare by the inventors Robert Fulton
and William Bauer. But it concluded by doubting the military
usefulness of torpedoes. For good measure, it also asserted that
"an efficient submarine propeller [boat] for war purposes has
not yet been invented." Tellingly, the article's reference to attacks upon "blockading ships" presumed that, of the Civil War's
two warring parties, only the Confederacy would deploy either
of the inventions.

Widespread prejudices against submarine boats and torpedoes—both often stigmatized during the war as "infernal machines"—stretched back to the Middle Ages. During that long
twilight era, the epithet, at various times in its most general
usage, applied to any weapon—be it explosives, cannon, or
smaller firearms—that used gunpowder. During that era, such
weaponry, widely viewed as a rebuke of the medieval code
of chivalry, was associated, quite literally, with supernatural
forces—particularly Satan. Indeed, even today, the exclamation
son of a gun survives in English as a linguistic relic of an era
which saw Old Scratch's hand behind every shot fired, every
bomb detonated.

By 1861 the literal association of gunpowder with Satan had receded. Moreover, prejudices against weapons that used gunpowder had narrowed; artillery, muskets, and the like had won status as morally legitimate "usages of war." But moral qualms still surrounded the use of hidden explosives, on land and at sea, intended to harm unsuspecting soldiers, sailors, or civilians. At the outbreak of the American Civil War, no submarine boat had yet succeeded in sinking an enemy ship. Even so, because of their contemplated role in delivering those explosives, such underwater vessels (also called "submarine batteries" or "submarine propellers") came to share the *infernal machine* epithet. More broadly, the term, during the American Civil War, became a catch-all pejorative applied to entities ranging from submarine boats and torpedoes to explosive shells disguised to look like pieces of coal that Confederate sailors often left behind in coal bins aboard steamships captured by Union sailors. For mid-nineteenth-century Americans, then, the term *infernal machine* no longer suggested a literal association with Satan. Even so, for many, perhaps most, Americans—both north and south of the Mason-Dixon line—the sobriquet still connoted a distinct association with evil.[1]

As it turned out, in Columbia, Tennessee, over a thousand miles southwest of the *Scientific American*'s New York offices, the Rev. Franklin Smith, an Episcopalian minister as well as a chemist and inventor, had also been contemplating how wars stimulate technological progress. Only his preoccupations focused on precisely those two technologies—the submarine boat and the torpedo—implicitly eschewed in the May 1861 *Scientific American*'s main roundup of wartime advances. A few weeks after *Scientific American* published its encomium to martial ingenuity, Smith published an open letter in the *Mobile*

(Alabama) *Advertiser and Register* calling for the development of submarine boats and torpedoes "capable of the destruction or capture of every blockading ship."

Smith's advocacy of submarines and torpedoes reflected attitudes that reached to the highest levels of the Confederacy's civilian and military leadership. Indeed, early in the Civil War, President Jefferson Davis and Navy Secretary Stephen Mallory—their later hesitations notwithstanding—revealed themselves as vigorous advocates of underwater warfare. Davis's support for such practices stretched back to his days as secretary of war for President Franklin Pierce. During that turn, he had been enthralled by reports on the Russian Navy's use of torpedoes in the Crimean War. Likewise, Mallory's enthusiasm for such technologies reached back to his days as a U.S. senator, representing Florida, during which he chaired that body's Naval Affairs Committee.

Fortunately for Davis and Mallory, the Confederate military soon won the expertise of other advocates of underwater warfare. During the spring of 1861, talented engineers, military and civilian, had been forced to decide whether to align themselves with the Union or the Confederate war efforts. Ultimately, decisions tended to be made on the basis of home state loyalty. And, serendipitously for the South, that winnowing awarded the Confederacy the services of several key soldier-scientists—chief among them Captain Francis D. Lee, a Charleston architect who, when the war came, became a Confederate Army captain and engineer specializing in the development of torpedoes. The Virginian scientist-engineer Matthew Fontaine Maury, formerly of the U.S. Navy but soon a commissioned captain in the Confederate Navy, was yet another enlistee beneficial to the South's war effort. And, like Lee, Maury soon busied himself developing torpedoes for the Confederacy.

Both men, in their research on torpedoes, built upon the

work of earlier inventors such as Robert Fulton. And both, reflecting a common rationalization across the South, justified the use of such weapons as a matter of practical, underdog necessity. Indeed, one of Matthew Fontaine Maury's daughters later recalled that her father even defended torpedoes on humanitarian grounds. "My mother was not in favor of the use of the submarine torpedoes and thought it barbarous to blow up men without giving them a chance to defend themselves," she recalled. The naval officer softly retorted that he hoped such weapons would reduce the war's duration. Interestingly, Maury was not the first inventor to make that self-serving argument. In 1797, Robert Fulton touted an armed submarine that he aspired to build, for a price, for Napoleon Bonaparte. While making his case, the inventor predicted that after word of "the terror of it [his armed submarine boat]" had spread across Europe, the news would allow France to abandon preparations for a planned invasion of England. In the end, Fulton predicted, his submarine boat would thus usher in an era of peaceable free trade on the world's oceans.

In October 1862, the Confederate Congress passed legislation establishing a torpedo bureau within the army as well as a navy submarine battery service. The U.S. Navy would not establish an equivalent division until 1869. For advocates of underwater warfare, the Confederate military's twin actions marked a signal moment. Past armies and navies had created ad hoc agencies to pursue limited torpedo projects. But this marked the first time that bureaus devoted to underwater warfare had been accorded official permanent status within a military hierarchy.

The sort of self-propelled and even self-guided exploding projectiles that later became associated with the word *torpedo* had yet to be developed when the American Civil War erupted.

The term that best fits these early torpedoes is the modern usage *mine*. Some Civil War–era torpedoes were conical-shaped and left behind to float like buoys to imperil enemy vessels. Still others, often more projectile-shaped, were dragged behind the aggressor ship's stern, or attached to a spar—a long pole—that stretched from the attacking vessel's bow. While these various torpedoes had an assortment of detonation methods, none moved through the water on its own power.

The Confederacy's confidence in torpedoes proved well founded. Ship-to-ship battles—of the sort, say, associated with Europe's Napoleonic Wars—seldom occurred in the American Civil War, and the few that did, even less often resulted in the actual sinking of enemy ships. By contrast, torpedoes— mines—destroyed or sank fifty ships. Testament to the Confederate emphasis on such warfare, torpedoes sank more Union vessels than were owned by the entire Confederate Navy. And testament to the emphasis that the Union *didn't* place on such warfare, during the entire conflict only one Confederate vessel—the CSS *Albemarle*—was sent to the bottom by an enemy torpedo.

During the war, President Lincoln, along with Secretary of the Navy Gideon Welles, Assistant Secretary of the Navy Gustavus Fox, and other high-ranking navy officials, proved themselves to be stalwart proponents of technological innovation. But, in most cases, they and other Union leaders reflected popular misgivings about torpedoes. Indeed, during the conflict, U.S. navy and army forces devoted far more energies to removing Confederate torpedoes from harbors and rivers than to deploying any of their own. A *Harper's Weekly* correspondent, after the destruction of the Union gunboat *Cairo* by a Confederate torpedo in December 1862, captured the U.S. military's ambivalence toward such weapons: "Since the destruction of the Cairo in the Yazoo River there have been fewer jests on the subject. These torpedoes are fired off in various ways—some by electricity, from a concealed station on shore—but more of them by friction . . . The business of seeking for torpedoes and fishing them up is one of the most exciting and perilous duties of our Western sailors."

By contrast, reflecting the Confederate enthusiasm for underwater warfare, the inventor Franklin Smith's newspaper article presented submarine boats and torpedoes as the means by which the South might compensate for its relative shortage of ships compared to those numbers already deployed by the Union Navy. At the Civil War's outset, after all, the Confederacy could claim but ten vessels. The Union Navy had ninety ships. Facing such superior firepower, the Confederacy, hoping to break the Union's blockade of its ports, searched for cheap alternatives to conventional warfare. Results of that search ranged from the deployment of defensive deceptions—*ruses de guerre*—such as the use of false flags by its commerce raiders and so-called Quaker guns, logs painted black to look like cannon. Mostly, however, this Confederate search for some underdog advantage—what a later age would call "asymmetrical warfare"—sought tactics and armaments designed to inflict maximum surprise and casualties among enemy forces.

Moreover, such tactics and armaments offered a psychological multiplier effect, a propaganda value, that often induced Union strategists to exaggerate the actual strength of Confederate forces. Reciprocally, Confederate strategists were aware of that effect and willingly exploited it. Horace Hunley himself, in 1863, wrote to an associate, "I am anxious first and above all for a dead silence on our part, that the enemy may be lost in uncertainty and mystery which is more dreadful than any understood evil of even the greatest magnitude." A submarine boat attack,

Hunley believed, could produce a "panic" among the enemy that could yield triumphs that transcended the destructive effects of any single explosive.

Historian Alex Roland, invoking a familiar biblical story, found in the Civil War duel between the Confederate and Union navies a maritime conflict which pitted the North's Goliath against the South's David. (In a measure of the analogy's aptness, Confederates—reputedly inspired by that same biblical story—gave the name David to a class of torpedo boats.) In the Old Testament story, Roland noted, David compensated for his disadvantages by the surprise use of an unexpected technology—his slingshot. Roland argued that the same Davidian approach to warfare—though without David's satisfaction of a final victory—also animated the Confederacy's war against the superior Union Navy.

And it was that same sort of David-versus-Goliath warfare to which Franklin Smith, in 1861, summoned his Confederate brethren: "From the Chesapeake to the mouth of the Rio Grande, our coast is better fitted to submarine warfare than any other in the world," he wrote. "I would have every hostile keel chased from our coast by submarine propellers." The minister-inventor then went on to venture—with remarkable and prescient specificity—some of his own ideas about the ideal design for such a craft. "The new vessel must be cigar shaped for speed—made of plate iron, joined without external rivets; about thirty feet long, with a central section about 4 x 3 feet—driven by a spiral propeller. The new Aneroid barometer made for increased pressure, will enable the adventurer easily to decide his exact distance below the surface."[2]

During mid- to late 1861 Horace Hunley might have read Franklin Smith's article calling for the Confederacy's development of submarine boats. To be sure, within that same period, Hunley met and befriended James McClintock, a man with whom, for the remainder of his life, his fate would be entwined.

McClintock, thirty-two years old, along with his partner Baxter Watson, co-owned a machine shop in New Orleans on Front Levee Street—near today's Warehouse District—a short walk upriver from Canal Street and the Custom House. During peacetime, the shop had built steam gauges for riverboats. But with the outbreak of war, the shop had won a contract to manufacture bullets for the Confederate Army.

Whether Hunley originated the idea of building a submarine boat and enlisted McClintock and Watson in the project, or vice versa, or whether the three men arrived at the idea simultaneously, will likely never be known. In contemporary letters Watson and McClintock each claimed credit as the project's chief designer. But McClintock, in a later, more modest moment, wrote to a correspondent, "I in connection with others was engaged in inventing and constructing a Sub Marine Boat."[3]

What does seem clear is that by the latter half of 1861, the three men had already begun work on a craft much like that which Franklin Smith had advocated. Moreover, it seems clear that regardless of which of the men conceived the idea of building the boat, during the early stages of work it was the sustaining drive, energy, and personal connections of Horace Hunley that propelled the project. Beyond that, among the three men, McClintock apparently possessed the most formidable background in engineering—certainly more than any that Hunley could have claimed. And based on available evidence—of professional background as well as actual work—McClintock best warrants credit as the project's chief inventor and designer.

Earlier in his life, McClintock—a lean man originally from Cincinnati—had been one of the youngest riverboat pilots on the Mississippi. He was also an engineer, talented and entirely self-taught, with a lively curiosity about advances in science and technology. Within weeks of winning the Confederate government contract job for his and Watson's shop, McClintock, displaying his usual initiative, had plunged into the work and designed and built two bullet-making machines.[4]

Horace Hunley's friendship with James McClintock turned on a shared interest in submarine boats. But the factor that, by the fall of 1861, had transformed Hunley's passion into a resolve to join McClintock and Watson in building such a craft was yet another mutual interest—a hunger for fortune and fame. In April 1861, Confederate president Jefferson Davis, aware of his navy's paltry size, had issued a proclamation offering "letters of marque and reprisal" to private citizens willing to arm private ships and hunt down or capture enemy vessels—either military or civilian ships. Letters of marque were assigned to specific vessels and to their owners. To obtain the document, prospective holders were required to post bonds: $5,000 or $10,000, depending upon whether the vessel's complement was over or under 150 men.

Privateering enjoyed a storied pedigree in U.S. history, reaching back to its use against the British Navy in both the American Revolution and the War of 1812. But by 1856, the practice had fallen into general disrepute internationally. That year, diplomats representing the Ottoman Empire, France, Prussia, Great Britain, Austria, and Sardinia gathered in Paris and signed a treaty banning its use. But U.S. leaders—aware of their own navy's feeble size when compared to those of other great nations—correctly recognized the underdog advantages that accrued from privateering. As a consequence, they declined to join the ban.

In early 1861, however, upon learning that the Confederacy intended to unleash privateers against U.S. ships, President Lincoln dispatched a delegation to Europe with instructions to make the United States a signatory to the 1856 Paris agreement. But the delegation was rebuffed. Too late, they were told. For the time being, the European diplomats insisted, the United States would have to live with the consequences of its earlier refusal to join the ban.

That U.S. diplomatic defeat set the stage for the Confederacy's deployment of privateers and, still later, of armed Confederate Navy commerce raiders acting against U.S. merchant ships. The irony, of course—not lost on Confederate officials— was that the Union's leaders, through diplomatic means, had tried and failed to prevent the South from employing a practice once frequently used by the United States.

In fact, the Confederate Congressional legislation, implementing President Davis's April 1861 proclamation, differed little from privateering bills enacted by the U.S. Congress in 1776 and 1812. Even the amount of the bonds required for letters of marque remained the same. In the U.S. versions of the legislation, however, the vessel's tonnage—whether the craft weighed more or less than one hundred tons—determined whether the prospective privateer paid $5,000 or $10,000.

Like earlier U.S. versions of the practice, Confederate privateering held out lucrative prospects for holders of letters of marque, as well as for the ship's officers and crew. Indeed, almost the entire value of captured ships and their cargoes went, in proportional shares determined by contract, to those responsible for each capture of an enemy vessel.

In accord with international maritime law, tribunals established by the Confederate government—prize courts—were to assess the value of the "prizes"—the captured ships and their cargoes. And because the value of many prizes reached $50,000 and higher, privateering held an obvious appeal for ambitious and adventurous young men such as Hunley and McClintock. Certainly, it dangled the lure of more money than McClintock and his partner Watson could ever reap from their bullet-making enterprise.

While the Confederate government, early in the war, took up calls for torpedo warfare, it seldom encouraged submarine boat construction. Inadvertently, however, such encouragement—at least for a few clusters of private Confederate citizens across the South—came about through Davis's call for privateers.

Torpedoes and submarine boats hardly lent themselves to the *capture* of ships. Therefore, Hunley, McClintock, and Watson assumed—even before their work commenced—that their privateering would perforce be devoted to the violent, take-no-prisoners *destruction* of U.S. Navy warships on Federal blockade duty.

Privateering in its usual course had entailed the capturing of unarmed, civilian merchant ships. Even so, the Confederacy's leaders, in formulating their privateering program, had hoped to encourage at least some of their citizens to attempt attacks on armed military ships. And in tacit recognition that such attacks, if successful, would likely lead to the destruction, rather than the capture, of such armed U.S. Navy vessels, the Confederacy had codified a series of financial incentives tailored to encourage the capture, rather than the killing, of Union sailors.

The government promised to pay a bounty of twenty dollars for each person aboard the defeated vessel at the outset of the attack, plus another twenty-five dollars for each prisoner taken and brought back to port from the same vessel. Additionally, the government promised to pay yet another bounty—of 20 percent of the value of each destroyed ship and her armaments.

But after public response to the call for privateers proved disappointing, the Confederate government soon began commissioning its own raiding ships, vessels such as the CSS *Alabama*, CSS *Florida*, and CSS *Shenandoah*, owned and commanded by the Confederate Navy.[5]

In contemplating their own privateering adventures, Hunley, McClintock, and Watson hoped to win acclaim by punching a hole in the Federal blockade. But given the method of their planned assaults—a torpedo delivered by a small underwater boat—the three hardly expected to take any prisoners. Even so, thanks to the government rewards promised for sinking armed ships, they began their venture with heady expectations of tidy profits. And if their submarine boat proved truly formidable—who knew?—might not the Confederate Navy, in the wake of the partners' initial success, commission these hearty civilian entrepreneurs to build an entire fleet of Hunley-and-McClintock-class submarine boats?

Little is known of Baxter Watson; few documents associated with him exist and his role in the project remains something of a mystery. What is known, however, is that the project's other two partners, Horace Hunley and James McClintock, each brought a lively intelligence to the task of designing and building a submarine boat. But each also possessed distinct assets: Hunley, his vision, his business acumen, and his circle of potential investors; and McClintock, his background in engineering and his sheer joy in tinkering.

The Southern-born Hunley brought a nominal degree of Confederate patriotism to the project. McClintock, however, was a native of Ohio and—at least at the war's outset—presumably burned with no particular passion for the Confederacy. But like Hunley, he did savor the prospects of winning a fortune. He also relished the challenge of designing and building the world's first submarine boat to destroy an enemy vessel. The catch, of course, was that, until they bagged their first prey, these prideful extroverts would have to keep their labors a closely held secret.

3

Men Who Would Practice Assassinations
at the Bottom of the Sea

TAKING THE LEAD in designing the submarine boat envisioned by his two partners, James McClintock hardly began with a tabula rasa. Despite long-standing biases against such vessels and their armaments, world history abounded with efforts to devise what were then widely looked upon as devilish craft capable of defying both gravity and the limitations of human lungs to target with lethal bombs unsuspecting surface ships.

Over the years, designers and inventors had wrestled with the same problems that McClintock soon confronted: Most obviously, for example, once below the water's surface, how does a crew replenish sustaining air to breathe? And after the crew is breathing underwater, how does one navigate that three-dimensional environment? How does the boat's commander orient the craft—and set a course over horizontal and vertical distances within a medium where even routine visual observation is greatly restricted or eliminated?

Moreover, once a course is set, how does a commander adhere to it? How does an underwater craft gain speedy and reliable lateral movement both above and below the water's surface? And how does one control and supply power to, and moderate the velocity of, dives and ascents? Does one use appendages—dive planes and the like—and try to regulate vertical movement exclusively through the manipulation of hydrodynamic factors? Or does one employ ballast tanks and pumps to take in and expel water, and thus control vertical movement through alterations of the craft's weight as it moves through the ocean? Or does one employ some combination of those two approaches?

And what sort of torpedo does one use? Any explosive deployed, after all, must be sufficiently reliable to inspire confidence in its timely detonation, yet deadly enough to sink an enemy ship. And just what sort of system does one employ to deliver that torpedo? Any system implemented, of course, would have to be able to deliver the torpedo against, and destroy, its target. But the system also needed to be safe enough, for those deploying it, to allow the submarine boat and its crew to escape afterward in a single piece.

Moreover—and beyond all of those specific considerations—the submarine boat would have to possess stability. It must be able to stay trimmed, and to withstand all possible problems related to water pressure weighing on itself and its crew. And any design created would need to incorporate sufficient stealth and cunning to take advantage of, and preserve, the singular advantage on which all fears of, and admiration for, all underwater boats originate—the element of surprise. And finally, the boat would need to incorporate safety features—means by which its crew members could escape the craft in the event of a looming catastrophe.

By now it's difficult, if not impossible, for citizens of the twenty-first century to appreciate the chimerical quality of early notions of underwater travel and warfare. Moderns—their images of underwater warfare stoked by generations of popular novels, and films such as *Run Silent, Run Deep, The Enemy Below, Up Periscope, The Hunt for Red October, Das Boot,* and, yes, *20,000 Leagues Under the Sea*—tend to think of submarines as, if not quite speedy, then at least quiet, dependable, and stealthful. And even if the underwater craft presented in such novels and films lack a minnowlike speed and agility, they nonetheless tend to be depicted as reasonably reliable modes of transportation and efficient killing machines.

Prior to World War I, however, submarines, or submarine boats, were anything but efficient. In fact, when they worked at all, they were at best lumbering affairs that created vexing challenges to those who dared to descend into the ocean inside of them. And, finally, with few exceptions, most of those early submarine boats, eschewing grandiose ambitions of science and exploration, had but one single and limited goal: to stay underwater only deep enough and long enough to surprise an enemy ship.

In short, most such craft were designed for one purpose, to kill other mariners. And the limited scope of that singular ambition, meshing with those early vessels' intrinsic mechanical shortcomings, meant that in most cases they operated in relatively safe—often estuarine—environments. Most never dived, nor aspired to dive, to depths greater than twenty or so feet from the water's surface. Thus, the designers of most early submarine boats were exempt from at least one problem that would bedevil their successors: the challenge of designing craft capable of withstanding the tons of water pressure that modern submarines encounter at great oceanic depths.

In 1870—a mere five years after the conclusion of the American Civil War—the French author Jules Verne, in his novel

Twenty Thousand Leagues Under the Sea, captured perfectly that century's ambivalence toward—its repulsion by and fascination with—submarine boats. Verne, after all, presents his novel's protagonist, Captain Nemo, as a bona fide misanthrope. Cynically and cowardly, inside his submarine boat the *Nautilus*, he revels in sneaking up on his prey, conventional surface ships—and, for no good reason, sending them to Davy Jones's locker. But Verne's Captain Nemo is also a beneficent visionary with a richly prescient—and ultimately laudable—appreciation for underwater vessels and all forms of ocean life.

For centuries, inventors had faced the myriad challenges—from breathing and propulsion to the regulation of water pressure and the maintenance of stability and buoyancy—entailed by humankind's long-held Promethean dreams of descending in underwater vessels toward the ocean's briny depths. According to legend, Alexander the Great, prior to his siege of the Phoenician city of Tyre, in today's Lebanon, ordered his army to destroy any underwater obstructions protecting that island port. To better watch his soldiers' activities, Alexander supposedly descended into the sea inside a diving bell whose construction he had ordered—a submarine vessel capable of admitting light and keeping its one-man crew dry.

During the Renaissance, Leonardo da Vinci designed but never constructed a diving suit and snorkel capable, he claimed, of allowing a person to remain underwater for a "protracted period of time." As revealed by the posthumous publication of his notebooks, Leonardo's proposed invention took the form of a diving apparatus that uses cane tubes for underwater breathing. The tubes are attached by leather to steel rings to prevent the tubes from being crushed by water pressure. A face mask is attached to the tubes, which, in turn, are attached to a bell-shaped float designed to keep the pipes' openings above water. Leonardo also claimed to have designed a submarine boat capable of destroying other vessels. Typically, the artist-inventor took an amoral approach toward his military inventions. He suffered no qualms about designing an offensive weapon, and then inventing countermeasures to protect against it. But when it came to his underwater boat, Leonardo drew a line. "I do not publish or divulge my method," he wrote, "because of the evil nature of men who would practice assassinations at the bottom of the sea by breaking the ships in their lower parts and sinking them together with the crews who are on them."

The sixteenth-century English mathematician William Bourne designed but never built what is often considered the first true submarine boat. In his book *Inventions and Devises*, published in 1578, Bourne, a self-educated former gunner in the English Navy, presented plans for a vessel with an enclosed wooden hull, waterproofed by leather hides. The boat's descent beneath the waves was to be regulated by air pumped into or released from leather ballast tanks controlled by screws. Oars manned by a small crew would provide lateral propulsion both above and below the water's surface.

Bourne's basic design was later embraced and improved upon by Cornelis Jacobszoon Drebbel, a Dutch alchemist and inventor. Like Bourne's original design, Drebbel's craft relied on oars for both underwater and surface propulsion. It also featured leather gaskets to prevent water from leaking into the boat. With support from the English government, it was built between 1620 and 1626 and tested on London's River Thames. Although the craft reportedly dived to depths of twelve to fifteen feet, it likely traveled incompletely submerged and, at least on its first test, leaked badly.

Several other attempts to design submarine boats followed in the wake of Drebbel's effort, including those by the Englishman John Day, the Italian Abbe Giovanni Borelli, and three Frenchmen—the priests Marin Mersenne and George

Fournier and an inventor known only as "M.T." Following Bourne and Drebbel, the next major advance in submarine technology came in 1775 during the American Revolution.

That year, David Bushnell, a thirty-four-year-old Yale University graduate, designed and built the *Turtle*, a one-man, pear-shaped, wooden submarine craft. Built in Saybrook, Connecticut, the boat was seven feet high and six feet in diameter. It was constructed from tar-caulked oak staves and reinforced with bands of iron—much like a wooden barrel—and it was the first sub to use screw propellers. Two hand-cranked propellers, on its top and its fore section, provided the *Turtle*'s vertical and horizontal propulsion. An aft rudder, also operated by hand, controlled the boat's direction. Two ballast tanks, each fitted with foot-operated pumps to force water out, regulated buoyancy. Designed to affix a torpedo—a stationary mine—to enemy vessels, it moved across the water's surface with about six inches of exposure.

The *Turtle* swims through the annals of nautical history as the first submarine boat to dive and then successfully return to the surface. It is also remembered as the first underwater craft to attempt—albeit without success—to sink an enemy ship. The episode occurred on September 6, 1776, when the *Turtle*, manned by army sergeant Ezra Lee, was dispatched to insert a torpedo into the hull of the British warship HMS *Eagle*, anchored in New York Harbor. Bushnell's craft was designed to deliver its armament—a 150-gunpower mine—by diving under its prey and, using an augur attached to its top propeller, drilling a hole in the enemy ship's hull. Once the mine was screwed into the hull, the *Turtle* was to move clear of the target. A crude clockwork timer would then detonate the explosive.

However, perhaps due to the curvature of the *Eagle*'s hull, or a possible copper lining attached to it, or simply fatigue, Lee failed to attach the torpedo. In the meantime, British soldiers ashore soon spotted the *Turtle* and dispatched a rowboat to investigate. Fleeing, Sergeant Lee released his bomb, which, due to a malfunction, exploded about an hour later, far clear of the *Eagle*.

Later during the Revolution, again without success, Bushnell himself in his *Turtle*, in Long Island Sound, tried to sink the British frigate *Cerberus*. Still later, during the War of 1812, reports—probably false—persisted of attacks by a second *Turtle* against British ships. Despite the *Turtle*'s mishaps, George Washington, among other national leaders, never lost faith in its inventor's brilliance. "One accident or another was always intervening," Washington wrote to Thomas Jefferson in 1787. "I then thought and still think that it was an effort of genius."[1]

Bushnell's *Turtle* had failed to sink an enemy vessel, but it had affirmed hopes for the offensive value of submarine boats. American inventor Robert Fulton, with the sailing of his Hudson River steamboat the *Clermont* in 1807, won widespread renown as the first entrepreneur to establish a line of commercial passenger ships. Less well known are Fulton's earlier efforts to develop torpedoes and submarine boats for the French and British governments.

The winter of 1799–1800 found Fulton in France at work on a submarine boat. Those labors eventually resulted in the *Nautilus*—namesake of, among other vessels, Captain Nemo's craft in *Twenty Thousand Leagues Under the Sea*. Fulton derived the name from the chambered nautilus, *Nautilus pompilius*, a species of marine mollusk that regulates its ascent and descent in the oceans by taking in and then expelling gases from its segmented chambers. In a December 1797 letter to Revolutionary France's Executive Directory, seeking funds for the boat's development, the inventor wrote of having devised "a Mechanical Nautulus."

Fulton's *Nautilus* stretched twenty-one feet and four inches in length. It possessed a copper-sheathed hull, a collapsible sail, two masts for surface propulsion, and two hand-cranked propellers for underwater power—one propeller for vertical, the other for horizontal movement. An onboard barometer indicated depth of descent. The *Nautilus's* four-man crew, when submerged, was supplied with oxygen by flasks of compressed air.

The *Nautilus* was successfully tested in Paris on the Seine River, then at the Atlantic port of Brest. During the latter trial, the craft, crewed by Fulton and three other hardy souls, reputedly stayed underwater for over an hour. The *Nautilus*— possibly reflecting successive modifications of its weapon system—is variously described as possessing a *Turtle*-like torpedo that it attached to the hull of its prey or as using a torpedo mounted on a spar attached to the submarine boat's bow. Whatever weapon system, or systems, it used, Fulton's craft during its trial at Brest is credited with sinking a forty-foot sloop supplied by none other than France's first consul, Napoleon Bonaparte.

But neither of those feats—nor subsequent equally impressive demonstrations for the British government of the *Nautilus's* abilities—persuaded either state to provide what Fulton considered adequate financial compensation for his invention. Spurned in Europe, Fulton in 1806 returned to the United States, where he soon advised the U.S. Navy on the development of underwater guns. Still later, in New York, with support from the U.S. government, he began work on another submarine boat. This one, the *Mute*, was to have been powered by a steam engine and would have carried a crew of a hundred men. Its length of eighty feet would have been almost four times that of his *Nautilus*. But Fulton's death in 1815 ended construction on the *Mute*, which was left to rot and sink in its moorings.

In the years after Fulton's death, his designs were improved upon by other inventors, among them the American shoemaker Lodner Phillips and the French engineer Brutus de Villeroi. In 1850 the Bavarian Wilhelm Bauer, an officer in that era's German Confederation Army, designed and built the *Brandtaucher* (Fire Diver). Like that of Hunley and his partners, Bauer's initial foray into submarine boat construction was inspired by his desire to pierce an enemy blockade of his country—in his case, Denmark's blockade of northern German ports during the First War of Schleswig (1848–51). As it turned out, the conflict ended with the German Confederation surrendering the state of Schleswig-Holstein to Denmark, before Bauer could enlist. But, determined to develop his submarine boat, Bauer soon joined the army of Schleswig-Holstein.

Twenty-seven feet long, the *Brandtaucher* carried a three-man crew and, like the *Turtle* and *Nautilus*, relied on human muscle to spin its two propellers. A ballast tank took on water when the crew sought to dive. A hand-cranked pump expelled the water when it came time to surface. A sliding weight mounted on an iron track was adjusted to maintain the craft's trimness. The *Brandtaucher* had a short, sausage-shaped hull and a low conning tower at its bow that offered on either side two portholes to admit light.

Bauer's boat made a promising start, diving in tests in the Baltic Sea's Bay of Kiel to depths of more than fifty feet. In 1851, however, during one of those tests, the boat malfunctioned. The *Brandtaucher* plunged fifty-four vertical feet and refused to ascend from the seafloor. After five harrowing hours underwater, Bauer and his crew—leaving their craft on the bottom—barely escaped with their lives.

Four years later, Bauer, on a commission for the Russian Navy, built the submarine boat *Seeteufel* (Sea Devil), which carried a crew of thirteen. Similar in design to the *Brandtaucher*, but with a length of fifty-two feet and beam (its greatest width) of twelve feet, the *Seeteufel* was almost twice the length of Bauer's earlier craft. The *Seeteufel* completed 133 successful dives—including, most memorably, one off Kronstadt, on September 6, 1856, during the coronation of Czar Alexander II. During the dive, musicians aboard for the occasion performed the national anthem. Its 134th dive, however, proved fatal for the *Seeteufel*, as it foundered and sank. Once again, however, Bauer and his crew managed to escape.

Contemporaneous with Bauer's experiments were those of the Spanish inventor Narcís Monturiol i Estarriol. By training, Monturiol was a lawyer; by occupation, a political activist and organizer and publisher of radical journals. So, however improbably, Monturiol came to his passion for submarine boats by way of his revolutionary politics.

That activism gave Monturiol a utopian worldview. And at the core of that vision lay a faith in the humanistic benefits of scientific inquiry. "To comprehend nature in all its parts is the ideal of Science," he would later write, "and it will be the ideal of Humanity just as soon as humankind can break the fetters that keep it subject to the limited atmosphere on earth." In that spirit, he believed that a craft capable of exploring the depths of the world's oceans might unlock secrets of nature beneficial to all humankind. But what specifically propelled Monturiol to design his underwater boat was his observation of the plight of Spain's coral divers—a group sufficiently proletarian to inspire his radical sympathies.

In accord with the benign purposes of Monturiol's imagined boat—to explore the world's oceans and to help those who dive for a living—the craft would be required to travel farther and dive deeper than any other submarine boat then either designed or built. As Monturiol later condemned what he regarded as the limited goals of previous underwater boat inventors, "The most to which they have been able to aspire has been to destroy enemy boats."

But with Monturiol's nominally altruistic objectives came unique design challenges. His craft would require an engine powerful enough to sustain voyages of long, even indefinite, duration. The boat would also have to be designed to allow its hull and crew to withstand the tons of water pressure that bedevil dives to extreme depths. Moreover, the craft's interior would need an air system capable of sustaining human life at great depths and over long periods.

Funding his venture through publicly sold subscriptions, Monturiol eventually designed and built a double-hulled submarine, twenty-three feet in length and eight feet in height, with space for up to six crewmen. Monturiol's creation, the *Ictineo*, was launched from Barcelona in 1859. The boat's name playfully combined the ancient Greek word for *fish* (*icthus*) and Monturiol's own punning alteration of the Greek word for *boat* (*naus*) into *neo*, the Latin word for *new*. Translated, *Ictineo* thus meant "new fish boat."

During trials, the *Ictineo* performed impressively. "The problem of underwater navigation has been completely solved," exclaimed one newspaper. "If this invention can be applied on a large scale, there will be no more shipwrecks," added *El Museo Universal*, an influential journal of culture and science. Indeed, the *Ictineo* soon won Monturiol government patronage for his second submarine boat, the *Ictineo II*, eventually launched in 1864. By then, however, Monturiol's utopian vision of benign underwater navigation had become entangled with the politics and military objectives of his government sponsors—patrons who, in the end, viewed the *Ictineo II* as simply another means for advancing Spain's naval power.

Yearning to reconcile the original utopian spirit of his fascination with underwater navigation with his newly compromised circumstances, Monturiol soon found himself—à la Robert Fulton and Matthew Fontaine Maury—hypocritically espousing the antiwar powers of his designs. "This machine," he wrote of one proposed but never-built craft, "would resolve the difficult problem of equalising the maritime forces of nations, and consequently would have taken a step towards the peace and concord that should rule among civilized peoples." In 1862, a collision with a freighter in Barcelona harbor destroyed the original *Ictineo*. In 1868, the *Ictineo II*, after falling victim to a reduction in government funding, was sold for scrap at public auction.[2]

Perhaps straining credulity, James McClintock later claimed that, at the outset of his efforts in New Orleans to design a submarine boat, he was unfamiliar with similar attempts by David Bushnell, Robert Fulton, and others. Even if that is true, Hunley, McClintock, and Watson were likely aware—at least in a general sense—of earlier efforts to develop such vessels. They also were likely cognizant, if only vaguely, of contemporary projects afoot in civilian and military quarters, in both the Union and the Confederacy, to develop submarine boats. Indeed, by embarking upon the construction of a torpedo-armed underwater vessel, Hunley, McClintock, and Watson had, however unwittingly, become party to an arms race of sorts—a barely, when at all, acknowledged competition between the North and South to become the first state to deploy a submarine boat capable of destroying an enemy ship.

The Confederacy had eagerly taken up the challenge—the U.S. Navy, but reluctantly and ambivalently. Indeed, the Union only joined the race after an opportunity, too promising to decline, had literally washed up on its shores. The French inventor Brutus de Villeroi's first effort to design and build a submarine boat had come in 1832, in Nantes, France. Almost three decades later, in 1859, he arrived in America with plans to build a craft in which he hoped to salvage shipwrecks off the Atlantic seaboard. But before the product of that resolve—an iron boat thirty-three feet in length—could be put to that use, it and its inventor became involved with the American Civil War and the U.S. Navy.

On the evening of May 17, 1861—four weeks after the Confederate shelling of Fort Sumter—observers alerted Philadelphia police to a suspicious-looking craft moving past the city in the Delaware River. But by the time the police got the report the mystery vessel had run aground on Smith Island, close to Philadelphia. The boat's four-man crew was arrested. The next day, reports of the mysterious boat captivated newspaper readers across the country. The Philadelphia *Evening Bulletin* described the craft as "presenting the shape and appearance of an enormous cigar with a boiler iron wrapper."

Inventor Brutus de Villeroi was not among those arrested that day. But within days, local reporters found him extolling the virtues of his submarine boat and yet another craft that he proposed to build for the Union war effort. By then, the arrested crew members had been released, and de Villeroi had delivered his boat to the Philadelphia Navy Yard for inspection by U.S. Navy engineers dispatched by Secretary of the Navy Gideon Welles.

Shortly thereafter, a report by those engineers, endorsing the virtues of the boat they had inspected and the likely military value of the one that de Villeroi proposed to build, reached Secretary Welles. And when Welles failed to take immediate action on the recommendation, de Villeroi, on September 4, penned a letter to President Lincoln. Detailing his proposed vessel's features, his missive concluded, "Sir, should you judge my services to be profitable to the Union[,] I could place myself at your disposal with my boat and a well-practiced crew. And should several boats be deemed necessary[,] I could have them promptly built and their respective crews could be made to practice [on] the original one"—the prototype boat seized on the Delaware River—"during the construction of the others."

President Lincoln, as commander in chief, always kept an eye out for any new weapons that might give the Union an edge over the Confederacy. Beyond that, he was fascinated with new technologies and considered himself an inventor. In 1849, he had patented a design for a device for lifting boats over shoals. Although the device was never manufactured, the experience of designing it had left him with a soft spot in his heart for inventors. Thus, throughout the war, the president relished opportunities to meet, on the back lawn of the White House or at the Washington Navy Yard, with inventors and join them in testing their various new weapons or explosives.

De Villeroi's offer thus impressed Lincoln. On the back of the Frenchman's letter, the president scrawled: "Respectfully submitted to the Navy Department, Sept 7, 1861[.] A. Lincoln." Then he sent the missive down the chain of command. By November, the U.S. Navy had accepted de Villeroi's proposal. Details of the agreement remain murky but, according to one contemporary account, the federal government agreed to pay de Villeroi $10,000 for the use of his concept. The deal also called for him to supervise the boat's construction and, upon its completion, to be its commander. The contract also stipulated that, due to the exigencies of war, de Villeroi's boat must be completed within forty days and at a cost not to exceed $14,000. With de Villeroi supervising, the work would be done by Philadelphia's Neafle & Levy shipbuilding firm.

In the end, however, de Villeroi's submarine boat proved a disappointment for all concerned. By setting a tight deadline for the completion of the Frenchman's craft, the U.S. Navy had hoped to deploy it against the much feared Confederate iron-clad *Virginia*, then nearing completion at Norfolk's Gosport Naval Shipyard. But when the Confederate Navy, on March 8,

1862, finally deployed the *Virginia*, de Villeroi's boat, missing its forty-days-to-completion deadline, was nowhere close to being ready. On June 19, towed by a steam tug, de Villeroi's boat—later named the *Alligator* but never formally commissioned—finally left Philadelphia.

On its maiden voyage, the boat departed Philadelphia carrying orders to destroy a bridge that spanned Virginia's Appomattox River and to assist in clearing the James River of enemy obstructions. In anticipation of such tasks, de Villeroi had equipped his oar-propelled craft with an air lock, a sort of submarine anteroom, a watertight chamber designed to allow divers to enter and leave the craft.

But by June 24, when the *Alligator* finally reached its destination, the proximity of enemy forces on the river's shore and the river's shallow depth, combined with the poor performance of the boat's oar-driven propulsion system and other shortcomings, prevented it from performing any of its tasks. In the wake of the fiasco, the *Alligator* was towed to the Washington Naval Yard to be refitted, prepatory to its next mission, with a hand-cranked propeller.[3]

Still later in the war, in 1863, after the U.S. Congress passed a law allowing for the arming of privateers, a consortium of investors organized the American Submarine Company to take advantage of the new legislation. But President Lincoln subsequently declined to sign the bill into law. And the underwater craft the company commissioned, the *Intelligent Whale*, remained incomplete until 1866—too late to be deployed in the war. Not until 1900, with the gasoline- and electricity-powered USS *Holland*, would the U.S. Navy officially commission its first submarine boat.[4]

By April 1861, when the Civil War erupted, expertise in torpedo construction had become widespread within military and civilian circles on both sides of the Mason-Dixon line. The proliferation of that expertise, if not its actual use—even among Union civilians—is underscored by an incident that occurred in Melbourne, Australia, in January 1864. The crew of the *Mustang*, a visiting U.S. merchant bark from New York, attempted, albeit unsuccessfully, to destroy the also visiting Confederate raider *Shenandoah*, then swinging at anchor in the same harbor, with an improvised torpedo loaded with 250 pounds of gunpowder.

If torpedo-building skills in the North were widely disseminated but seldom used, knowledge of the construction of submarine boats found even fewer avenues for deployment. And in the end, within Union circles, government and private, the building of underwater boats during the war remained fleeting, isolated endeavors.

By contrast, in the Confederacy, the construction of underwater craft, though never widespread, proceeded far more robustly. The activity tended to be concentrated in five key areas: Mobile and Selma, Alabama; New Orleans and Shreveport, Louisiana; and Richmond, Virginia. Though Confederate submarine boat construction often received informal or even official government assistance, it nonetheless remained largely a domain of private citizens. An exception to that trend occurred in Richmond, early in the war, when the Confederate government proceeded with its own attempt to develop an underwater vessel.

The Confederate boat was built in 1861 at Richmond's Tredegar Iron Works and tested in the James River that fall. Designed by William L. Cheeney, a New York–born former U.S. Navy officer who later joined the Confederate Navy, the craft, even now, remains something of a mystery. Though its size and features apparently resembled those of Brutus de Villeroi's *Alligator*, the precise dimensions of Cheeney's boat remain unknown. Nor is it even known whether its construction was ever completed. Much of what is known about this Confederate craft comes from reports of a Union spy: that fall, the spy, a Mrs. E. H. Baker, witnessed a successful test of what she was told "was but a small working model of a much larger one, that was now nearly completed, and would be finished in about two weeks."

A crew of "two or three men" operated the craft. The men, she was told, "are provided with submarine diving armor, which enables them to work under the water and attach the magazine [the torpedo] to the ship intended to be blown up. They then have only to quickly move away to a safe distance, fire their fuse, and the work is done." The object of the attack, she was told, "was to break the blockade and allow the steamers 'Patrick Henry' and 'Thomas Jefferson' out to sea, these vessels being loaded with cotton and bound for England."

During the test witnessed by Mrs. Baker, a scow was towed into the James River. The submarine boat made its way underwater toward the target, and the divers successfully attached a torpedo to the scow. Minutes later, the scow exploded. As the Union spymaster James Pinkerton later recalled Mrs. Baker's account, "The only visible sign of its [the submarine boat's] existence was a large float that rested on the surface of the water, and which was connected with the vessel below." Apparently the "float," painted dark green for camouflage, supplied air to the boat's crew—an ostensible lifeline that would later prove to be the craft's undoing.

Soon after the test run witnessed by Mrs. Baker, the same experimental boat—or a fully realized vessel based upon that smaller prototype—was towed to the mouth of the James River. There, on October 9, 1861, its crew attempted an attack on the USS *Minnesota*, flagship of the North Atlantic Blockading Squadron. But—replicating the *Turtle*'s similar failure—its crew, this time, was unable to attach their torpedo to their target's hull. They skulked back to port empty-handed.

Upon learning of the failed assault, Louis M. Goldsborough, commander of the North Atlantic Blockading Squadron, issued an order demanding that all ships of the squadron be on watch for "submarine infernal machines." The Confederates, he warned, "are said to possess one calculated to be used underwater, and thus to attach a torpedo with a time fuze to a ship's bottom. It is, I understand, to be first towed tolerably near a ship by means of a tug, or else by boats with muffled oars, then to be submerged and so navigated to the vessel against which it is to operate."

Later in the war, according to the spymaster Pinkerton, the crew of the Rebel submarine boat met a nightmarish death after Union sailors happened to notice the craft's green snorkel-like "float" in the water. "I was informed that one of the vessels of the blockading fleet off the mouth of the James River had discovered the float, and putting out drag-rope, had caught the air-tubes and thus effectually disabled the vessel from doing any harm, and no doubt drowning all who were on board of her."[5]

As naval officers on both sides of the conflict eventually realized, the threats posed by submarine craft, and the actual numbers of such boats, often proved more imagined than real. Even today, secrecy shrouds the scattered reports of other submarine boats rumored to have been built both north and south of the Mason-Dixon. Then and now, for instance, vague reports circulated around New Orleans concerning the possible construction there of at least one other Civil War–era underwater craft. However, for Hunley, McClintock, and Watson, the failure of other competitors, real and imagined, to build and deploy such boats only increased their urgency to complete their own vessel.

Generating still more urgency for Hunley, McClintock, and Watson, by the winter of 1862, concerns in New Orleans were increasingly shifting from the Union naval blockade, still in place, to fears of an outright invasion. By late February, ships under the direction of Flag Officer—soon to be Rear Admiral—David Farragut, commander of the recently created West Gulf Blockading Squadron, were gathering at Ship Island, Mississippi, a narrow and barren, seven-mile-long barrier island about one hundred miles southeast of New Orleans.

The West Gulf squadron had been created by a decision in late December 1861 to break the old Gulf squadron into two parts. That action had followed a decision by Secretary of the Navy Welles to try to capture New Orleans via the Gulf of Mexico. Until then, conventional wisdom in U.S. military circles held that because of two downriver fortifications, New Orleans could only be taken by a military assault *down* the Mississippi River, launched from strategic points north of the city. Once the idea of capturing the Crescent City via a naval invasion from the Gulf and up the Mississippi River had been embraced, Welles had named Farragut to lead the invading flotilla.

Flag Officer Farragut—carrying invasion orders from Navy Secretary Welles and sailing aboard his flagship the USS *Hartford*—had reached Ship Island on February 20, expecting to be joined there by a formidable flotilla. Instead, there were only three steamers, all "so disabled" as to be scantly seaworthy. Welles had promised Farragut a squadron of more than thirty vessels. But as Farragut soon learned, most of the promised vessels lay scattered across thousands of square miles of ocean. In the meantime, he could only bide his time until they arrived.[6]

For Horace Hunley and his band of submariners, meanwhile, Farragut's misfortune had won them more time to complete their boat. And who knew? Perhaps in conjunction with the *Manassas* and other Rebel ironclads based, and under construction, in and around New Orleans, and the downriver Confederate guns of Forts Jackson and St. Philip, maybe they could defeat this rumored Union invasion. But that hope rested on an increasingly questionable proposition—that they had sufficient time to complete the boat by which they aspired to overturn all past assumptions about naval warfare.

4

The CSS *Pioneer*

IN THE WINTER OF 1862, James McClintock, Baxter Watson, and Horace Hunley were well on their way toward completing their submarine boat. On the eve of the Civil War, New Orleans—with its total population of 169,000 (144,000 free whites, 11,000 free blacks, 13,000 slaves)—had ranked as the nation's sixth-largest city and the South's largest. Indeed, it was the only Confederate city with a population exceeding 100,000.

Throughout its long, gaudy history, New Orleans had been a city of abundant opportunities. The chance for a fresh start, after all, had drawn Horace Hunley's own father there. Testament to the presence of those opportunities, by 1860 foreign-born immigrants constituted about a third of the city's free population. And by 1862, they and others were scrambling to exploit the latest boom, sparked by the Civil War, to impel the city's capital and energies.[1]

Sweeping up Hunley and his partners, a surge in shipbuilding by private entrepreneurs had been produced by ongoing outrage over what was widely viewed as President Davis and Navy Secretary Mallory's failure to mount a serious naval challenge to the Federal blockade of Louisiana's coast. At least in part, that failure had resulted from the shortage of oceangoing ships available to the Confederate Navy. But it also arose from Confederate assumptions that any Federal attempt to capture New Orleans likely would come downriver, from the north—an assumption that had led to a reluctance by Southern naval strategists to deploy many of their few oceangoing vessels off the Louisiana coast.

Local protests against the Richmond government's perceived quietism soon stirred New Orleans's civic boosters to action. Indeed, spotting what he considered an ironic blessing in the tightening Federal blockade, the publisher-journalist James De Bow naively allowed himself to believe that the blockade would realize his long-cherished dream of a diversified Southern economy. "Every branch of manufacturing is springing up," he wrote to a friend in February 1861.

Focusing on a more specific activity but in a similar spirit of civic celebration, Henry Leovy's New Orleans *Daily Delta*, in October 1861, reported that "some of our wealthiest and most public spirited citizens" hoped to construct a fleet of ironclad boats that would be deployed against the Federal blockaders: "It is proposed to effect a subscription of $2,000,000, and with that sum construct ten steamships . . . here at New Orleans and in the Mississippi River. . . . It is contemplated, after building the steamships to tender them to the Confederate government for the war, with the condition that they should be employed at the mouth of the Mississippi River or in the neighboring waters of the Gulf."

The vague verb *tender* leaves it unclear as to whether the local shipbuilders were trolling for an outright purchase, replete with windfall profits, of their ironclads by the Richmond government, or whether their motives were purely patriotic. But it also seems doubtful that such a project would have gotten far in the New Orleans of that era without the prospects of pecuniary gain for at least some of its involved parties.

Reinforcing the city's swirling laissez-faire ambience, New Orleans claimed a long history of blurring distinctions between military and civilian enterprises, and the political and the pecuniary. Whether it be cotton, sugar, or the latest paramilitary venture, legal or otherwise, setting out from the Crescent City, New Orleans investors—lawyers, bankers, newspaper owners and editors, dockside brokers, and others—were always ready to put their money on a winning horse. In 1836 local investors had purchased bonds to finance the revolt against the Mexican government by U.S. citizens living in the then Mexican province of Texas. And in 1850 they had gladly purchased bonds that supported Narciso López's ultimately ill-fated filibuster to invade Cuba.

Reaching even further back into New Orleans history, the city's business leaders fondly recalled, and romanticized, the privateering escapades of the buccaneer Jean Lafitte. In 1815, during the Battle of New Orleans, the Breton pirate had interrupted his plundering of British and Spanish vessels long enough to come to the aid of General Andrew Jackson's forces.

Amid that rollicking municipal tradition, for many in New Orleans, the American Civil War arrived in the city as just another investment opportunity—a perception demonstrated by the business community's instant and robust response to the Confederacy's call for the outfitting of privateers.[2]

Work on the submarine boat's design had commenced in late 1861, at McClintock and Watson's machine shop at 31 Front Levee Street, not far from the French Quarter. Later, as the actual construction progressed, the work outgrew the Front Levee Street shop. The project then moved to the nearby, and much larger, Leeds Foundry, at the corner of Delord and Constance streets—a few blocks from the waterfront and just upriver of Canal Street—in the district long known as the American Quarter and known today as the Warehouse District.

There were times when it seemed that the boat would never be finished. The Union naval blockade of New Orleans rendered it difficult if not impossible to obtain imported materials and specialized parts for the boat. Adding to difficulties, the labor proved grueling. To render iron malleable, metalsmiths fired it to white-hot temperatures. Only then could workers bend the metal to a desired shape. Workers used hoists and pulleys to lift the resultant iron plates into place. But even with the hoists and pulleys, such tasks in that era still largely depended upon human muscle. Afterward, the workers beat the plates with heavy hammers to complete any shaping or detailing that remained to be done.

The Leeds Foundry spread over an entire city block. In addition to a three-story main building, the operation consisted of sheds and yards, whose openness mitigated some of the heat's discomforts. But those open features at the foundry also created security risks. Most, after all, who engaged in such activities knew that unwanted disclosures were anathema to the business of outfitting privateers. As the New Orleans *Daily Crescent* mused, "Just allow us to hint to the many inquirers, privateering is a private business, and they who embark in it are sufficiently wise and prudent to keep their movements to themselves. . . . Therefore, it will be well to restrain free talk at this moment." Union spies, of course, posed threats. Much of what we know about Civil War–era construction of submarine boats, after all, derives from accounts from spies and deserters. But commercial spies—pro-Confederate private, domestic competitors—also posed a threat to private ventures like Hunley's. Indeed, the speculation continues to persist that at least one other submarine boat was constructed in New Orleans during the Civil War.[3]

No doubt the partners behind Hunley's submarine boat agreed from the start on the need for secrecy around their work. But, its largeness notwithstanding, New Orleans was a hard place to keep secrets secret—particularly if one was a well-known public figure. By virtue of his law practice, his brokerage businesses, and his successive governmental posts, Horace Hunley enjoyed just such local status. But even James McClintock and Baxter Watson by then enjoyed a certain renown, particularly as their wartime bullet-making operation continued to thrive. By the summer of 1861, Henry Leovy's _Daily Delta_ was praising the "inventive genius" the two had brought to their Confederate Army contract work. "They have," the _Delta_ reported on August 17, "built their own machine, and have brought it to such perfection that they can now turn out 10,000 Minie balls of perfect and uniform shape per hour."

All three of the principals in the submarine boat project were cocky young men, aware of the potential historical importance of their venture and the opportunities for personal wealth it presented. Put another way, all three were—by age and circumstances—just the sort who were destined to find it difficult to resist temptations to engage in imprudent braggadocio about their ostensible secret. Reflecting such indiscretion, in that same August 17 _Daily Delta_ story that praised their "inventive genius," the writer—likely Leovy himself—after detailing McClintock and Watson's minié-ball manufacturing operation and other technical achievements, coyly added, presumably with their acquiescence, "There are many others, notice of which we shall defer to another time. We might also say that the ingenuity and enterprise of our citizens have been developed to a degree which will enable us to raise the blockade of our port at will."

Secret or not, as the work on the submarine boat went forward, it proved to be grueling labor. An urgency attended the operation, driven partly by the competitive instincts of the partners, but also by the exigencies of war. Inevitably rumors had reached New Orleans of the imminent conversion of Flag Officer Farragut's squadron from a blockading fleet into a New Orleans–bound invasion force.

Later accounts of the Leeds Foundry activity asserted that the submarine boat was constructed from quarter-inch iron plates cut from old boilers. Those plates, by the same accounts, were then attached to an iron frame. McClintock later described the boat as possessing "a cigar shape." And, according to a later U.S. Navy drawing of the craft, the vessel was thirty-five feet in length with a beam of four feet. An application for the boat's letter of marque put its height at four feet. The craft's middle section, cylindrical in shape, stretched ten feet; the bow and stern were tapered. A manhole at the top of the boat's small conning tower allowed a two- or three-man crew to enter and exit the boat.

A screw propeller cranked by one or two men allegedly powered the craft. Accounts also refer to a vertically hung aft rudder that controlled horizontal direction and side-mounted diving planes on the hull that regulated vertical direction. The latter were said to resemble the pectoral fins of fish. Indeed, contemporary wags—possibly familiar with the work of Narcís Monturiol i Estarriol—dubbed Hunley's craft the "fish-boat."

Allegedly, the ship's commander, who kneeled in the boat's midsection with his head poking into the conning tower, controlled the rudder and the two diving planes. A ballast keel—weighted and detachable from the inside—reputedly allowed the boat to float with its conning tower barely awash. A pump for taking in water and expelling it from a ballast compartment provided additional control over descent and ascent.

The boat apparently carried, as Franklin Smith had advocated, a barometer to indicate depth of descent. But no instrument aboard measured speed. Beyond that, when the crew descended, they found it difficult to know whether they were moving at all. Once underwater, with no way of reliably seeing and no passing objects to visually reveal movement, the men were, for all purposes, blinded. During several tests, the propeller operators continued turning the boat's crankshaft for long periods, only to later discover that the boat, as McClintock recalled in a postwar interview, was "hard and fast in the mud." Indeed, a report, whose facts cannot be confirmed, by William H. Shock, fleet engineer for the U.S. Navy's West Gulf Blockading Squadron, asserted that during those tests, "two contrabands [slaves] . . . were smothered to death" inside the craft.

Unlike other underwater vessels of that era, this boat featured no snorkel-like device for securing fresh air. Nor, for that matter, did it contain, as did Fulton's first *Nautilus*, flasks of compressed air. The crew of this craft would have to survive solely on the ambient air left inside the crew chamber after the boat's hatches were closed.

Of that supply, McClintock later recalled that initially he and an assistant found that the boat contained air sufficient to last them for no more than fifteen minutes. But, he added, "increased confidence came with increased experience." In time— presumably as their cardiovascular systems became acclimated to underwater conditions—they suffered less stress and thereby consumed less oxygen. Soon enough, McClintock claimed, the two "were able to remain below for a period of two hours without suffering any serious inconvenience."[4]

It was in the design of their craft's system for delivering its torpedo that the builders of the submarine boat faced their most

daunting challenge. For in that realm, none of the early pio-
neers of submarine technology—from Bourne to Bushnell, Fulton to Bauer—had managed to develop an entirely satisfactory
method for delivering the torpedo to an enemy ship's bottom—
or, for that matter, for detonating the bomb.

At the Civil War's outset, those who sought to engage in underwater warfare faced three choices among torpedo delivery
systems. The torpedo could be mounted at the end of a "spar"
(a long pole); it could be attached by mechanical means, such as
an augur, as conceived by Bushnell; or—probably the most dangerous of the three systems—the torpedo could be towed by
rope behind the submarine's stern. The idea behind the latter
system was that while the boat dived beneath the enemy ship,
the torpedo would trail behind and rise by natural buoyancy to
strike the hull of its target.

Beyond the selection of a torpedo delivery system, a decision had to be made between torpedoes that detonated on
impact—fitted with a contact fuse—or those ignited by an electrical charge. Or, declining those two options, one could use a
torpedo that employed clockwork to trigger its detonation following a set passage of time.

In the end, the partners in New Orleans apparently elected
to employ for their craft a torpedo that was dragged by a rope
behind the boat's stern. The method by which that torpedo was
detonated, however, remains unclear.

Initial tests of the craft in the nearby New Basin Canal revealed
some leaks that were easily plugged. But by early February 1862, the boat—by then painted obsidian black to conceal
its presence underwater—was ready for more thoroughgoing
tests. John K. Scott, a former riverboat captain and a friend of
Hunley's from the Custom House, had already been recruited

as the craft's commander. Scott's apparent background as a naval commander presumably gave him a panic-proof ability to handle any emergencies that might befall the craft. He also possessed a handy expertise in diving and was comfortable in that era's "submarine armor," a forerunner to modern scuba gear.

For further trials, the partners towed their craft down the three-mile-long New Basin Canal (later filled in to create an earlier version of what is now Interstate 10) to the waters of spartina-marsh-encircled Lake Ponchartrain. As much tidal lagoon as lake, Ponchartrain's shallow, brackish waters—no more than fourteen feet deep in most places—spread over more than six hundred square miles. The lake was connected to Lake Borgne at its eastern end; and Lake Borgne, in turn, had a direct opening to the Gulf of Mexico. Put another way, Lake Ponchartrain offered as benign a test environment as the partners were likely to find.

Even so, the trials on Ponchartrain soon revealed problems with the craft more intractable than simple water leakage. Fundamental shortcomings plagued the boat's design. Among other vexations, if any member of the craft's two- or three-man crew left his assigned position and moved a few inches fore or aft, it slipped off keel. Still other problems bedeviled navigation and propulsion. Despite those difficulties—though woefully little is now known about the craft—McClintock later claimed in a postwar letter that "the Boat demonstrated to us that we could construct a Boat, that would move at will in any direction desired, and at any distance from the surface."

Its shortcomings notwithstanding, Hunley, McClintock, Watson, and Scott considered the boat, eventually christened the *Pioneer*, seaworthy. Or, more accurately, lakeworthy: performance shortcomings rendered the vessel ill suited for running in the open ocean with its depths and tidal challenges—or for that matter in the Mississippi River with its confounding, forceful currents. Conveniently, however, the *Pioneer*'s test waters, Lake Ponchartrain, offered at least two lucrative targets: the Union steamers *New London* and *Calhoun*, which, as McClintock recalled, had both "been a menace on the lake."[5]

Accordingly that spring of 1862, Captain Scott applied to the Confederate government for a letter of marque. Scott's letter referred to "a submarine boat called the Pioneer." The partners, one assumes, were aware that their craft would, in all likelihood, get no closer to any ocean than its usual Lake Ponchartrain domain. Even so, in his letter seeking the privateering license, Scott expressed an expansive vision of the *Pioneer*'s future, seeking "authority to cruise the high seas, bays, rivers, estuaries, etc. in the name of the Government." The *Pioneer* would "aid said Government by the destruction or capture of any and all vessels opposed to or at war with said Confederate States, and . . . aid in repelling its enemies."

To assure that his letter reached the proper authorities in Richmond, Scott sent it to the Confederacy's recently installed secretary of state, Judah Benjamin, the former New Orleans lawyer, former U.S. senator for Louisiana, and former law partner of Leovy's *Daily Delta* co-owner, Pierre Bonford. (It was indeed a small world in which these men operated, and within it all roads led back to Canal Street.) Then, leaving nothing to chance, Scott—doubtless at Hunley's behest—arranged for the application letter to be sent as an enclosure within a missive from a mutual friend of Hunley and Benjamin, Francis Hatch, that reliable political wire-puller of the Canal Street Custom House. Confederate officials granted the *Pioneer*'s letter of marque on March 31, 1862. Eschewing the boat's actual name, the commission referred to it only as a "submarine propeller" armed with a "Magazine of powder." The designation made the *Pioneer* an official government-sanctioned privateer and thus entitled it to append the prefix *CSS*—Confederate States Ship—before its name. As it turned out—with doleful portent for techno-nautical dreamers across the Confederacy—the *Pioneer* would be the only submarine boat during the entire war to be accorded a letter of marque and its attendant authorization to employ the *CSS* prefix.

Officials granted the letter of marque after the *Pioneer*'s owners posted a $5,000 bond. Listed as sureties on the bond were Horace Hunley and another, newer investor, Hunley's friend Henry Leovy. Earlier documents associated with the application had listed Hunley's wealthy brother-in-law Robert Barrow along with McClintock and Watson as the boat's "owners." But their names failed to appear on the actual letter of marque issued by the Confederate government.

McClintock's and Watson's names failed to appear on the final document, probably because neither man was wealthy, and in the end, both likely found themselves unable to deliver on their promised financial commitments to the project. The disappearance of Barrow's name, however, is likely due to another cause, one unrelated to finances.

True to the tenets of the Whig Party to which Barrow formerly belonged, he had a personal history of supporting what that age quaintly called "internal improvements." His canal investments bore witness to that faith. In short, he was receptive to new technologies, particularly those he deemed likely to yield him personal profits. Moreover, he possessed sufficient wealth to fund a hundred submarine boats as a sole investor.

Why then did Barrow apparently have second thoughts about the *Pioneer*? We can only speculate. Perhaps the ongoing antipathy of this philosopher-king to the secessionists who had brought on this war led him to withdraw his commitment to the

project. Or, then again, perhaps Barrow the businessman simply had lost faith in the boat as a venture worthy of his money.

Little is known about the activities of the *Pioneer* before or
after it received its letter of marque. There are, of course, those
unconfirmed reports of the deaths of two crew members during
the craft's early trials. And another contemporary source attests
that—before or shortly after winning its privateer status—the
little boat blew up a barge on one of its Lake Ponchartrain tests.
But it seems unlikely that the *Pioneer* ever attempted to attack
an actual enemy ship, if for no other reason than there simply
wasn't enough time.[6]

The other warships of Flag Officer David Farragut's invasion
squadron eventually reached Ship Island. And, in late April
1862, his ships easily defeated the once feared guns, downriver
from New Orleans, of Forts St. Philip and Jackson. The
squadron that Volumnia Hunley called "the Invincible Armada
of Lincoln" soon sailed, unmolested, toward New Orleans.
Leading a combined force of more than forty vessels, Farragut—along with soldiers commanded by General Benjamin F.
Butler—captured New Orleans on April 28, a mere four weeks
after the *Pioneer* had received its letter of marque.

On the eve of Farragut's arrival in New Orleans, Horace
Hunley, James McClintock, and Baxter Watson, fearing their
invention might fall into enemy hands, scuttled the *Pioneer*
in the New Basin Canal. Then—determined to renew their
venture—they set off overland for the next major Confederate
port east of New Orleans: Mobile, Alabama.[7]

PART II

MOBILE

Spring 1862–Summer 1863

5

The *American Diver*

HORACE HUNLEY, James McClintock, and Baxter Watson reached Mobile in the spring of 1862. For the three, the Gulf port promised, if nothing else, a fresh start. Reinforcing that perception, the stream of refugees arriving in Mobile soon also included the partners' old wire-puller friend from the New Orleans Custom House, Francis Hanson Hatch, who, in turn, retained all of his ties to powerful leaders across the Confederacy.

In Mobile, all three partners plunged into their work. Hunley's characteristic self-confidence even led him into military matters only barely related to submarine boat building. An April 30 Hunley letter finds him proffering advice for improving the city's defenses along the Alabama River. In his suggestions, Hunley gave free rein to the same quixotic spirit of technological improvisation—and delight in basic geometry— that had enlivened earlier projects such as his ledger book dream of building an octagonal brick tower in New Orleans. Taking a page from recent design innovations incorporated into Confederate ironclads such as the *Manassas* and the *Virginia*, he urged those in charge of the city's river defenses to ponder "the use of iron walls that cannot be penetrated instead of brick or sand that can be"; and along those walls to consider "the presentation of an <u>obtuse</u> angle to the fire of an enemy by which balls are glanced, losing nearly all of their effective force."

But, Hunley's enthusiasm and the presence of Francis Hanson Hatch notwithstanding, Mobile did present problems for the three young men from New Orleans. In many ways, after all, the Crescent City had been Hunley, McClintock, and Watson's oyster. But this was a different city. More to the point, Mobile had its own cabal of Confederate political and military leaders. And for these newcomers from New Orleans, suddenly plopped down in Mobile, this Alabama port presented formidable challenges. Here, so close to and yet so far from New Orleans, the three would have to fend for themselves. They would have to make new friends, new allies, and new deals.

Mobile traced its origins back to a French settlement founded along the Mobile River in 1702. Following a series of floods, the town moved to a location along the northwestern edge of Mobile Bay. In 1763, at the end of the French and Indian War, Mobile became a British possession. During the American Revolution, Spanish forces seized the town. Not until 1813, after its capture by American forces, did Mobile fall under Old Glory's dominion. During the 1850s and '60s, the Deep South's cotton boom made Mobile, thirty miles from the Gulf of Mexico, one of the four busiest U.S. ports. And by 1860, that same surge had also boosted the city's population to 29,000—21,000 whites, 800 free blacks, and 7,500 slaves.

Mobile was a fifth the size of New Orleans. But in its polyglot diversity, the coastal Alabama port mirrored that of the larger port to its west. Indeed, to this day, Mobile hosts a Mardi Gras celebration that, local boosters insist, antedates that of New Orleans. An English visitor in 1861 described Mobile as "the most foreign looking city I have yet seen in the States." In the city's market, he saw "Negroes, mulattoes, quadroons, and mestizos of all sort, Spanish, Italian, and French, [all] speaking their own tongues, or a quaint lingua franca, and dressed in very striking and pretty costumes."

More to the point, for Hunley and his partners, Mobile, after New Orleans's capture, was the only remaining major Confederate port still open on the Gulf, with functioning rail and river links to the South's interior. Even so, unlike New Orleans, Mobile did not loom large as an industrial center. And, for that reason, Union strategists considered the act of blockading the city's namesake bay of more importance than any occupation of the actual city.

North to south, Mobile Bay stretched some thirty-two miles. East to west, at its widest breadth, it reached twenty-two miles. In most places it was no more than twelve feet deep. The bay's dredged main shipping channel, used by deep-draft oceangoing ships, passed through an opening along the estuary's eastern edge. Three forts guarded the bay, but the sturdy, pentagonal-shaped Fort Morgan, which guarded that main shipping channel, posed the most formidable threat to Union ships.[1]

As events turned out, it was well for them that Horace Hunley and his partners had fled New Orleans. Indicative of the new order established by the Union occupation of the Crescent City, by that May General Benjamin F. Butler, commander of those U.S. forces, had established his headquarters in a suite of second-floor offices in the same Custom House building in which Horace Hunley and Francis Hatch once toiled.

Lest New Orleanians should fail to understand that a new regime reigned over the city, days after its capture by the Union, General Butler set an example for the local citizenry. He ordered the hanging, from the Federal Mint Building, of a Confederate partisan who had removed Old Glory after it had been raised over that and other public buildings, including the Custom House. Adding further insult to Rebel pride, the top— the third—floor of the Custom House, previously unoccupied, became Federal Prison No. 6—home, during one stretch, to as many as two thousand Confederate soldiers.

Equally devastating, the Federal occupation brought to ruin Louisiana's sugar and cotton economy. Union forces confiscated or otherwise disrupted productive operations on lands belonging to Barrow, Hunley, and the state's other planters. In 1861, before the Union naval blockade had become truly effective and before the Federal invasion, the state's sugar planters, from the cultivation to the marketing of their crop, had experienced a bumper harvest. Indeed, that year, the combined yield of Louisiana's 1,291 plantations had come to 495,410 hogsheads of sugar, with a total value of $25 million. By contrast, the 1862 sugar harvest—reflecting the impact of the Federal invasion— would come to a paltry 87,000 hogsheads, with a value of $8 million, roughly a two-thirds drop in total value over the previous year.

But even before New Orleans fell to the forces of Flag Officer Farragut and General Butler, Horace Hunley had already grown disenchanted with the Confederacy. Weeks before Union forces captured New Orleans, in a letter to her husband Robert Barrow, Horace's sister had chastised her husband and brother for joining the "the decriers of our [Confederate] President," who to her mind "are doing wrong": "When I hear Horace or yourself speak against our President and Government and 'others too' it hurts me worse than for us to lose a battle," she wrote. "I wish I could convince yourself and Horace of what my own instinctive sense of right teaches me in this regard but if I cannot, at least let me beg of you to cease talking against our President and Government."[2]

No doubt some of Horace Hunley's antipathy toward the Confederate government may be attributed to the influence of Robert Ruffin Barrow. Hunley was, after all, like his brother-in-law, a sugar planter—albeit on a far more modest scale—and thus would have been receptive to Barrow's self-interested arguments about the dangers the Confederacy posed for import tariffs protecting the South's sugar crop and for slavery itself.

Hunley's hostility toward the Confederacy also likely resulted from what the partners early on perceived as governmental indifference, and later as hostility, toward their queries seeking support for their submarine boat project. Such attitudes within civilian and military circles resulted from the technological novelty, in that era, of submarine boats, as well as the presumed violations by such vessels of traditional codes of warfare.

Compounding problems for the submarine boat partners was the fact that the craft that they advocated—a privateer submarine boat—failed to fit squarely into the domains of either the Confederate Army or Navy. From their project's commencement, the partners were destined to be swept into the interservice rivalries that bedeviled relations between the Confederate Army and Navy. Exacerbating such tensions, the Confederate Army operated the so-called brown-water navy, which generally controlled all operations on the Confederacy's rivers. The navy, by contrast, oversaw most operations on the Confederacy's coast and on the high seas.

It was thus at Mobile and the Confederacy's other ports—in most cases, estuaries where rivers met the sea and where the army's and navy's theaters overlapped—that tensions grew most intense. Creating further difficulties for the three men, except for Hunley's experience commanding the *Adela* on its trip to Cuba, none of the submarine boat partners, so far as any located records attest, had any experience commanding, or even sailing aboard, oceangoing vessels. So far as records indicate, even the career of McClintock, the most seasoned sailor among the partners, had been confined to rivers. And the Confederate Navy officers whom the partners entreated for support surely took due notice of that deficiency in experience. Perhaps more pertinently, none of the submarine boat partners had, or had managed to enlist a commander for their proposed craft who could claim, knowledge of Mobile's *local* waters—river, estuary, or Gulf.

The identities of the investors in the partners' second submarine boat venture remain unknown. Whether the three original partners simply drew on the same funding sources who had capitalized the *Pioneer* or whether they reached out to other investors remains unknown. But soon after reaching Mobile, the three men did receive their first bona fide official Confederate government assistance. Any help, of course, would have been welcome. But, in this case, its source made it doubly so. The offer came from Major General Dabney Herndon Maury, the recently appointed commander of Confederate Army troops in and around Mobile and the surrounding Department of the Gulf.

Forty years old, Maury was a generational peer of Hunley and his partners. He had close-cropped hair, a bushy goatee, and a mustache. A native of Virginia and a graduate of the University of Virginia, Maury had also studied at West Point. He had seen military action in the Mexican War and, as a member of the Confederate Army, fought in places such as Pea Ridge, Arkansas, and Corinth and Vicksburg, Mississippi. A man of lively and varied interests, he was the author of *Tactics for Mounted Rifles*, a standard textbook on that topic. Further endearing the general to the submarine partners, Dabney Maury was a nephew of Matthew Fontaine Maury, the Confederate naval officer and scientist renowned for his devotion to the development of torpedoes. In fact, upon the death by yellow fever of Dabney's father—U.S. Navy officer John Minor Maury—when Dabney was just two years old, Matthew Maury had stepped in to bring up the boy.

At least partially then, Dabney Maury's enthusiasm for underwater warfare resulted from interests stirred by his famous uncle. But other, more immediate circumstances also prompted Dabney Maury's receptivity to the ideas presented by the three refugees from New Orleans. Like them, General Maury was new to Mobile, having only arrived that May, but it had not taken him long to acclimate himself to his new command.

Confederate forces in Mobile in May 1862 had reasonably feared an imminent repetition of the Union naval invasion that, weeks earlier, had captured New Orleans. But, unbeknownst to most Southerners, the same orders from U.S. Secretary of the Navy Gideon Welles that had sent Farragut to New Orleans had also commanded him to reduce the Confederate redoubt at Vicksburg, Mississippi, and then—and only then—to capture Mobile. Welles's orders failed to appreciate the immensity of each of those three tasks. Nor did they recognize the time and resources that each demanded.

For his part, had Flag Officer Farragut had his way, after securing New Orleans, his armada would have immediately sailed for Mobile. But instead, obeying Welles, Farragut and most of the vessels under his command—operating above New Orleans on the Mississippi River—squandered the coming months on a series of futile attempts to capture Vicksburg.

In Mobile, meanwhile, as it became clear that Farragut had been dispatched to Vicksburg, his fleet's movements lured many Confederate strategists into a false confidence. They came to believe that Mobile—at least for the foreseeable future—faced no threat of capture. To be sure, a sufficient number of Farragut's vessels remained along the Gulf coast to keep the Union blockade in place. No Rebel steamer, civilian or military, entered or exited the bay that season. But other than that, all seemed calm. "I cannot perceive in any direction hereabouts indications of an early attack upon Mobile," General Maury wrote to a fellow officer.

Free of such concerns, many Confederate strategists had, over those months, allowed themselves to nourish bold dreams of taking the offensive against the Union's land and naval forces. Some—including Dabney Maury—even contemplated a Confederate recapture of New Orleans. Integral to such bravura visions was the edge, many Confederate strategists believed, that new naval technologies afforded the South.

More specifically, the commanders at Mobile eagerly anticipated the completion of a series of ironclads then under construction. In particular, Maury awaited the delivery of two ironclads then being built at nearby Selma, two hundred miles northeast of Mobile up the Alabama River. "Were the two ironclads, the Nashville and the Tennessee, now ready for service," Maury boasted, "we could probably capture and hold New Orleans."

If—as one report later claimed—two men had died during the tests of the *Pioneer*, Hunley, McClintock, and Watson apparently never mentioned those deaths to General Maury. Certainly, however, they told the general of their successes with the boat "for running under the water, at any required depth from the surface." And in the end, Maury, whatever they told him, liked what he heard.

Though a civilian vessel, the *Pioneer*, as a registered privateer, had fallen squarely under the domain of the Confederate Navy. This new boat for which the partners attempted to enlist support in Mobile not only had no registration, it also remained unclear whether it would enjoy army or navy affiliation. Further complicating matters, as an unbuilt, essentially hypothetical craft, it lacked even the physical tangibility—the presence—that might have elicited a prompt decision about its status.

Lines of authority ran a muddled course through the Byzantine civilian and military bureaucracies of the Confederacy. In that murky milieu, it could be difficult, if not impossible, to determine where one command ended and another began. Army versus navy—land versus sea—turf battles only thickened the muddiness. Logic and protocol, for instance, would have suggested that Horace Hunley and his associates make their entreaty concerning the construction of a submarine boat to the naval officer who commanded Mobile's naval forces.

But in this case and so many others, politics trumped logic and protocol. Typifying a tendency of the civilian-controlled Confederate War Department to give precedence to land over naval forces, Maury enjoyed broader powers than did his naval counterpart in Mobile, Admiral Franklin Buchanan. Exercising that advantage, General Maury—bestowing his blessings and more upon their project—eventually dispatched the New Orleans trio to the Park and Lyons Machine Shop, at the corner of State and Water Streets, close to Mobile's harbor.[3]

There, Hunley, McClintock, and Watson met the shop's owners, Thomas W. Park and Thomas B. Lyons. And inside that shop, McClintock and Watson found men at work on labors that must have conjured memories of their own New Orleans shop's government-contract manufacturing of minié balls. The Park and Lyons shop was busy with its own government-ordered work—in this case, the boring out of the barrels of hundreds of old rifles to make them compatible with larger-caliber ammunition already in Confederate hands.

For McClintock and Watson, observing this shop, however hot and humid, humming with government-funded work must have served as a bittersweet reminder of their own more prosperous days. And Horace Hunley too, that day, likely had finances on his mind. In New Orleans, by dispatching the *Pioneer* to a watery grave, the three men had also effectively scuttled any immediate prospects of finding a fresh batch of investors for the submarine boat they hoped to build in Mobile. Whether or not they asked for Confederate financial assistance during their meeting with General Maury is unknown. What *is* known, however, is that no money was forthcoming.

But while General Maury offered no financial support for the submarine boat, he did offer the partners the loan of a technically gifted army officer under his command, as well as a group of stalwart subordinates. The officer, whom the three soon met, was Lieutenant William A. Alexander, a British-born mechanical engineer. The London native had emigrated to the United States in 1859 and soon found his way to Mobile. In 1861, when the Civil War commenced, he enlisted in an Alabama regiment. Later—along with members of the Twenty-first Alabama Infantry Regiment, which had suffered heavy losses at the Battle of Shiloh—Alexander had been assigned to temporary duty on the rifle conversion project at the Park and Lyons Machine Shop. Upon meeting the three newcomers from New Orleans, however, General Maury ordered Alexander to end his supervision of the rifle-boring work and to devote himself and the labors of his men to the submarine boat.[4]

At the Park and Lyons shop, Hunley, McClintock, and Watson were thus joined by their three new collaborators: Thomas W. Park, Thomas B. Lyons, and William A. Alexander. The expanded group proved to be an efficient team. Even so, work conditions were far from ideal. As had been the case in New Orleans, in Mobile, the demands of war forced the submarine boat partners onto a schedule that rushed the craft's construction and afforded them little time to conduct necessary trial runs.

As they finalized a design for their boat and burrowed into the labors of building it, William Alexander, with his background in mechanical engineering, proved a particularly gifted member of the team. Likewise, the Park and Lyons shop proved well suited for the work. Like the Leeds Foundry in New Orleans, the Park and Lyons shop offered, beyond its main building, a cluster of roofed but open-sided structures and open yards. And like the New Orleans operation, the Park and Lyons shop's architectural configuration mitigated some of the grueling heat that attended the construction process.[5]

Unlike those associated with the *Pioneer*, all descriptions and images of the partners' second craft—even its dimensions—must be regarded as suspect. No contemporary, working plans for or images of the boat have been located. Even so, we do have a reasonably sound idea of what the craft looked like and how it worked.

Like the *Pioneer*, the new submarine boat—generally called the *American Diver* and less frequently the *Pioneer II*—used a screw propeller for lateral propulsion and, to guide that lateral course, a vertical-hung aft rudder. But as the new craft took shape in Mobile, its designers sought to incorporate into it improvements over its predecessor.

James McClintock later recalled the *American Diver* as being thirty-six feet long. That would have made it a foot longer than the *Pioneer*. At four feet at its highest level, the craft would have matched the height of its predecessor. But with a width of three feet, it would have been a foot narrower than the *Pioneer*.

Elliptical in shape, the *American Diver*'s twelve-foot midsection flowed into tapered end sections of that same length. And, according to McClintock, it was through that hydrodynamic design that the *American Diver* trumped its predecessor: "Twelve feet of each end was built tapering or molded, to make her easy to pass through the water." And while narrower than the *Pioneer*, the new boat's design apparently created more interior space for the crew than the *Pioneer* offered. And that enlarged interior chamber allowed the new boat to accommodate a larger crew—five men, as opposed to the *Pioneer*'s two or three.

Among the New Orleans refugees who found their way to Mobile that spring was John K. Scott, Hunley's old customhouse friend and, more recently, captain of the late CSS *Pioneer*. In Mobile, Scott soon resumed his command role aboard the partners' new craft. In the eventual tests of the *American Diver* conducted in Mobile Bay, Captain Scott found that, when running near the surface, he could visually orient himself by gazing out the two circular glass windows on either side of the craft's conning tower. But once the boat descended, he found it difficult, if not impossible, to determine direction. Fully developed periscopes for submarines, after all, would not appear until 1902.

McClintock in a postwar letter to Matthew Maury recalled the problem: "As we was unable to see objects, after passing under the water, the Boat was steered by a compass, which at times acted so slow, that the Boat, would at times alter her course for one or two minutes before it would be discovered." Such misdirection, McClintock recalled, forced Scott to resurface "more frequent[ly] than he otherwise would."

The *Pioneer* had suffered from its reliance on human propulsion. To remedy that shortcoming, McClintock soon began trying to install or build (accounts of the effort are vague) what he called an "Electro Magnetic" engine for the *American Diver*. Reliable electric motors did not appear until the early twentieth century. Even so, nineteenth-century scientists—reaching back to English physicist Michael Faraday during the 1820s—had experimented with such engines powered by electrical current produced by chemical batteries. Records of McClintock's own apparent efforts in that realm are long lost, and the extant evidence, however tantalizing, is exasperatingly scant and vague.

To be sure, the Union's naval blockade of Southern ports rendered it difficult to obtain the specialized parts needed to build such an engine. In a postwar interview, McClintock complained of how "every necessary commodity was only attainable at an enormous expense and with great difficulty." And in a postwar letter to Matthew Maury, McClintock recounted how he had wanted the *American Diver* to overcome the propulsion problem that had hindered its predecessor vessel. "Our chief difficulty [with the *Pioneer*] was [a] want of speed, and to obtain this I spent much time and money, upon an Electro Magnetic Engine, but was unable to get sufficient power to be useful." Yet another source, Admiral Franklin Buchanan, alluded in a contemporary letter to "getting a man from New Orleans who was to have made the 'Magnetic Engine.' "

The paper trail of McClintock's activities that season is now lost to posterity. But—curiously, given Buchanan's reference to "a man from New Orleans"—it so happens that J. G. Wire, a New Orleans inventor, had registered a "Machine for operating Submarine Batteries" that December with the Confederate Patent Office in Richmond. The term *battery* preceded by the word *submarine* in that era tended to connote battery as in ordnance rather than electricity. But in this case, the phrase, rendered in its entirety ("a machine for operating . . ."), clearly seems to refer to an underwater boat. Given that, it seems reasonable to presume a likely—though for now unproven—link between the New Orleans inventor and McClintock's efforts in Mobile.

After the failure of McClintock's efforts to install an electric motor in the *American Diver*, he apparently attempted to outfit the vessel with a steam engine. But that effort also proved unsuccessful. The records of McClintock's steam engine efforts remain as obscure as those of his electric motor gambits. But practical steam engines were, of course, well developed by the 1860s. They propelled many of the world's ships. Admiral Buchanan, writing of that period, recalled a steam engine being "removed" from the *American Diver*. McClintock apparently failed to install a steam engine because the boat's construction was already substantially complete and its shape and dimensions, as well as its propulsion and ventilation systems, had been fashioned for a very different sort of engine. In frustration, seeking a workable propulsion system, McClintock—with the demands of war pressing on him—reverted to the tried and true. "I afterwards fitted cranks, to turn the propeller by hand, working four men at a time." Contemporary documents offer scant information on the intended torpedo modus operandi of the *American Diver*. But in a February 1863 letter, Admiral Buchanan noted that the "torpedo or explosive machine was to have been towed by a rope from the Boat [the *American Diver*] and when under the vessel [the enemy ship] was to have been exploded."[6]

By the winter of 1863 the *American Diver*'s sponsors were ready to test their new boat. In constructing their craft, Hunley,

Watson, and McClintock had found an eager ally in General Dabney Maury. But now, six months later, seeking to deploy their completed boat, the men's expanded partnership would have to pass muster before the officer who commanded Mobile's naval defenses. And as they soon discovered, in Admiral Franklin Buchanan they faced a far tougher, more skeptical, judge of their project than General Maury.

At sixty, Buchanan was more than a generation older than Hunley and his partners. Put bluntly, the admiral, unlike General Maury, was old enough to consider the young men foolishly naive. Even so, a cursory perusal of Buchanan's career might have given the partners confidence that he would ultimately approve the *American Diver*'s deployment. Buchanan—his friends called him Buck—was a gruff, no-nonsense, clean-shaven, balding man with a hawkish nose. Irascible, he tended to perceive matters in black and white: a person or an idea was either good or bad. Prior to his Confederate naval service, Buchanan had served for forty-four years in the U.S. Navy. He had been the founding superintendent of the U.S. Naval Academy at Annapolis, had served as second in command on Matthew Perry's expedition to Japan, and had been commanding officer at the Washington Navy Yard.

While officers of his vintage often resisted innovations in naval technology and weaponry, that generalization seemed not to apply to Buchanan. In the winter of 1862—before his promotion to admiral's rank—he had sought and won the coveted command of the state-of-the-art ironclad *Virginia*, then emerging at the Norfolk navy yard from the burnt hull of the Union frigate *Merrimack*.

On March 8, Buchanan commanded the *Virginia* in Hampton Roads on its first day of action. Over those hours, the Confederate ironclad sank two Union warships, the *Cumberland* and *Congress*. A wound suffered that day—later determined to be non-life-threatening—persuaded Buchanan, reluctantly, to relinquish his command of the *Virginia*. Otherwise he would have commanded the ironclad the next day during its duel with the Union ironclad, the *Monitor*—certainly the most celebrated naval battle of the entire war.

Buchanan spent two months in a Norfolk hospital recovering from his wounds, all the while basking in universal praise from across the Confederacy for the heroism he had shown in the Battle of Hampton Roads. Promoted to the rank of admiral in August, he reported the following month to his new command in Mobile. There he was placed in charge of the naval squadron in Mobile Bay as well as the naval district of the Gulf—roles in which he oversaw a tiny squadron never composed of more than a few vessels. Narrowing his focus still more, soon after assuming his new command, Buchanan found himself preoccupied with a single ship, the 209-foot-long ironclad *Tennessee*, newly constructed and widely perceived to be a technological marvel. In fact, many considered the *Tennessee* to be the key to vanquishing the Federal blockading squadron off Mobile—and even recapturing New Orleans.

Knowing only that background, Hunley and his partners—proffering the services of their own technological marvel to the crusty old admiral—might have reasonably expected Buchanan to offer them a welcoming reception. But those bare facts of his recent days and months concealed a more complex, even tortured, personal history. Even the origins of Buchanan's service in the Confederate Navy had followed a circuitous course. Like many U.S. Navy officers on the eve of the war, Buchanan had elected to allow home state loyalty to dictate which side he joined.

Expecting that his native Maryland, a slave state, would join the Confederacy, Buchanan submitted his resignation to U.S. Navy Secretary Gideon Welles in April 1861. But when Maryland's pro-Union leaders subsequently managed to defeat the state's secessionists, Buchanan sought to have his U.S. Navy resignation rescinded. Indignantly, Welles refused the request. Not until the following September did Buchanan, swallowing his pride, finally join the Confederate Navy.

His heroism commanding an ironclad at Hampton Roads notwithstanding, Buchanan was known for possessing a prickly, conservative bent. He was quick to react to perceived slights— and to the inevitable public doubts about his loyalty to the Confederate cause. Indeed, Buchanan's receptivity to innovations, tactical as well as technological, often resulted more from his eagerness to prove those loyalties than from any authentic interest, or confidence, in the alleged advances.

An episode that occurred later in the war, in 1864, amply illustrated that tendency. The ironclad *Tennessee* had been touted unrealistically by its advocates as a miracle vessel capable of sinking a multitude of Union warships. But when, following radical modifications, it was finally tested in Mobile Bay, the ironclad, as Buchanan had expected, delivered a mediocre performance. For those trials the admiral had found an able commander to put in charge of the craft. But—aware of the Confederate national pride invested in the ironclad—Buchanan was equally cognizant of what another age would call the public relations aspects of that first cruise. Thus, during its trials, Buchanan insisted on serving aboard the *Tennessee* as the craft's titular commander, right alongside the actual commander. In a subsequent private letter to a colleague, the admiral put his cards on the table: "Every body has taken it into their heads that <u>one</u> ship can whip a <u>dozen</u>, and if the trial is <u>not made</u>, we who are in her, are d——d for life, consequently the <u>trial must</u> be made."[7]

Buchanan's resentment against what he perceived as civilian meddling in military affairs also darkened his dealings with

Hunley and his partners. For starters, the admiral considered
most civilian-conceived inventions the stuff of folly. A letter, for
instance, to Alabama governor John Shorter found Buchanan
rejecting—as ill-conceived—two inventions, a torpedo ram and
a "Fire Ship," submitted on behalf of constituents. The latter
vessel's precise modus operandi is now lost to posterity. But
Buchanan's objections suggest that, at least in that case, he
probably had a point: "As to the 'Fire Ship' I think from the explanation of Mr. Patterson, she would soon destroy herself with
the burning turpentine."

The admiral likewise saw all manner of privateering ventures as a drain on his resources. To Navy Secretary Mallory he
complained, "Frequent applications are made to me for guns,
small arms, and ammunition to carry out private expeditions,
but I do not feel authorized to supply them, as my own means
are limited." In that same spirit, he also viewed privateering
forays as disruptive to his command and potentially fatal to the
naive civilians who participated in them. "If these private expeditions are fitted out without being controlled by me, or subject
to my orders, their authority will be abused, and those concerned, if captured, will be treated as pirates."[8]

In the end, true to form, Buchanan, as an arbiter of the *American Diver*'s practical value as a vessel of war, proved every bit as
rough as anyone familiar with the darker aspects of his background might have expected. Further sealing the submarine
boat's fate was its own actual performance, as witnessed by
Buchanan. During the first half of February 1863, the crew of
the *American Diver* conducted a series of trial runs inside Mobile Bay. In one instance, venturing to the far ends of the bay,
the little boat possibly even attempted an actual attack on a
Union blockading ship.[9]

Sadly, for Hunley and company, as the *American Diver's* crew cranked heartily away inside, the craft never obtained a consistent speed of more than two miles per hour throughout all its trials in Mobile Bay. And, in early 1863, on what turned out to be its final run, the boat sank into the bay. The men inside, Buchanan soon wrote Navy Secretary Mallory, "came very near being lost."

The boat's sponsors were crestfallen. Twice in less than twelve months they had watched their submarine boats disappear into watery graves. Admiral Buchanan, by contrast, was predictably unsympathetic. "I never entertained but one opinion as to the result of this Boat, that it would prove a failure," he wrote on February 14 to Navy Secretary Mallory. "I considered the whole affair as impracticable from the Commencement."

In the wake of the *American Diver* debacle, Baxter Watson—apparently having been rebuffed by Admiral Buchanan—wrote to the Confederate Navy in Richmond seeking assistance in salvaging the lost craft. But Navy Secretary Mallory kicked the matter straight back to Buchanan. In response, the admiral in a March 3 letter to Mallory reiterated his doubts about the *American Diver's* practical value and, for good measure, added one more objection. It focused on the vessel's torpedo delivery system: "The boat cannot possibly be of any practical use in Mobile Bay in consequence of its shoalness [shallowness, or prevalence of shoals], nor do I think it could be made effective against the enemy off the harbor as the blockading vessels are anchored in water too shoal to permit the boat to pass under them."[10]

6

The *Fish Boat*

HORACE LAWSON HUNLEY, thirty-nine years old that winter of 1863 in Mobile, had embarked upon his submarine-boat-building career almost two years earlier. He had begun the quest intoxicated with dreams of the fortunes that he and his partners would reap from the Union ships they would dispatch to the ocean floor—up to $50,000 or more per ship.

But now, looking back, he saw only a nagging flotsam of financial losses. Hunley had been one of several investors in the *Pioneer*, and more recently he had presumably been among those who defrayed the cost of building the *American Diver*, the craft now sitting somewhere on the bottom of Mobile Bay. All totaled, this latest venture had cost its sponsors at least $15,000.

But, if they were to persist in their efforts and seek to build another craft, to whom could Hunley and the other investors now go for the requisite capital? Under ordinary circumstances—before this war had changed everything—Hunley could have asked his wealthy brother-in-law Robert Barrow for a loan. Hunley, after all, had done that in the past.

But that option was by now long foreclosed. A year earlier, Barrow had even reneged on his promised funding for the *Pio-*

neer. And—given Barrow's ongoing hostility toward secession and the Confederate state that it had created—how could Hunley consider his brother-in-law as a patron for this latest initiative? And beyond that, yet another circumstance foreclosed any further largesse from Barrow: with his crops and plantations subject to outright Federal seizure, and his slave labor force now subject to his worst fears, Robert Ruffin Barrow's once great fortune was rapidly becoming a fond memory.[1]

As he pondered the dire circumstances of Robert and Volumnia back in Louisiana, Horace Hunley knew one thing. If he and his partners were to build yet another submarine boat, they would need new investors to share the financial risks.

Ultimately a new group of investors did step forward. And so, twice within a dizzyingly brief span of months, Hunley, McClintock, and Watson—the three original submarine boat partners from New Orleans—brought new colleagues into their project. And, at least initially, all signs boded well for a solid working relationship within the expanded, and freshly recapitalized, team. Edgar Collins Singer, a mechanical engineer from Ohio who had moved to tiny Port Lavaca, Texas, led the new investors. Another prominent member of this fresh ensemble was A. A. "Gus" Whitney. Others in the group—variously called the Singer Submarine Corps or the Singer Secret Service Corps—included J. D. Breaman, R. W. Dunn, James Jones, and D. Bradbury.

Joined by a cadre of fellow Texans with backgrounds in artillery warfare, Singer and Whitney manufactured contact torpedoes for the Confederacy. Since the war's start, citizen inventors and entrepreneurs across the South had welcomed the Confederate government's official encouragement of underwater warfare. Inventors designed and, in a few cases, actually manufactured a wide range of explosive devices intended for deployment in the battle theater's harbors and rivers, and even on land. In the end, most of the designs and devices were adjudged by Confederate officials to be crude, unreliable, or both. Few of the torpedo designs were even deemed worthy of consideration by the Confederate military.

By 1863, however, a handful of citizen torpedo inventors and manufacturers, owing to their work's high quality, had managed to stand out among the crowd. And the Confederate military, supplementing its own internal ordnance resources, increasingly did business with these private entrepreneurs—Edgar Singer among them. The "Singer torpedo" (or "Fretwell-Singer torpedo," after codesigner John Fretwell), as it came to be known, possessed a deadly simplicity: the mine itself consisted of a buoylike floating cone, two-thirds full of gunpowder— typically about sixty pounds. The weight of a saucerlike plate falling from a platform inside the cone jostled a safety pin, which, in turn, released a spring-loaded plunger. The plunger then struck a percussion cap, which detonated the gunpowder.

A Richmond ordnance commission would conclude in the summer of 1863 that the Singer torpedo was reliable, required minimal human tinkering to work, and—closing the sale—it was also hard for approaching ships to see: "One great advantage the torpedo possesses over many others is that its explosion does not depend upon the action or judgment of an individual; that it is safe from premature ignition, and at the same time is cheap and portable, while its position in river or harbor can not be readily ascertained by an enemy's vessel."

The Texans' torpedo business eventually brought them to Mobile, where they had contracted with the Confederate Navy to mine the city's bay with Singer torpedoes. And it was while the torpedo manufacturers were meeting the demands of that contract that they were solicited by Hunley, Alexander, McClintock, and Watson. The submarine boat partners told Singer and the other Texans about the boat they hoped to build. No doubt they also reminded the ordnance manufacturers of the Confederate government's standing offer to pay private citizens a bounty of 20 percent of the value of any ships they sank.

Hunley and his partners possibly also enticed the Texans with another opportunity: the chance for Singer and his men to incorporate their torpedo into the design of a submarine boat that had the potential to revolutionize naval warfare. Standard torpedoes had to wait for unsuspecting enemy vessels to sail over them. Hunley's proposal presented a more dynamic use for Singer's explosives—their delivery via an aggressive underwater vessel.

More generally, after venturing out of Texas and east of the Mississippi, as Singer's associate J. D. Breaman soon wrote his wife, he and the other Texans had taken it upon themselves to invest in "many new schemes." In the carefree spirit of roving gamblers, the torpedo makers thus welcomed the submarine boat partners' invitation to invest in their next craft. As always in surveying the paper trail of such ventures, hard figures are scarce. At least one document, however, does shed light on the scale of the next boat's costs. Breaman soon wrote to his wife that he and Whitney had "bought one-fifth [interest in the boat] for $3,000." Horace Hunley, by contrast, his finances now greatly reduced, had—as later probate documents revealed—to content himself with a relatively paltry $400 share in the next boat, whose total budget, based on Breaman's letter, presumably came to $15,000.[2]

With fresh funding, Hunley and the partners seemed headed for success. But another development, hundreds of miles away, assuming they read of it, surely must have served at once as both a boon to their hopes and a cautionary tale. On April 18, Savannah, Georgia's *Daily Morning News* greeted readers with a jubilant headline: "Another Yanker Devil Gone Home." The story—originating with *The New York Times* and soon disseminated on both sides of the Mason-Dixon—reported that the U.S. Navy's *Alligator*, designed by Brutus de Villeroi, had on April 2 fallen victim to a storm off North Carolina's treacherous Outer Banks.

The *Alligator*—having been refitted with a hand-cranked propeller at the Washington Naval Yard—was, at the moment of its demise, being towed to Port Royal, South Carolina, for service in the South Atlantic Blockading Squadron. But when, during that southward cruise, a fierce storm arose off the Outer Banks, the captain of the towing ship, the USS *Sumpter*—seeking to save his own vessel—had been forced to release the towlines linking his craft with the unmanned *Alligator*.[3]

As a consequence, in spring 1863, with the *Alligator* now resting on the floor of the Atlantic Ocean, Horace Hunley and his partners faced a less crowded field in their quest to deploy the world's first militarily successful submarine boat.

Oddly enough, as it turned out, Horace Hunley elected that same season to take leave of Mobile. Abdicating whatever leadership role he still played in the submarine boat project, he retreated from coastal Mobile into a series of itinerant journeys through the South's hinterlands. Exactly what motivated those travels—covert government assignments, business, a falling-out with the new partners, perhaps even mental depression—remains a mystery.

Whatever motivations impelled Hunley's wanderings, his precise whereabouts that season remain largely unknown. One thing, however, appears certain. During the spring of 1863, Horace Hunley had fallen into the sort of melancholy which that age called a "brown study." By spring 1863, of course, anyone

supporting the Confederacy would have been experiencing a
sense of desperation. The Confederacy's heady days during the
early Civil War were past. But Hunley's woes during those
months seemed to well up from deeper, more personal origins.
Doleful, his own mortality weighed much on his mind. "I have
some idea of joining our forces in defence of Vicksburg," he
confided in a letter that May, from Canton, Mississippi, to his
"dear friend Henry" Leovy. "Should any accident befall me, I
wish you to take charge of my affairs." In his letter and in a will
written that same day—May 4—in Canton, Hunley named
Leovy executor of his estate and gave his friend specific instructions, in the event of his death, for settling his affairs.

In retrospect, Horace Hunley's stated idea of throwing in with
the Confederate soldiers defending Vicksburg seems, at first
glance, oddly inexplicable—particularly coming from a man ostensibly advancing a project that he hoped would culminate in a
decisive technological breakthrough for the Confederacy's faltering war effort. The Vicksburg option takes on a still more
startling quality when one ponders its timing. On April 30, four
days before Hunley's letter to Leovy, Federal forces under
General Ulysses S. Grant, determined to capture Vicksburg,
had crossed from the Mississippi River's western to eastern
bank, just below that strategically critical Confederate redoubt.
Grant's maneuver, combined with those of other Union field
commanders, effectively rendered the defense of Vicksburg a
doomed cause.

Suffice it to say that, by then, the spring of 1863, Horace
Hunley, in spirit, had fallen a long distance from those halcyon
days of his youth when his ledger book had teemed with hopeful, if idolatrous, musings about the world's "great men." Put
another way, by contemplating "joining our forces in defence of

Vicksburg," Hunley was effectively pondering the abdication of his recent role as a principal member of a team devoted to developing a technological advance that, by his professed belief, might well rescue the Confederacy's faltering war effort. Still more curiously, Hunley—thirty-nine years old, with no field command experience—was pondering leaving that role in the boat project in order to assume an uncertain but certainly lesser role in another cause, the protection of Vicksburg, in which his contribution could be nowhere nearly as substantial. That Hunley—a shrewd gambler of long standing—would ponder such long odds seems even odder when one considers the fact that, after so many months of foiled and costly efforts, he had every reason to believe that he finally stood on the eve of seeing his submarine dreams fully realized.

How to explain Hunley's wanderings over those months? "My poor brother, where is he now?" a woeful Volumnia Barrow rhetorically asked her husband in a letter that season. Blazing a trail for later chroniclers, an early biographer, while acknowledging that the documentation is scant, found solace in the assumption that Hunley faced, during those months, unspecified "grave responsibility" and was "engaged in various capacities for the Confederate Government, as a Secret Agent." And that, of course, may have been the case. During his absence from his submarine boat partners, Hunley, in fact, may have been acting as a sort of James Bond in gray for the Confederate government. After all, in at least one episode of which we're aware—the *Adela*'s cruise to Cuba—he had acted on nominally secret orders from officials in Richmond. But beyond that jaunt, evidence of other, ongoing secret work by Hunley for the Confederate government is scant, piecemeal, and in the end unconvincing.

Stronger evidence suggests that during that period, matters of a less romantic bent preoccupied the broker and planter

Hunley—specifically, the selling of sugar crops that he and Barrow seem to have stashed away in unoccupied Georgia and Mississippi. The paper trail of Hunley and Barrow's business records from those months grows faint quickly, and it offers often contradictory hints as to the status of the two men's holdings. However, that trail does suggest that the crops and lands of both men were subject to confiscation and occupation by both Confederate and Union troops.

More tangibly, however, the somberness of Hunley's letters of that period suggests a concretely simple explanation for his odd behavior: a despondency caused by business reversals brought on by the war and by his abrupt relegation to a $400-share, minority-partner status in a $15,000 enterprise in which only recently he had been a principal partner. Moreover, perhaps the brooding Hunley's growing despair had been compounded by some now unknown disagreement with the apparently self-confident Singer and the other Texans who now held great sway over the submarine boat project.[4]

Meanwhile, back in Mobile that spring—with accounts settled among the partners and with assistance from the Confederate military—work on the new boat speedily progressed. Like its two predecessors, this new boat would rely on a screw propeller and a vertically hung aft rudder to empower and guide lateral movement. But it also possessed an advance over the *Pioneer* and the *American Diver*. Its vertical movement would be further aided by diving planes—set forward along its hull and operated from within—that could be manipulated, as desired, to assist diving and resurfacing.

In a key way, however, McClintock's design for this new boat marked a retreat from an earlier ambition. With this latest design, McClintock abandoned his quest to equip a craft with either an electromagnetic or a steam engine. Too much time and money, he reasoned, had already been squandered on those ambitions during the partners' *American Diver* days. And, in the end, they had been forced to settle on mere human propulsion. No—this time around, things would be different: to conserve time and money, McClintock and his partners resolved that, from the start, they would settle on a more modest aspiration. This next craft would be powered by human muscle and human muscle alone.

McClintock soon produced a design for the new boat. In dimensions and features, it would duplicate many aspects of its two predecessors. But it would be larger and—though powered by human muscle—incorporate technological advances over the CSS *Pioneer* and the *American Diver*.

Soon enough, with McClintock's latest design in hand, the partners, assisted by a detail from the Confederate military, repaired once again to the Park and Lyons Machine Shop, at the corner of State and Water Streets in Mobile. Construction on the new boat soon commenced.

Like the Leeds Foundry in New Orleans, the architectural openness of the Park and Lyons shop had, from the time of the partners' arrival in Mobile, posed security risks—both from Union spies and local business competitors. At least one other submarine boat was completed in Mobile during the war; and both Mobile and nearby Selma were centers for the building of torpedo boats. Thus to reduce security risks posed by political and industrial spies—and out of practical necessity—the partners, at some point during their turn in Mobile, moved their construction activities to the Seamen's Bethel Church, an empty former house of worship on Church Street. And it was there that the main construction of the partners' third craft— and possibly the *American Diver*—took place.[5]

About forty-two wrought iron plates were used to construct

the main section of the new boat's hull. To create additional height and interior crew space, two iron strakes—longitudinal plates, each eight inches wide—were inserted into the hull and ran along the full length of both its port and its starboard sides. The caps that formed the new boat's bow and stern were of cast iron. And because the designers wanted a vessel that could slip smoothly through the water, the plates were not overlapped as with many vessels, but instead butted up against each other. Inside the boat—holding the entire assemblage together—were a series of butt straps, flat metal strap pieces to which the plates were riveted.

In the end, this new craft was forty feet long—five feet longer than the *Pioneer*, four feet longer than the *American Diver*'s reputed length. It rose four feet high at midship and reached three and a half feet at its beam. This latest incarnation of the partners' vision of a submarine boat surpassed in size its two predecessors. The new craft was equally, perhaps more so, conducive to provoking what a later age would call claustrophobia among its passengers. The *Pioneer* had accommodated two or three men—accounts differ. And five men, it was said, could squeeze into the *American Diver*. But this new boat was designed to accommodate—albeit just barely—eight men!

The crew would enter and exit the craft—one at a time, perforce with arms stretched over their heads—through two narrow oval-shaped fore and aft hatchways, each about twenty inches wide, a snug maneuver not unlike squeezing through the hole in a modern rubber tire. The hatches' hinged covers could be locked from the inside. Watertight rubber gaskets secured them from leakage. The two hatches sat atop the boat's two conning towers, spaced about eighteen feet from one another. Measured from the top of the hull's curvature, the two conning towers rose to about fourteen and a half inches in height.

The design required the boat's captain to command the ship

and steer the leverlike device that controlled its rudder from a forward position inside the boat's narrow crew compartment. A wooden bench extending from the crew chamber's port side offered the captain a place to sit. The captain was thus forced to navigate from a hunched position or with his head poking into the forward conning tower, where he could squint outward through four circular view ports, each a mere two inches in diameter—two looking forward, one on the port, and one on the starboard. The aft conning tower featured two more viewing ports—one on each side. The craft also had twelve "deadlights"—five sets of side-by-side glass ports running down the top of the chamber, and one apiece atop the forward and aft conning towers. The deadlights were designed less for allowing the crew to look out than for admitting natural light into the chamber's otherwise dark recesses.

To power the craft, seven crewmen sat along a plank affixed to the boat's port side. From their shared bench, the men turned a zigzag crank mounted to the hull's starboard side, which—indirectly via a set of differential gears—spun the boat's screw propeller. The differential gears, installed in the boat's propulsion system, multiplied the crew's cranking force—thus giving the boat a faster, smoother-running propeller.

The vessel's dark interior constituted an ergonomic nightmare. Cramped, it was too narrow to allow one man to pass by another. Never able to fully straighten their backs, the seven men who manually powered the propeller were forced to sit along a bench, hunched over their shared zigzagged crankshaft at their individual stations. Perversely, though ingeniously, that hardship for the crew, as it turns out, also solved a potential problem in the boat's physics.

Despite the fact that the seven men assigned to cranking stations sat along a bench on the same side—the port side—of the boat, their center of gravity remained just above the boat's keel. Put another way, the men's uncomfortable position inside the cramped boat—all seated on the same side but hunched over a shared center of gravity—deftly solved a weight displacement problem that otherwise would have required the presence of counterweights on the boat's other side—a solution which, in turn, would have brought its own challenges to the vessel's trimness.

McClintock's cleverness didn't stop there. In emergency situations, the crew, through actions taken inside the crew chamber, could drop sections of the boat's weighted keel. And to create ballast tanks in the fore and aft sections, McClintock designed bulkheads with eight-and-a-half-inch gaps at their top and riveted where the boat's main section gave way to its cast iron, tapered bow and stern sections.

To descend, the crew member seated immediately behind the captain and the most aft crew member opened the two ballast tanks. A pair of sea cocks—below-the-waterline valves— took in water. To ascend, the same crewmen cranked pumps that forced water out of the tanks. Had the tanks been sealed— had they lacked the gaps at their top—the submarine boat would have required other means, likely more complicated, for displacing air as seawater poured in. Instead, air from the two tanks was simply dispersed into the crew compartment. In the ballast tank's design, McClintock fashioned a simple solution to a potentially complex problem. But that solution would later have fatal consequences for the boat.

To further control dives and ascents, the captain moved a counterweighted lever to manipulate the pair of diving planes mounted on the outside hull just behind the captain's station. The diving planes could be angled upward and downward. And to prevent the planes from becoming "fouled"—entangled with ropes, seaweed, or other debris—tiny wedgelike iron appendages were mounted slightly forward of them. The boat carried a compass and, to measure depth, a barometer. For their new craft's weapon system, the partners—embracing the tried and true—ultimately decided to replicate the rope-towed torpedo that had been used by the *American Diver*.

During this new boat's early unofficial trials in Mobile Bay, its crew discovered that even without surfacing for fresh air, they could remain below for long periods. Even so, to lengthen that duration, McClintock designed and installed a crude snorkel system for the craft: attached to a bellows inside the boat were two pipes that projected from a box just behind the forward conning tower.[6]

Winter gave way to spring and spring to summer; and by mid-July the new boat was ready for its official trials before the local Confederate brass. Borrowing a moniker occasionally applied to the *Pioneer*, the partners called this new craft the *Fish Boat*. (Only later would it be called the *H. L. Hunley*.) But despite the moment's auspiciousness, when it came time to formally release the *Fish Boat* into the Mobile River and Bay, Horace Hunley—still rambling about the South—was nowhere to be found. (For instance, a July 27 letter from him—one of the few extant letters of his from that period—places him, at least on that particular day, in Rome, Georgia.) But even with Hunley absent, the tests of the new boat went well.

Despite the boat builders' faint resolve to guard their work from public exposure, their enterprise was never much of a secret around Mobile. A Confederate deserter later boasted to U.S. Navy officials that he "saw her"—the *Fish Boat*—"in all stages of construction at Mobile." And, in mid-July, when the craft was finally launched on its first official trial from Mobile's Theater Street dock, a crowd of curious onlookers gathered to witness the event. Indeed, the event was so public that years

later, one witness—a "small boy" at the time—still vividly recalled the hoopla when the boat slipped into the Mobile River.[7]

In New Orleans, Horace Hunley, James McClintock, and Baxter Watson on occasion had committed indiscretions while
building the CSS *Pioneer*. For instance, in discussing their project with visiting journalists at the Leeds Foundry, they had exercised more candor than prudence. But the public launch of
the *Fish Boat* from Mobile's Theater Street Dock inaugurated a
dangerous new level of flirtation with forces potentially injurious to their project's security.

Perhaps that lack of caution was deliberate. Possibly it belonged to a strategy, however desperate, of the partners to use
public opinion to overcome the political and military obstacles
that still thwarted the successful deployment of their boat. Or,
perhaps, this brazen public trial was simply yet another link in a
growing chain of indiscretions. Whatever the origins of this latest incident, one thing was clear: never before had the partners
been so unabashedly seduced by the temptation to gather a
crowd.

If, on the other hand, the partners deliberately sought to use
public acclaim to vanquish their critics, their strategy, arguably,
served its purpose. Over the next few days, as successive crowds
watched this new boat put through its trials, it became clear
that this craft performed better than its two predecessors. The
concluding demonstration came on Friday, July 31. Numerous
high-ranking Confederate officers attended—including Admiral Buchanan, General Maury, Captain J. D. Johnston, then
commanding the CSS *Selma*, and General James E. Slaughter,
a frequent visitor to the Park and Lyons shop. All were impressed with what they saw that day: the submarine boat dived
under a barge placed in the river as a dummy target, used a

floating torpedo to blow it up, and then successfully resurfaced some four hundred yards beyond where the raft had been destroyed.

Even stubborn Admiral Buchanan was impressed. Having observed along with others the *Fish Boat*'s destruction of the barge, he was in no position to defend his past opinion—as applied to the *American Diver*—that such boats were wholly "impracticable" for military purposes. But Buchanan remained unprepared to acknowledge their practicality for use in Mobile Bay.

In the end, Buchanan—searching for a politic, official response to that day's successful demonstration of the *Fish Boat*'s firepower—found a solution of cunning brilliance. It was a response that, at once, acknowledged the boat's abilities but insinuated its practical limitations for use in the shallow and already well-defended Mobile Bay. And not coincidentally, Buchanan's double-edged flattery, even as it praised the *Fish Boat*, also schemed to consign it to another port, another commander.

The following day, Buchanan wrote to Flag Officer John Randolph Tucker, commander of Confederate naval forces in Charleston. Buchanan described the previous day's demonstration and wrote of how impressed he had been with the *Fish Boat*'s destruction of the barge. Moreover, the admiral added, during that demonstration, he had personally witnessed the craft reaching a speed of four knots—twice that of the *American Diver*. "To judge from the experiment of yesterday[,] I am fully satisfied it can be used successfully in blowing up one or more of the enemy's Iron Clads in your harbor."

More to the point, he informed Tucker that two of the boat's civilian sponsors, Baxter Watson and Gus Whitney, would soon be arriving in Charleston "for the purpose of consulting General Beauregard and yourself" about the possible deployment of the "sub-marine iron boat" in Charleston. "They will explain

all its advantages," Buchanan promised. "And if it can be operated in smooth waters where the current is not strong as was
the case yesterday, I can recommend it to your favorable consideration." Buchanan closed the dispatch by asking Flag Officer Tucker to show his letter to Tucker's army counterpart in
Charleston, General Pierre G. T. Beauregard, newly returned
to Charleston following his turn in the war's Western theater.

Watson and Whitney, traveling by train, arrived in Charleston
shortly after Buchanan's letter reached Flag Officer Tucker.
Greeting the two men from Mobile, the navy commander
welcomed Buchanan's proposal. Then, as requested by Buchanan, Tucker passed the letter on to General Beauregard;
afterward, Watson and Whitney met with the general. A talented engineer and a gifted artillerist going back to his West
Point days, Beauregard found himself impressed as he studied
the plans and sketches that Watson and Whitney laid before
him.[8]

Quite possibly Beauregard was already familiar with the basic features of the submarine boat. In June 1862, between his
stint in the West and his return to Charleston, an ailing Beauregard had stopped en route at the resort of Bladon Springs,
north of Mobile, for a week or so of recuperation. During that
period, he also spent time in Mobile. He was there on June 20
to receive a dispatch from President Davis, and also on the
twenty-fifth to advise General John H. Forney, then commander of the Department of Alabama and West Florida.

Did Beauregard during that stopover learn anything about
the submarine boat project? Details of those visits have never
surfaced, and the wording of a later letter Horace Hunley wrote
to Beauregard, in which he introduced himself to the general,
suggests no prior meeting between the two—even reaching
back to their days in Louisiana.

Even so, it seems unlikely that Beauregard could have left south Alabama and his meeting with General Forney—and in all likelihood other officers—that summer of 1862 without gaining some familiarity, direct or secondhand, with the novel craft that a handful of then freshly arrived, and far from discreet, fellow Louisianans were scheming to build in Mobile. Indeed, the timing of the stopover and subsequent events—Beauregard's enthusiasm for the craft and his swiftness in embracing it— argue that, prior to his return to Charleston, the general, himself an engineer, already possessed knowledge of the submarine boat project.[9]

Beyond the realm of historical conjecture, however, certainly Beauregard *needed* the craft that Watson and Whitney discussed with him that August of 1863 in Charleston. With the ever tightening Federal blockade around Charleston's harbor, Beauregard faced a worsening military predicament. Early in the war, the Union fleet had won a handy base of operations at nearby Port Royal, midway between Charleston and Savannah, to the south. And by that summer, Charleston, along with Wilmington, North Carolina, was the Confederacy's two last remaining uncaptured major Atlantic ports.

In Charleston's harbor and offshore, the Confederates faced a formidable Union armada of twenty-four vessels armed with 190 guns, many of them high-caliber weapons. One of those vessels was a double-turreted monitor, seven were single-turreted monitors (a class of Union ironclad based on the original *Monitor*). Beyond those guns, Union forces boasted another twelve land batteries, mounting forty-one heavy guns and mortars. All totaled, the Union arsenal around Charleston came to 231 pieces of artillery.[10]

Defending Charleston and its harbor against those Yankee armaments, the Rebels countered with approximately two hundred pieces of heavy artillery scattered throughout several forts across the estuary—but none as powerful as the heaviest of the Union weapons.

Facing that situation, Beauregard's available options and time were dwindling. Put bluntly, he was in no position to decline any remotely plausible offer of assistance. Wasting no time, on August 5 he wired General Dabney Maury, his army counterpart in Mobile:

HAVE SEEN WHITNEY AND WATSON. HAVE ACCEPTED THEIR SUBMARINE BOAT. PLEASE ASSIST THEM TO GET IT HERE AS SOON AS POSSIBLE.

Beauregard's assent to the proposal was apparently expected, for arrangements for the shipment of the *Fish Boat* to Charleston had already been made. Likely aware of the unlucky fate of the Union Navy submarine boat *Alligator* as it was being towed that spring from Washington to Port Royal, Confederate authorities apparently never considered any means of transport other than rail to get the *Fish Boat* from Mobile to Charleston. Drawing on experience, Confederate strategists generally considered inland rail routes to be more secure than coastal water routes. Equally important, in this particular case, the rail option promised a delivery many times faster than any water route could offer.

In an August 8 letter to his fiancée, Lieutenant George Washington Gift recalled supervising the men who—over a two-day period, using hoists and levers—lifted the heavy boat out of Mobile Harbor and loaded it onto two linked flatcars for that trip. In the letter, Gift expressed his awe before "a very curious machine for destroying vessels . . . which I certainly regard as the most important invention to us that could have been made." He also wrote that he entertained no doubts as to this wondrous craft's illustrious future: "It will become in a very short time," he predicted, "one of the great celebrities in the art of defense and attack on floating objects." Three days after Beauregard's telegram reached Mobile, the hulking underwater craft—a *Fish Boat* out of water—began its distinctly terrestrial, northeasterly journey toward Charleston.[11]

PART III

CHARLESTON

Summer 1863–Winter 1864

7

The Consequences of Faltering
in the Hour of Success

FOR MORE THAN TWO DAYS, the locomotive pulling the two flatcars that cradled the *Fish Boat* rolled northeasterly across the coastal plains and Piedmont of Alabama and Georgia, and eventually into South Carolina. During the entire trip, the boat likely remained covered by a tarp of canvas. The shroud would have been draped over the *Fish Boat* less because the craft constituted any sort of secret weapon—public exposure in Mobile had already compromised that advantage—than simply to protect it from weather and coal embers from the train's engine.

By Wednesday, August 12, 1863, the locomotive had reached Charleston. Upon arriving in the city, the engine pulling the flatcars on which the boat rested ended its journey at the North Eastern Railroad Depot's harborside tracks. There, at the rail depot that sprawled between the end of Chapel Street and the Cooper River, workers hoisted the *Fish Boat* down from the flatcars to the depot's wharf. At the dock, several men associated with the *Fish Boat*—in all likelihood including Baxter Watson and Gus Whitney, who were already in town—fidgeted with their boat until well into the evening.

Over the coming days and weeks, meanwhile, curious Charlestonians gathered around the boat's temporary resting place to gaze upon the odd-looking craft, greeting the city's new arrival with a mixture of skepticism and hopefulness. The Charleston diarist and socialite Emma Holmes noted, "It certainly is a wonderful thing, & we hope for its success." However, a friend of Holmes—one with a military background—took a less sanguine view of the boat's chances at destroying an enemy ship. Noting her friend's skepticism, Holmes wrote, "Col. [Delaware] Kemper said he doubted its success, as it was not a new invention, &, if good, would have been used before."[1]

After the war, General Ulysses S. Grant, in his *Personal Memoirs*, recalled that "I always admired the South, as bad as I thought their cause, for the boldness with which they silenced all opposition and all croaking, by press or individuals, within their control." Yes, the New Orleans papers, during the war's early months, had indulged themselves with coy references to the activities of Hunley and his partners. But as the war wore on, Confederate newspapers, unlike their Northern counterparts, seldom revealed information that might have endangered military operations.

But that discretion, exercised in official and institutional quarters, rarely extended to the activities of the partners themselves. A case in point: two months after the boat's arrival in Charleston, the author Edmund Ruffin, venturing to the North Eastern Railroad dock, encountered no trouble in gaining access to the craft, by then returned to that same wharf where it had earlier rested. And despite Ruffin's disclaimer that he "could not understand any thing of the apparatus and management" of the *Fish Boat*, his diary entry for that evening— October 12—nonetheless recorded a vivid physical description of the boat, both in and out of the water—its dimensions, its shape, its draft while running on the surface, its diving abilities, and the size of its torpedo. Likewise, it was through such public observation that Emma Holmes's watchful friend Colonel

Kemper learned enough about what he called the *Porpoise*— her diary recounts his detailed description of the boat—to form an opinion of the craft and to dismiss it as "not a new invention."

In his own October 12 diary entry, Ruffin would note that, standing alongside him, that evening, were "8 or 10 persons looking on, for curiosity" at what he called the "Diving Torpedo boat." Despite his curiosity, Ruffin also exhibited a reflexive patriotic deference to the need for secrecy in shrouding this technological wonder from potentially dangerous disclosures: Hence his recollection of having "asked no questions & heard none from others."

But the details offered in Ruffin's own description of the submarine boat belied the nominal secrecy with which he and others professed to shroud its wonders. Any casual observer with eyes and ears in Charleston over those months could have easily obtained just the sort of information on the *Fish Boat*— specific in details—that a Union Navy intelligence officer would have welcomed. Indeed, on the evening that an awed Ruffin stood on the dock and admired the craft's capabilities, surely any of the other "8 or 10 persons looking on, for curiosity" standing beside him could have recorded the same information. And, as Ruffin's studied silence that night ironically attested, all of that information was easily obtainable without the observer asking a single question. In Charleston, as in New Orleans and Mobile before, this submarine boat was already well on its way to becoming—to borrow a phrase from the poet Leonard Cohen—"a secret all over the block."[2]

With the *Fish Boat* in Charleston, by then, were its designer James McClintock and at least two other partners in the submarine boat venture—Baxter Watson and Gus Whitney. Another

two partners, Edgar Singer and J. D. Breaman, reached
Charleston over the next few days. In the city, Singer and Breaman quickly settled into their construction of the torpedoes
with which the *Fish Boat*'s partners hoped to destroy enemy
ships, and thus win both public acclaim and their long-sought
fortune.

For his part, General Pierre G. T. Beauregard had high
hopes for the newly arrived submarine boat from Mobile. Indeed, according to a subordinate officer, he considered it "the
most formidable engine of war for the defense of Charleston
now at his disposition."

His enthusiasm for the *Fish Boat* typified the general's attitude toward technological innovations. Forty-three years old,
Beauregard had a long background in engineering, stretching
back to the late 1840s. And—lucky for the submarine boat partners—he also had deep Louisiana roots. The dashing officer
had been born to a family of Gallic origins in St. Bernard
Parish, just south of New Orleans. Indeed, Beauregard grew up
speaking French and likely did not learn English until the age
of twelve, when he went off to a boarding school in New York
City. He later attended and, in 1838, graduated from the
United States Military Academy at West Point, New York.

As a young officer, Beauregard served in the Mexican War.
Later he returned to Louisiana and served as a supervising en-
gineer for the New Orleans Custom House and other federal
construction projects around the state. On December 31, 1860,
Beauregard had resigned his post as supervisor of the Custom
House construction to take a new position, as commander at
the West Point academy—a position he held for only five days.
As his native region's future political course became clear,
Beauregard resigned his post at West Point to offer his services
to the Confederacy.

Since the start of the Civil War, it seemed that there were

few places in which Beauregard hadn't served: he'd been in Charleston and presided over the first shots against Fort Sumter. And along with Joseph E. Johnston, he'd been one of the two victorious Confederate brigadier generals at Manassas, the First Battle of Bull Run—the war's first significant engagement. Later, Beauregard led Confederate forces in the war's Western theater. During that period, he'd performed heroically, if controversially, as second in command in the first major engagement of that theater—the Battle of Shiloh. In September 1862 he had been brought back to Charleston, from which he soon oversaw Confederate Army coastal defenses for South Carolina, Georgia, and, later, parts of Florida. But it would be Charleston where the general would be based and which would dominate most of his time and attention. In that city, as the South Carolina diarist Mary Boykin Chesnut wrote, "Beauregard is a demigod here to most of the natives."

More than most Confederate generals, Beauregard enjoyed a reputation as a romantic. He was handsome, and he spoke French. He was a talented raconteur and a gifted horseman. Moreover, he enjoyed a reputation as a ladies' man. Indeed, as a young West Point cadet, he had even conducted a romance with the daughter of General Winfield Scott—later the author of the Union's Anaconda strategy and thus, intellectually, the creator of the very blockade that Beauregard, day and night, was doing his utmost to defeat.

Throughout his career's various turns, in and outside of Louisiana, Beauregard maintained close ties with his native state's key political leaders, many of whom, in 1861, took up service with the new Confederate government. And many of those leaders were the same men that Horace Hunley, James McClintock, and Baxter Watson had turned to that same year as they began construction of the *Pioneer*.

Hunley's mentor Francis Hanson Hatch, for example, remained close to former U.S. senator and more recently Confederate diplomat John Slidell—who just happened to be General Beauregard's brother-in-law. On top of that, in Charleston, as in Mobile and other Confederate ports, the lines of authority between navy and army were often muddled. While the army was charged with harbor defenses, most of the ships in that harbor were under navy command. But unlike in Mobile, where senior army and navy commanders vied for authority over the other, in Charleston—aside from occasional squabbles over cannon and matériel—such contests seldom occurred.

General Beauregard of the Confederate States Army enjoyed generally good working relationships with the two key naval officers in Charleston. Beyond that, by every measure—rank, seniority, experience, military and civilian politics, and public acclaim—Beauregard possessed far more power than did those two naval officers, station commander Duncan M. Ingraham and Ingraham's nominal subordinate, squadron commander John Randolph Tucker.

Indicative of that circumstance as well as the general's broader, more aesthetic interests, in 1863 he ordered the young Confederate soldier-artist Conrad Wise Chapman to execute a series of works depicting the various defenses guarding Charleston Harbor. More pertinently for the *Fish Boat*'s partners, Beauregard had no ill will toward civilians and the projects they proposed to him. When the submarine boat partners reached Charleston in August 1863, Beauregard was already well into negotiations with a group of local civilian entrepreneurs who were building the *David*, an ironclad torpedo boat. The *David*, designed to run with a shallow draft, just barely below the waterline, had been proposed by the entrepreneurs as a deadly countermeasure against the Federal blockade strangling Charleston's economic and material sustenance.

Given that background, it's not difficult to fathom why Beauregard, on August 12, soon after the *Fish Boat* reached Charleston, issued orders to his quartermaster, Major Hutson Lee, to accord Gus Whitney carte blanche to obtain any "articles he may need for placing his submarine vessel in condition for service."

Whitney and the partners got another shot of encouragement when General Thomas Jordan relayed to them a message from John Fraser & Co., one of Charleston's leading trading firms. At once a measure of Charleston's growing desperation but also good news for the *Fish Boat*'s owners, the message announced a startling series of bounties: $100,000 to any enterprising nautical warrior who destroyed the Federal ironclad *New Ironsides*; the same amount for the destruction of the wooden frigate *Wabash*; and $50,000 for every destroyed monitor.[3]

By August 1863, when the *Fish Boat* rolled into town, Charleston, with its population of 41,000, was, after the Union's capture of New Orleans, the South's largest city still under Confederate control. Moreover, the city continued to constitute a yawning sieve in the Federal blockade—an entrepôt where blockade runners operated with relative freedom, running both in and out of the port. Populating Charleston were 23,000 whites, 3,000 free blacks, and 14,000 slaves. With its skyline punctuated by the myriad steeples that conferred upon the port its epithet "the Holy City," Charleston spread across a peninsula formed by the confluence of the Ashley and Cooper Rivers.

The island citadel of Fort Sumter, only three miles southeast of Charleston, dominated sea approaches to the city and its har-

bor. It had been the 1861 shelling by secessionists of Fort
Sumter—by August 1863 securely in Confederate hands but
then occupied by Federal forces—that had sounded the first
shots of this war. And it was for that reason that Union strategists, eager to take revenge on Charleston, reviled the city as
the "cradle of secession."

In addition to Fort Sumter, two other substantial military
landmarks—Fort Moultrie and Castle Pinckney—guarded the
sea approaches to Charleston Harbor and the city itself. Beyond those, the harbor and city were ringed by fourteen other
smaller forts and floating batteries. All totaled, some 240 guns
manned by some six thousand soldiers guarded the harbor and
city.

Indeed, in the summer of 1863, after two years of stubborn
efforts, the Union's army and navy—confronting those armaments—had still not captured Charleston. And so, that July,
President Lincoln dispatched new leadership to the Charleston
theater: Rear Admiral John Adolphus Bernard Dahlgren and
Major General Quincy A. Gillmore. The shared strategy of the
two officers was to attack and capture Morris Island, along the
southern edge of Charleston Harbor. Once they were in control
of Morris Island, they would use it as a base from which to
bombard Fort Sumter. And with the reduction of Sumter, the
way would be cleared for the Union's capture of Charleston.

Upon assuming their new commands, Dahlgren and Gillmore had quickly embarked upon their strategy's first phase—
the capture of Morris Island. By mid-July, however, following
fierce Union naval and land actions, that phase had stalled at
Battery Wagner, a redoubt of sand, logs, and earth on Morris Island, still in Rebel hands. Determined to press ahead with a
siege of Fort Sumter, Gillmore ordered the construction of four
Union batteries and the mounting of over forty guns on those
parts of Morris Island his troops already occupied. And by mid-

August, when the *Fish Boat* reached Charleston, the Federal assault on Fort Sumter, soon joined by a flotilla of Union ironclads, was in full motion.

For the submarine boat's partners, meanwhile, there was still the dispiriting matter of Horace Hunley's ongoing distance from their project. General Beauregard's letter to Whitney giving carte blanche for any supplies he asked for had contained a telling reference. In the letter, Beauregard referred to the *Fish Boat* as "his"—Whitney's—"submarine vessel." The letter thus tacitly recognized Whitney as the new, at least nominally, lead partner in the enterprise. Horace Hunley, still away on his travels around the South, had failed to join the other partners in Charleston.

On August 15—mere days after the *Fish Boat* arrived in Charleston—Hunley, from Enterprise, Mississippi, wrote his friend James McClintock a letter teeming with encouraging bromides: "Remind your crew of Manassas & Shiloh and the consequences of faltering in the hour of success." But left unstated in the letter was any suggestion as to why Hunley at that most propitious moment in his own life—and that of the submarine boat project—would be anywhere else but Charleston. Indeed, in retrospect, the letter's most striking aspect was the depth of detachment it revealed on Hunley's part from a project he once held close—even referring at one point to "your experiment at Charleston."[4]

In time, however, second thoughts about his aloofness from the venture seem to have agitated the brooding Hunley. And by August 21, he had found his way to Charleston. He was also apparently feeling concerns, if not about the boat's tactics, then about the fate that the craft's crew would possibly suffer because of those tactics should they fall into enemy hands. The stigma, after all, attached to "infernal machines" remained strong in most military quarters.

Thus, as he assisted in preparing the *Fish Boat*'s crew for their first sortie against an enemy vessel, Hunley pondered the possibility—even the likelihood—that, in the event of their capture, the men might be treated as cold-blooded murderers rather than gallant soldiers or sailors. For that reason, he insisted that they be attired in official uniforms. To the quartermaster in Charleston, he placed an order for "nine grey jackets, three to be trimmed with gold braid." Hunley wanted the crew's appearance to bespeak nothing if not military legitimacy. Explaining his order, he wrote, "the men for whom they [the uniforms] are ordered, are on special secret service & . . . it is necessary that they be clothed in the Confederate Army uniform."

Likely unbeknownst to Hunley, his request mirrored one made sixty-six years earlier, by another submarine boat pioneer, the inventor Robert Fulton. That request came in December 1797, as Fulton was seeking to sell Napoleon Bonaparte's navy on his "Mechanical Nautulus." Recognizing the stigma attached to underwater warfare, Fulton had asked the Directory for formal "Commissions Specifying that all persons taken in the *Nautulus or Submarine expedition* Shall be treated as Prisoners of War."[5]

With uniforms for the crew and Singer's freshly assembled torpedo attached to the rope that trailed behind their craft, the *Fish Boat*'s partners wasted no time in deploying their vessel. This time around, however, James McClintock, replacing John Scott, would command the boat. In assuming that role, McClintock drew not only on his knowledge of the craft as its designer, but also his years of experience as a river pilot and as an engineer. Joining him inside the boat were seven other crew members who, over the previous weeks, had trickled in from Mobile to Charleston.

It was always assumed that the *Fish Boat* and the torpedo that trailed behind it at the end of a length of rope would be easy for an enemy ship to spot. Thus, to preserve the element of surprise, the partners concluded that any assault by the submarine boat must be made at night. For that reason, the *Fish Boat*'s initial test runs and its subsequent actual sorties in Charleston Harbor always took place after darkness fell across the water.

On those initial cruises in Charleston Harbor, the *Fish Boat* apparently functioned well enough. Seven crewmen, hunched along their cramped port-side bench, turned their zigzag crank that spun the boat's propeller. Meanwhile, Captain McClintock—forward of the other crewmen and facing forward while seated on the commander's bench—controlled the boat's rudder with the joysticklike lever that rose before him from the compartment's floor. Yet another lever, mounted on the commander's left, controlled the boat's outside diving planes. Periodically, when it came time to dive, the crew member stationed behind McClintock and the man at the aftermost station—the station closest to the stern—would simultaneously open their respective sea cocks, which, exploiting the force of gravity, brought water into the forward and aft ballast tanks. And when McClintock decided it was time to ascend, each of those men would reverse that process—closing the sea cocks and then cranking the pumps at their respective stations to expel the water from the tanks. Periodically, McClintock would poke his head upward into the forward conning tower and, when there was a view to see, peer out of one of the tower's four circular view ports.

The *Fish Boat* would remain a few feet underwater for periods of roughly a half hour, then resurface for fresh air and a visual reorientation. The moon was waxing over those weeks, and through the four view ports in his forward conning tower, McClintock could gaze at a silhouetted display of the enemy's formidable—and, for the Rebels, target-rich—squadron of ironclads and frigates. But despite the embarrassment of riches that each night dangled before the Confederates, the *Fish Boat* that August failed to engage—much less sink—any Union ships.

Reflecting on McClintock's failure to engage the enemy, one assumes that the same qualities that made him such a gifted expert in what an impressed British naval officer later termed "all sorts of submarine engineering" may also have led to timidity in his command of the *Fish Boat*. In essence, the very qualities that made him a superb engineer—patience, the technological and scientific breadth of his expertises, and his attention to detail—may have inhibited him in a role where intuitive boldness often trumped more contemplative virtues.

The worsening military situation around Charleston—coupled with the *Fish Boat*'s failure to engage a single enemy vessel—frustrated General Beauregard, Flag Officer John Tucker, and the other Confederate officers who had invested such high hopes in the submarine boat. Triggering further exasperation, during that same period McClintock also rebuffed a request that a Confederate Navy officer be placed aboard the *Fish Boat*. A seaman unfamiliar with the boat's operations, McClintock answered, could only get in the way.

Confederate officials, meanwhile, grew more concerned after Charleston's residents, in the wee hours of Saturday morning, August 22, were awakened by a deafening explosion. The blast—the first of a barrage of thirty-six exploding shells over the next two days—came from a large Union cannon. The eight-inch Parrott rifle, nicknamed the Swamp Angel, was based on Morris Island, more than four miles distant from downtown Charleston. Even more startling, the cannon fire was not aimed at Fort Sumter. Union forces—raising the ante in the Charleston theater—were deliberately targeting the city of Charleston.

The siege of Charleston blazed over the days and weeks ahead. And events were hardly more encouraging for the Confederacy in the war's other theaters. A month earlier—that July—General Robert E. Lee, frustrated by a slew of debilitating defeats on Southern soil, had decided to bring the war onto enemy terrain. But the effort had foundered badly; at a small Pennsylvania town called Gettysburg, his northern advance had ended in a massive Rebel defeat. And about a thousand miles to the west, on the same July 4 that witnessed the start of Lee's retreat back to Virginia, Confederate forces had suffered a second major defeat: following a series of Union naval and land offenses that had begun in May 1862, fifteen months earlier, the town of Vicksburg, Mississippi—"the Gibraltar of the Confederacy," on a high bluff above the east bank of the Mississippi River, once believed impregnable—had finally been captured.

The defeat gave Union forces unfettered control of the entire Mississippi River, sundering vital railroad supply lines between east and west and deepening strategic challenges. It also effectively split the Confederacy into two parts. Together, the defeats at Gettysburg and Vicksburg, along with other military setbacks and increasingly debilitating conditions on the home front, caused a staggering loss of morale across the entire Confederacy.

Of course, those Confederate defeats only emboldened Union morale. For the thousands of blue-clad soldiers and sailors scattered across this conflict's vast domain, there was now reason to believe that their long-sought victory might be close at hand.

In Charleston Harbor, meanwhile, those Confederate setbacks only placed new pressures to perform on the submarine boat that Beauregard, only weeks earlier, had called, according to a subordinate, "the most formidable engine of war for the defense of Charleston now at his disposition." All along, the growing irritations of the Confederate officers in Charleston focused on what they perceived as a lack of aggressiveness in James McClintock's command of the craft he had designed. By August 23, exasperation with McClintock's evident timidity led General Thomas Lanier Clingman, commander of Confederate forces on Sullivan's Island, to complain to a subordinate officer: "The torpedo boat started at sunset but returned as they state because of an accident. [Gus] Whitney says though McClintock is timid it shall go tonight unless the weather is bad." Within hours, on that same evening of the twenty-third, Clingman's anger glowed white-hot. In a second note to the same subordinate, he inveighed, "The torpedo boat has not gone out. I do not think it will render any service under its present management."

The *Fish Boat*'s inaction disappointed General Beauregard. And ultimately, he decided that he had no other option than the one which seemed the most obvious: in the wake of the *Fish Boat*'s failure to engage any enemy vessels, orders were issued for the craft to be seized by the Confederate Army, and for it to be manned with a crew recruited from the Confederate Navy.[6]

8

In Other Hands

DURING THE SAME MONTH, August 1863, that culminated in the *Fish Boat*'s seizure by the Confederate Navy, yet another stroke of ill fortune befell the craft. In Charleston, as in Mobile, a nominal secrecy still shrouded this strange-looking, attention-provoking vessel. But—thanks in part to the partners' preening desire for public attention—its existence was hardly a secret. And sometime that August, the *Fish Boat* became an object of surveillance by two pro-Union informers.

The two men, their Union sympathies notwithstanding, were engaged in blockade running between Charleston and Nassau. And via a third-party letter—from S. G. Haynes, the U.S. consul in Nassau—what the two informants had observed soon found its way to U.S. Navy Secretary Gideon Welles. Haynes's letter described "a party of Engineers in Charleston who have completed a Submarine boat of Boiler-iron in the shape of a Spanish sigar." The letter possibly erred in at least one detail; the craft's construction may or may not have involved any boiler iron. But Haynes was correct in describing the intentions of the boat's crew, warning that they "plan to attack, and blow up, with torpedoes[,] first the ironclads, and then all the blockading squadron that comes with in reach." He closed the dispatch with a chilling endorsement of the *Fish Boat*'s lethal powers: "My informants inform me that they have examined the machine in all its parts, and have no doubt of its capability of accomplishing all their purpose. This infernal machine is all ready. And my only fear is that this mail will not reach you in time to put the squadron on their guard."[1]

Welles relayed the intelligence to Rear Admiral A. B. John Dahlgren, commander of the South Atlantic Blockading Squadron. Dahlgren, however, apparently having heard the false reports that the Confederate submarine boat had already sunk in an accident, never acted on the warning.

Not that John Dahlgren lacked interest in the latest advances in naval technologies. Fifty-three years old, he had spent most of his navy years as an engineer and inventor, serving as director of the U.S. Navy's Bureau of Ordnance. Among his many contributions, the Dahlgren gun—since 1856 one of that era's standard armaments aboard U.S. Navy ships—was his invention. His elevation to rear admiral, for which he had vigorously lobbied, had come about only seven months earlier. But truth be known, Dahlgren's current position, leading the South Atlantic Blockading Squadron, was his first field command.

Dahlgren, the son of a Swedish naval officer who had emigrated to Philadelphia, was at his core an engineer. When reacting to the informants' disclosures, he was eager to safeguard his squadron. That fall, he would threaten to hang a group of enemy prisoners suspected of using a torpedo, which he regarded "as an engine of war not recognized by civilized nations." But his engineer's curiosity also betrayed a fascination, even a grudging admiration, for his enemys' ability to incorporate stealthful cunning into their engines of war. His own squadron, after all, included ironclads and other weaponry that drew on recent advances in naval design.

Ironically, on August 11, during the same period that the *Fish Boat* reached Charleston, Dahlgren had written a letter to Welles, arguing for the usefulness of both torpedoes and submarine boats in Charleston Harbor. It was not the first time that Welles had heard such an entreaty. It had, after all, been Rear Admiral Samuel DuPont, Dahlgren's predecessor as commander of the South Atlantic Blockading Squadron, who had requested the services of the *Alligator* in this theater. But, in April 1863, when it sank en route to Port Royal, that ill-fated craft had lost its chance to prove its mettle in these waters.

In his letter to Welles, Dahlgren argued that submarine boats and torpedoes could still advance the Union's cause. But neither, he asserted, would be deployed around Charleston for the purpose of killing soldiers or civilians. Instead, they would be used to remove obstructions placed in the harbor by the Confederates. Over the past few months, the Rebels had stretched a series of floating booms—physical barriers—across the harbor. These booms consisted of logs linked to one another by ropes and cables. They were intended to block enemy ships and also to foul—to become entangled with—the propellers of steam vessels that tried to cross them. In the end, however, nothing substantive came of Dahlgren's request.[2]

In the wake of the *Fish Boat*'s confiscation, the partners were presumably promised financial compensation for their loss. The boat was later assessed to have a value of $27,500, a figure almost double what they had budgeted during its construction. Efforts, meanwhile, moved forward to place a new crew aboard the *Fish Boat*. To command the craft, navy officials settled on Lieutenant John A. Payne, who, most recently, had served aboard the ironclad CSS *Chicora*, based in Charleston. Joining Payne in the *Fish Boat* crew was yet another Confederate Navy lieutenant, Charles Hazelwood Hasker, a former U.S. Navy seaman, who had served as boatswain aboard the CSS *Virginia* during the Battle of Hampton Roads. Rounding out the boat's eight-man complement were six other seamen, recruited from the *Chicora* and the *Palmetto State*. And assisting the boat's crew in the devising and mounting of its torpedo was a civilian, the explosives expert Charles L. Sprague.

Strongly recommended to Beauregard, Sprague, with his expertise in torpedo warfare, filled in for Edgar Singer and Gus Whitney. Singer and his partner J. D. Breaman, with their boat now in navy hands, had already left Charleston to confer with officials in Richmond about other projects.

Wasting no time in taking charge of their new craft, Lieutenant Payne and his crew, during test trials, began familiarizing themselves with the intricacies of the *Fish Boat*'s operations. As their confidence soared, they shed the prohibition against daytime tests that had previously been imposed upon the submarine boat. In the process, Payne and his crew soon found themselves winning large crowds of impressed onlookers, enthralled with the boat's wondrous maneuvers.

Weeks earlier, the *Fish Boat*'s designer and, by then, commander, James McClintock, had declined a request from the Confederate Navy to detail an officer aboard the submarine boat. In rebuffing the request, McClintock had asserted that the presence of a single man unfamiliar with the craft could be disruptive to its smooth operations. But now—giving the lie to what in retrospect appeared to many to have been McClintock's needless arrogance—the *Fish Boat* seemed fine in other hands. In an almost playful way, Payne and his crew, in plain daylight, performed public rehearsals for their prospective assaults on enemy vessels. Over several days, as Payne carefully angled the lever that controlled the boat's two diving planes, the *Fish Boat* would approach the broadsides of various Confederate ships swinging at anchor in Charleston Harbor, dive under them, and then—to the delight of successive crowds—resurface on the other side.

It was just such a demonstration that Lieutenant Payne, on the morning of August 29, was preparing to make when something went awry. The accident took place near the dock at Fort Johnson, on James Island, southeast of Charleston. At the time the *Fish Boat* was astern of, and tied by a towline to, the Confederate ship *Etowah*. What exactly happened next remains unclear.

According to one account, while entering the *Fish Boat*'s forward hatch, Payne became entangled in the towline that attached his craft to the *Etowah*. Struggling to free himself, he accidentally fell into the *Fish Boat*'s crew chamber, where his foot inadvertently pressed the lever that controlled the craft's two diving planes. At that point—with its two hatches wide open—the *Fish Boat* began sinking. Yet another account suggests that the wake of a passing ship precipitated Payne's stumble. Or that Payne never stumbled at all—that his foot never fell against the diving plane. The wake simply swamped the boat, causing water to flood the crew compartment, sending the *Fish Boat* to the harbor floor.

Finally, a *Chicora* crewman, C. L. Stanton—albeit not a witness to the incident—later claimed that the accident was occasioned by the sudden headway of the *Etowah* away from its wharf. The *Fish Boat*, following a series of demonstration dives, had been "fastened [to the *Etowah*] with a light line with the fins in position for diving," recalled Stanton. But the crew of the submarine boat had not expected, nor prepared for, that motion of the larger craft. Consequently, "the line by which the boat was attached to the steamer snapped, and she went down . . . like a lump of lead."

Whatever precisely caused the accident will likely never be known. But Lieutenant Charles Hasker later offered a vividly harrowing firsthand account of the catastrophe: "The boat made a dive while the manholes were open and filled rapidly. Payne got out of the forward hole and two others out of the aft hole. Six of us went down with the boat. I had to get out over the bar which connected the fins and through the manhole. This I did by forcing myself through the column of water which was rapidly filling the boat."

By then the boat was submerged and rapidly sinking toward the harbor floor. Still inside and fighting for his life, Hasker tried to escape through the hatch of the aft conning tower. Thrashing about, he eventually squeezed halfway through the open hatch. By then, the hatch's heavy iron lid, forced downward by the water pressure weighing on the boat, slammed against Hasker's back. Stunned but determined to free himself, he finally managed to get outside of the boat, only to realize that the calf of his left leg had become caught under the hatch's lid. "Held in this manner I was carried to the bottom," Hasker recalled. The harbor in that area was from twelve to twenty-five feet deep. "When the boat touched bottom I felt the pressure relax. Stooping down, I took hold of the manhole plate, drew out my wounded limb, and swam to the surface."

In the end, three men—Commander Payne, Lieutenant Hasker, and crewman William Robinson—survived the accident. The other five crewmen—Michael Cane, Nicholas Davis, Absolum Williams, Frank Doyle, and John Kelly—were all drowned or asphyxiated. To what star-crossed causation does one attribute the grim fate that befell the submarine boat and its crew? Was the incident a freak accident, a devilish turn of happenstance? Or, from a broader perspective, might McClintock have been acting prudently when he barred those lacking experience in submarine boats from even entering the craft? Perhaps, in the end, the *Fish Boat* wasn't as simple to operate as first appearances might have suggested.

In a postwar letter to Matthew Fontaine Maury, McClintock—duly respectful of the dead and mentioning no names but clearly handing up a mental indictment of those he considered responsible for the mishap—offered his own postmortem: "The boat and machinery was so very simple, that many persons at the first inspection believed that they could work the boat without practice or experience, and although I endeavored to prevent inexperienced persons from going underwater in the boat, I was not always successful in preventing them."

Because by then the *Fish Boat* had become such a widely witnessed curiosity, grieving over the lost seamen acquired a public dimension. Writing from aboard the CSS *Palmetto State*, which had furnished Absolum Williams, one of the *Fish Boat*'s volunteer crewmen, Confederate Signal Corps member Augustine Smythe felt a personal sense of loss. "We had quite a sad accident yesterday," he wrote to an aunt. "A 'machine' we had here & which carried eight or ten men, by some mismanagement filled with water & sank, drowning five men, one belonging to our vessel, & the others to the Chicora. They were all volunteers for the expedition & fine men too, the best we had. It has cast quite a gloom over us. Strange, isn't it, that while we hear with indifference of men being killed all around us, the drowning of one should affect us so."[3]

General Beauregard, for his part, could ill afford any prolonged grieving over the loss. Beset by a military predicament that seemed, each day, to be closing in on him, he had to decide—and quickly—whether or not to salvage the submarine boat. Soon after the accident, he wired his subordinate General Roswell Sabine Ripley, commanding army officer of the Charleston district: "Fish Torpedo still at bottom of bay, no one working on it. Adopt immediate measures to have it raised at once. Put proper person in charge of work. Inform Lieut Payne of my orders."

The *Fish Boat*, according to a later account, was found to be "lying at an angle of about 35 degrees, the bow deep in the mud." The Herculean task of raising the wreck from the harbor floor fell to Angus Smith and David Broadfoot, a civilian diving team that often worked in Charleston for the Confederate Navy. Gathering their support crew, heavy chains, submarine armor, and air pumps and hoses at the Fort Johnson dock, Smith and Broadfoot soon made their descent toward the craft. And eventually the *Fish Boat* was resurrected.

When the boat's hatches were pried open, they offered a grisly scene—the bodies of the five doomed crew members were grossly bloated. Indeed, Edmund Ruffin, in his diary, recounting a secondhand account, asserted that "the corpses were so swollen, & so offensive, that they could not be drawn out of the hold—& they were suffered to remain until the process of putrefaction had ceased." Indeed, in the end, to remove them through the *Fish Boat*'s two narrow hatches it became necessary to saw off the arms and legs of each corpse. The Smith and Broadfoot team were paid $7,000 for the boat's salvage and another $400 for the removal of the five bodies within. The burial of the five men—in Charleston's Seaman's Burial Ground—required coffins of a size that compelled Payne to pen a justifying note to his superior; with his September 22 invoice of $135 for the men's burial: "The amount is large but the bod[ies] had been under water and required larger coffins."[4]

The submarine boat, meanwhile, was pumped out and, after the removal of the corpses, given a thorough cleaning. And by September 14—sixteen days after the accident—the *Fish Boat* was reassigned to Lieutenant Payne. During that awkward interregnum, the *Fish Boat*, like some unwanted orphan, lay berthed at the North Eastern Railroad Depot's wharf in downtown Charleston. There—open to scrutiny by loyal Charlestonians and Union spies alike—the craft waited forlornly for its next assignment.

Then, on September 19, five days after the boat's reassignment to Lieutenant Payne, Horace Hunley, now in Charleston and suddenly bestirred to reengage with the project, penned a letter to General Beauregard. Little did Hunley then know of the dire personal consequences that the letter would eventually entail for its author:

> Sir:
>
> I am a part owner of the torpedo boat the Hunley. I have been interested in building this description of boat since the beginning of the war, and furnished the means entirely of building the predecessor of this boat, which was lost in an attempt to blow up a Federal vessel off fort Morgan [in] Mobile Harbor. I feel a deep interest in its success. I propose if you will place the boat in my hands to furnish a crew (in whole or in part) from Mobile who are well acquainted with its management, I [will] make the attempt to destroy a vessel of the enemy as early as practicable.

It was a bold move for Hunley. Though he had no prior relationship with the general, he was implicitly appealing to their shared Louisiana ties—a web of associations stretching from Francis Hatch to John Slidell to Henry Leovy. Moreover, Hunley's claim to have "furnished the means entirely of building the immediate predecessor" craft of the *Fish Boat*—the *American Diver*—was likely at best an exaggeration, at worst an outright lie. But among the letter's other noteworthy aspects, it includes one of the earliest, if not *the* earliest, reference to the *Fish Boat* by the name by which posterity would commemorate the craft—the *Hunley* or, more formally, the *H. L. Hunley*.

All previous names for the *Hunley* and its immediate predecessor, the *American Diver*, had been more generic and descriptive than formal and nominative, more fluid than fixed.

Indeed, except for the CSS *Pioneer*, all of the submarine boats with which Hunley had been associated—specifically, the *American Diver* and the *Fish Boat*—had remained unregistered with the Confederate government and possessed names of a provisional, ad hoc cast. Thus, just as the biblical Adam had asserted his dominion over the world by the effrontery of bestowing names upon its animals, so Horace Lawson Hunley—though on paper a mere $400 investor in the boat—was not only giving the craft its first formal name, he was also asserting his moral, if not financial, dominion over the craft.

Hunley's letter to Beauregard manifested a renewed sense of engagement with a project that, only weeks earlier, in Hunley's letter to McClintock, he had referred to as "your experiment" in Charleston. But then again, two of the key investors in the submarine boat were no longer even in town. The Texans Edgar Singer and J. D. Breaman were, by then, in Richmond—no doubt trying to scare up some fresh government contract work.

On top of that, weeks earlier, had not those two and all of the other partners stood by as General Beauregard confiscated this boat on which they had labored for so long and spent so much money? Reinforcing Hunley's sense of entitlement, more recently—in the wake of that terrible accident that killed five men—not a single one of those partners, so far as records indicate, had stepped forward to ask that the boat be returned to its original owners. Given those circumstances, who besides Horace Hunley enjoyed a stronger claim over the craft? And, for that matter, who else better deserved to have it bear his name? William Alexander, years later, when a correspondent asked how the craft, though built by others, ultimately came to bear Hunley's name, answered that it was Hunley who "first conceived the idea of this boat." But it should also be noted that, conceptually, the first incarnation of the underwater craft that

Alexander alluded to as "this boat" was actually the *Pioneer*—
conceived and constructed in New Orleans months before
Alexander, based in Mobile, had met Horace Hunley, James
McClintock, and Baxter Watson. Perhaps, then, the point to derive from Alexander's assertion has to do less with who actually
first conceived the idea of the boat than with Hunley's evident
success in enticing Alexander and, likely, others into believing
that Hunley had played that seminal role.

As it turned out, unbeknownst to Hunley when, on September 19, he penned his letter to Beauregard, the general had, at
least ten days earlier, already decided to dismiss Lieutenant
Payne from his command of the *Fish Boat*. Acting on Beauregard's decision, an order on September 9 from General Thomas
Jordan to a subordinate instructed that "Lieutenant Payne
should be relieved" of the command. Beyond dismissing Payne,
however, Beauregard found himself in a quandary about who
should command the submarine boat. Jordan's order of September 9 offered no hint of whom, if anyone, Beauregard had
in mind for the command.

Having already dismissed Payne, Beauregard, as he weighed
Hunley's request, likely pondered the cluster of associations
stretching back to New Orleans that connected him and Hunley. But while those bonds mattered, compared to other considerations, they likely resonated but faintly. The general knew he
was running low on options. And besides that, Hunley claimed
he had men in Mobile who were ready and willing—right
now—to come to Charleston and to squeeze into the dark in-
nards of this iron contraption.

And surely, Beauregard also must have surmised, given this
boat's recent history, that it would be difficult, if not impossible,
to find volunteers in Charleston willing to take that same risk.

And so, on September 22—three days after Beauregard received Hunley's offer—he issued orders to have the *Hunley*
turned over to Hunley and to provide him with any assistance
and supplies that he required, with "the understanding that said
boat shall be ready for service in two weeks" and that all costs
were to be made "at the expense of the Confederate States."[5]

9

The *H. L. Hunley*

By the first week of October 1863, the first members of the crew from Mobile that Horace Hunley had promised General Beauregard had reached Charleston. As Hunley had assured the general, all of these men, from Mobile's Park and Lyons Machine Shop, were "well acquainted" with the submarine boat.

The new crew had yielded to Hunley's entreaty only after he had persuaded them that the recent accident had resulted from the boat's operation by inexperienced men. By contrast, they—the men who had worked on the craft in Mobile—had a wealth of experience with such boats. So how great could the risks be? Beyond that—and it had been left unsaid in Hunley's letter to Beauregard—many of these men had also been acquainted with the *American Diver*, the predecessor boat that the original partners from New Orleans had constructed in Mobile. To any casual observer, it would have appeared that Horace Hunley was now in charge of the project. But lest the world miss that point, using a stencil he had kept with him since leaving New Orleans and with which he had created signs for his successive law offices, he soon painted a new name—*H. L. Hunley*—on the submarine craft.[1]

But appearances often deceive. In fact, Hunley exercised far less authority over the craft than that which he implicitly claimed. Yes, the boat—at least unofficially—now bore his name. And, though Beauregard had granted Hunley nominal custody of the craft, officially it remained under the *control* of the Confederate military.

Moreover—if for no other reason than the fact that he had spent the past few months away from the submarine boat project—H. L. Hunley had little if any experience at the helm of the *H. L. Hunley*. Fortunately, however, for all concerned parties, even before Hunley had made his offer to Beauregard, he knew of a suitable commander, then based in Mobile, who, Hunley was confident, was fully qualified to assume command of the *H. L. Hunley's* diving planes and its other newfangled intricacies.

The submarine boat's new commander was to be twenty-two-year-old First Lieutenant George E. Dixon, of the Confederate Army. According to varying accounts, when the *Hunley*—then still called the *Fish Boat*—had been in Mobile harbor, Dixon had "taken an active part in the construction of this vessel," or had "successfully experimented with the boat," or, at the least, had merely "taken a great interest" in the submarine boat. Whatever his prior experience with the vessel, the young officer clearly brought an informed and disciplined zeal to his new assignment.[2]

Dixon's origins are unclear. No confirmed image of him is known to exist. He was probably not a Southerner, and possibly he was a native of the Midwest. He had been serving as an engineer aboard a Mississippi riverboat when the war commenced. Apparently quite wealthy, his dandyish wardrobe and accoutrements—linen shirts, leghorn hat, diamond pin, and cashmere pants—seemed more suited to a riverboat gambler than to a riverboat engineer. When war came, Dixon enlisted in the Confederate Army. And, in April 1862, as a member of Company A of Alabama's Twenty-first Infantry Regiment, he suffered a severe wound to his upper left thigh from a musket ball during the Battle of Shiloh. The injury would have been more serious, even fatal, had it not been for a twenty-dollar U.S. gold coin that deflected the musket ball's trajectory. In May 1862, in recognition for his service at Shiloh, Dixon was promoted to the rank of first lieutenant.

After Shiloh, Dixon, still attached to the Twenty-first Alabama Infantry Regiment, returned to Mobile. There he soon became acquainted with the submarine boat project unfolding at the Park and Lyons shop. Presumably the lieutenant still limped from the wound he had suffered at Shiloh. But even if he didn't, one may assume, based on his subsequent actions, that he was growing weary of his life in Mobile, away from the war front. He longed for action.[3]

Through Hunley's beseeching of Beauregard, and Beauregard's requests to Dixon's superiors in Mobile, Dixon soon obtained a twenty-day leave of absence from General Maury. Good-luck coin in pocket, the young army officer found his way to Charleston. Joining him there were his second in command Thomas Park, one of the two partners in the Park and Lyons shop, and Charles Sprague, the torpedo expert already based in Charleston. Rounding out the *H. L. Hunley*'s complement— the so-called Hunley and Park crew—were five other men from Mobile: Robert Brookbank, Joseph Patterson, Charles McHugh, Henry Beard, and John Marshall.

With no time to squander, the new crew, under Captain Dixon's command, began familiarizing themselves—or reacquainting themselves—with the submarine boat's operations. To the delight of onlookers who, weeks earlier, had dismissed the boat as a death trap, the *H. L. Hunley* soon resumed its diving and resurfacing in Charleston Harbor with a porpoiselike aplomb. Crowds gathered on the Cooper River docks to watch the submarine boat as it made successive dives under the CSS *Indian Chief*, a three-masted schooner anchored in the harbor. Dragging a dummy torpedo—an empty canister—at the end of a hundred or so feet of rope, the *Hunley* would approach the Confederate ship, then abruptly slip beneath its wooden hull, only to reappear minutes later on the *Indian Chief*'s opposite side.

On October 15, however, Dixon was for some reason unavailable to command the boat. William Alexander—skewing the generally accepted *Hunley* chronology that places Dixon that day in Charleston—later claimed that Dixon was with him that day, in Mobile, and not yet assigned to the *Hunley*. Eager to participate, Dixon "would have been one of the Hunley and Parks [*sic*] crew had there been a vacancy." Whatever the case—whether Dixon was simply elsewhere in Charleston or back in Mobile—what happened next is beyond dispute.

Horace Hunley, on that overcast morning, somewhere near the mouth of the Cooper River, took the controls of his submarine boat. To entertain the awaiting crowd, he proceeded to execute the boat's usual mock attack on the *Indian Chief*. By initial appearances, all appeared to be going according to plan. The *Hunley* approached the *Indian Chief*. And several hundred feet off that larger vessel's starboard side, the underwater craft dived beneath the water's surface.

This time, however, as anxious minutes festered into a damning eternity of hours, the *H. L. Hunley* failed to reappear—not on the *Indian Chief*'s port side, nor anywhere else. Like some victim of one of the vengeful Furies of Greek mythology, the little boat had once again vindicated McClintock's caveat about the fatally deceptive simplicity of its operations. Only in this instance, the *H. L. Hunley*—eschewing nepotism—had managed, besides taking the lives of its other seven cranking crewmen, to even claim that of the man for which the boat had been recently renamed. Horace Hunley's pride had affixed his name to the submarine boat. But hubris put him, that day, at the boat's helm.

For the absent but still alive George Dixon, meanwhile, the mishap marked a bittersweet irony. Even so, his good luck gold coin had once again proven itself far more than double the worth of its weight in that precious metal.[4]

10

'Tis More Dangerous to Those Who Use It
Than to the Enemy

IN THE WAKE of the *H. L. Hunley's* latest sinking, General Pierre Beauregard could not help but question his faith in the potential blockade-piercing powers of the submarine boat. But despite those doubts, he remained intrigued by the craft's still untested military prowess. After all—so far as anyone could determine—it had been Horace Hunley's poor judgment in choosing to command the craft rather than any mechanical defect in the boat that had caused this latest mishap. Thus, by October 18, 1863—three days after the accident—orders had been issued, once again, to raise the boat from the harbor floor. By then, the diving team of Angus Smith and David Broadfoot—who once again had won the grisly recovery job—had already located the *H. L. Hunley* at a depth of some forty-two feet of water.

This latest submarine boat disaster was hardly a secret in and around Charleston. But the city's two major newspapers—acting with the same self-censorship they had exercised after the boat's initial sinking—avoided any immediate mention of the *Hunley*. By now, local editors were well aware of the sort of published revelations that were likely to win them a reprimand from local military officials. Indeed, on October 18, three days after the *Hunley*'s second sinking, the *Augusta* (Georgia) *Daily Constitutionalist* published a revealing and disparaging story, by a correspondent identified only as "W," on torpedo and submarine boats. The story implicitly referred to the *Hunley*'s recent mishap. "These crafts," W concluded, "have been more injurious to our people than to the enemy, and thus far have proved to be a humbug."

The following day, Beauregard—exercising the sort of "boldness," so admired by General Grant, by which the Confederate military "silenced all opposition and all croaking"—ordered his chief of staff, Jordan, to write a letter to the *Constitutionalist*'s editor. Jordan's missive complained about the offending story's comments on the "Submarine Torpedo Boat," as well as its references to new changes in the armaments at Fort Sumter. Such information, Jordan wrote, "is surely of benefit to the enemy, and it has been particularly the wish of the Commanding General that this matter be kept from their knowledge."

Jordan then came to the intent of his letter—brute press intimidation. "In view of these facts, he [Beauregard] trusts that you will have no objection to furnish him with the name of your correspondent 'W' and at the same time, he must request that you will in [the] future abstain from publishing any thing [*sic*] the knowledge of which would possibly be of the least service to the enemy."

For civilians in Charleston, a growing sense of isolation impinged upon their days, a sense of being cut off from the rest of the world and even from news originating in their own city. Indeed, yet another order from Beauregard soon compounded that sense of remove by imposing de facto martial law upon Charleston. On October 17, the *Mercury* published an edict originating from the general that required all civilians visiting or returning to the city to be prepared to show proper travel credentials that were to be issued by the office of Charleston's mayor.[1]

Storms delayed the salvage of the *Hunley* for three weeks. Not until November 7 did the wrecked boat breach the harbor's surface—a feat for which the Smith and Broadfoot salvage firm was promised $13,750, half of the boat's value as assessed by a team of military referees. That assessment of the craft's worth, in turn, represented an almost doubling of the original $15,000 budget that, a year earlier, had funded the boat's construction in Mobile. The diving team was also promised another $400 for removing the eight bodies from and cleaning the *Hunley*.

A Confederate military oversight board later second-guessed the $13,750 figure. Noting the government support that Smith and Broadfoot had received during the salvage operation, it decreed that the team should be paid $6,875—half that figure. But no one gainsayed the $400 figure for the body removal and the boat's cleaning.

That price proved, by any measure, a bargain. When hatches of the water-filled craft were pried open and its crew chamber was pumped out, those who crawled inside were unprepared for the scene they confronted. "The spectacle was indescribably ghastly," General Beauregard later recalled. "The unfortunate men were contorted into all kinds of horrible attitudes; some clutching candles, evidently endeavoring to force open the man-holes; others lying in the bottom[,] tightly grappled together, and the blackened faces of all presented the expression of their despair and agony."

Lieutenant William Alexander was an original member of the submarine boat's Hunley and Park crew, but at the last minute he had given his spot to Thomas Park, one of the co-owners of Mobile's Park and Lyons Machine Shop. Even so, Alexander eventually had followed his old Mobile friends to Charleston. And he was present when the freshly salvaged *Hunley* was opened.

In an article he wrote decades later, Alexander attributed the loss of the second crew—the Hunley and Park crew—not to any conscious error, to any mistake born of erroneous or insufficient information on Horace Hunley's part. Rather, Alexander saw the accident as issuing from what he viewed as Hunley's "forgetfulness"—a failure of memory born not of ignorance, but of excessive "familiarity"—complacency is perhaps a better word—with the boat's diving and resurfacing procedures.

While diving beneath the *Indian Chief*, Alexander speculated, Hunley had reflexively opened the boat's forward sea cock—the valve that allowed water to enter the forward ballast tank. Later, to resurface, he presumably intended to use the forward pump to expel whatever water had entered the tank. "It was found in practice to be easier on the crew to come to the surface by giving the pumps a few strokes and ejecting some of the water ballast, than by the momentum of the boat operating on the elevated fins." In Alexander's imagining of the accident, he forgot that it was the crewman seated immediately behind the commander, not the commander, who operated the forward ballast tank and pump. Given the cramped confines of the crew chamber, it would have been impossible for Hunley, occupying the commander's station, to operate either.

Modified with that correction, Alexander's replay of the accident carries a certain plausibility. As Hunley sought to resurface—forgetting he had not ordered the sea cock closed—he ordered the crewman immediately behind him to crank the pump that ejects water from that same forward ballast tank. As water flooded into the boat's crew chamber, it began plunging head first toward the harbor floor. Hunley, meanwhile, in the boat's darkness, ordered the crewman behind him to continue cranking the pump—both of them never realizing, or realizing only too late, that the sea cock remained open. Could the men have been saved from either drowning or asphyxiation? Alexander recalled that when the *Hunley* was brought to the surface, those inspecting the craft noticed that the bolts securing the two hatches had been unscrewed. Apparently, Alexander concluded, the men had tried to open the hatch lids, but water pressure had held both of them shut.

But three of the seven main ballast keel-blocks were removable, a safety feature. So why had they not been dropped? For that too, Alexander offered an explanation: yes, the men had tried to drop these blocks. Inspectors of the wreck determined that bolts, alleged by Alexander to have secured the removable blocks, had been partially turned. But the crew had simply run out of time—the boat had struck bottom—before the keel blocks could be dropped.

Like Beauregard, Alexander recalled the grisly scene that awaited those who opened the *H. L. Hunley*'s two hatches—a tableau that evoked Edgar Allan's Poe's macabre short story "The Premature Burial": "When the hatch covers were lifted considerable air and gas escaped. Captain Hunley's body was forward with his head in the forward hatchway, his right hand on top of his head (he had been trying, it would seem, to raise the hatch cover). In his left hand was a candle that had never been lighted, the sea cock on the forward end . . . was wide open."[2]

In Horace Hunley's pockets, the recovery team found $1,091 in Confederate currency and $25 in U.S. gold coins valued, due to the inflation bedeviling the South, at $250 in Confederate money. They also recovered a gold watch whose value was later assessed at $25 in Confederate money.

In the letter that Hunley had written to Henry Leovy, from Canton, Mississippi, on May 4—five months earlier—he had beseeched his old friend, "should any accident befall me," to take charge of his affairs. Specifically, Leovy was instructed to sell sugar and tobacco crops owned by Hunley—those crops which, stowed away for safekeeping, remained unconfiscated by Federal or Confederate forces—"and use the money for speculation or running the blockade till the end of the war." Whatever revenues those sales yielded, Hunley further instructed, should be used to pay off debts to his brother-in-law Barrow. And if the sales yielded any profits, Leovy was to divide those between himself and Barrow. Following that settling of accounts, Horace's sister Volumnia Barrow was to receive any and all remaining money and property.

In the will, written that same day, Hunley—expanding upon the instructions given in his letter—dictated that Leovy, after taking $5,000 from the estate, should distribute the remainder of its assets to Volumnia. The will also included a wistful "request" from Hunley to Volumnia that "if my property in Louisiana be recovered," she should "use at her discretion five thousand dollars for the benefit of my Aunt Mrs. L. E. Lawson."

An inventory of Horace Lawson Hunley's estate, filed a year later in St. Tammany Parish, listed its total value as $48,679.67—a figure woefully shy of the fortune he likely had dreamed of amassing. And even that assessed value likely overstated the estate's true worth. The bulk of Hunley's property, even by then, consisted of virtually worthless Confederate currency, along with assorted claims against the Confederate government and various individuals for sugar and other goods, claims that almost certainly would never be paid. Saddest of all among the will's itemized entries was the one for $400—for "Interest in Torpedo boat H. L. Hunley at Charleston."

On November 8—a day after the retrieval of his boat and body—Horace Hunley was laid to rest in Charleston's Magnolia Cemetery. In a two-sentence notice the following day, Charleston's *Daily Courier* eulogized him as a "devoted patriot to his country's cause." On November 9, a day after Hunley's funeral, the corpses of the other seven crew members were removed from the boat and buried in the same cemetery.

Hunley's friend—and now estate executor—Henry Leovy had journeyed to Charleston to attend Horace's funeral and tie up legal matters related to his properties. But the sad task of notifying Volumnia Hunley Barrow, still in Louisiana, of her brother's death fell to Gardner Smith, an inventor and engineer who had spent time in New Orleans and Mobile and who, apparently just recently, had become one of Horace's closest friends.

Volumnia had longed for Horace's return ever since he had fled New Orleans in spring 1862, just ahead of Flag Officer Farragut's squadron. And in the intervening months, she and her husband, Robert Ruffin Barrow, had done their utmost to entice him back to Louisiana. In April 1863, six months before Hunley's death, Robert Barrow had written to Horace pleading for his return. "This is the place for you & you ought to be here and you should be here," he wrote. "So come home."

But the Barrows' entreaties had failed to bring Horace back. And now he was gone. In his November 29 letter from Mobile, Gardner Smith related the circumstances of Horace's death, offered his sympathies, and described the "solemn and Impressive" Episcopal church service that had preceded his burial in Charleston. "I had a fine lined coffin ready," he wrote. "General Beauregard ordered a military escort, two companies and a band of music[ians]." Smith also transcribed the inscription on the stone tablet that marked the grave of Volumnia's only brother:

CAPT HORACE
L. HUNLEY
Aged 39 years
of Louisiana
A native of Tennessee
Who lost his life in the
Service of his Country
On the 15th of Oct. 1863

Smith told Volumnia of how the other seven crewmen aboard the *Hunley* had been recovered a day after Horace's body was retrieved, and buried in the same cemetery on the day after Horace's burial. Smith also wrote of how close he and Hunley had become. "I lost in him my best male friend." Likewise, he recalled, "my wife had also become much attached to him. He was so gentlemanly and kind. When I came home and related the death and burial, she wept as though it had been a dear relative. And said—Oh! That I could have been with you to have wept at the grave [in place of] an only sister whose heart must bleed for a brother lost & buried among strangers. But here I assure you, not without friends, for he was beloved by all who knew him." Enclosed with Smith's letter to Volumnia were three mementos of her brother: a lock of Horace's hair, a pair of officer's sleeve buttons, and two gold studs.[3]

Yet another show of deference—one of which Smith was possibly unaware—marked the funerals at Magnolia Cemetery. So that Horace and his crew might be buried in the same section of the graveyard, alongside one another, the Charleston novelist and historian William Gilmore Simms, an ardent supporter of the Confederacy, arranged to exchange a plot he owned in that part of Magnolia for another in a different area.[4]

Fate remains an ineffable proposition, and there are many vantages from which to ponder it. From one perspective, First Lieutenant George E. Dixon had been lucky. Sheer happenstance—the fact that he had, for whatever reason, not been at the boat's helm on a particular day—had saved him from the misfortune that befell the *H. L. Hunley's* Hunley and Park crew.

But from another perspective, chance had played no role in the accident. And it's possible that Dixon—his gold coin notwithstanding—took this latter, less superstitious view. Perhaps the cocky Dixon saw the accident as a logical consequence of what he possibly viewed as Horace Hunley's essential unfitness for command. Perhaps—viewed through Dixon's own diamond-hard regard for his own nautical prowess—the accident seemed an incident unlikely to be repeated, so long as a competent commander was at the boat's helm.

Whichever of those perspectives Dixon eventually embraced—or, more likely, whatever blend of those two views he finally adopted—nothing diminishes the startling quality of the next turn of events: by November 12—a mere four days after Horace Hunley's burial—Lieutenant Dixon was already beseeching General Beauregard and other senior Confederate officers in Charleston to let him and the *H. L. Hunley* have one more chance at sinking a Union ship![5]

In the end, Beauregard's growing isolation as the defender of a beleaguered city and his increasing alienation from his own political superiors probably aided those eager to see the *Hunley* resume its operations.

Supremely confident and possessed of a larger-than-life public persona, General Beauregard had never enjoyed good relations with Jefferson Davis, the often brooding and prickly president of the Confederate States of America. And if either of the two men needed a reminding of their poor rapport, it had come ten days earlier, on November 2, as Davis concluded a tour of the Confederacy. Davis had been passing through Charleston en route back to Richmond; and during a speech at City Hall he praised the city's defenders, but failed to mention Beauregard by name. Beauregard, perceiving a slight, retaliated by rescinding his prior agreement to attend a dinner held that evening to honor the president.

Moreover, that slight, real or imagined, came amid a season of discontent for the usually buoyant Beauregard. The previous March, news arrived from Louisiana of the death of the general's beloved wife, Caroline. Her passing and his continuing troubles with Davis and other Confederate leaders, military and civilian, produced a despondency so deep that Beauregard seriously considered resigning from the army.

In the end, the general, quite vividly, wore Charleston's deteriorating situation on his once dapper visage. As a consequence of the ongoing Federal blockade, Beauregard, unable to acquire the imported dye by which he had maintained the dashing darkness of his hair, mustache, and goatee, was forced to allow all three to grow gray.

As late as November 5—three weeks after the *H. L. Hunley*'s latest accident and three days after his latest dustup with President Davis—General Beauregard remained fixed in his position that the *Hunley* should never again be deployed. While Dixon was in Mobile beseeching General Dabney Maury for an extension of his detached duty in Charleston, Beauregard sent him a telegram: "I can have nothing more to do with that Submarine boat. 'Tis more dangerous to those who use it than to the enemy."

But Beauregard's telegram notwithstanding, over the coming days he faced relentless suasion from the submarine boat's advocates. Many of those calls came from two key *Hunley* supporters—Beauregard's chief-of-staff General Thomas Jordan and Lieutenant George E. Dixon.

Young Dixon possessed no proven credentials as a military leader. But Beauregard apparently saw something—some dash of resolve or self-confidence—in the soldier from Mobile that he admired. In a later letter, the general would call Dixon "a brave and determined man." Thus, that November 1863, Beauregard, acting on gut instinct, reversed his earlier decision and granted Dixon's request to be allowed to resume his command of the *Hunley*.

Afterward Beauregard completed arrangements with General Maury for an extension of Dixon's detached detail away from Mobile. And, on November 14, through Thomas Jordan, Beauregard also granted Dixon's request for assistance in cleaning the craft. He ordered the services of ten slaves armed with brushes, soap, and lime to thoroughly scour what Beauregard in his official order now referred to as the "sub marine Torpedo Boat H L Hunley." Beyond that, Beauregard ordered that all necessary assistance be accorded to Dixon to make the needed repairs to the craft.[6]

Still other events involving torpedoes in Charleston Harbor, meanwhile, were transforming attitudes inside both Union and Confederate circles. Earlier that fall, on the night of October 5, the torpedo boat *David* had attacked the Union ironclad *New Ironsides*. Rear Admiral John Dahlgren was outraged. Indeed, the assault so angered him that—overcoming his own moral qualms about torpedoes—he even proposed their use by his own forces. Writing on October 7 to Navy Secretary Welles, a furious Dahlgren argued that Union ships should match and raise the Confederates' bet: "If 60 pounds of powder, why not 600 pounds? . . . By all means let us have a quantity of these torpedoes, and thus turn them against the enemy. We can make them faster than they can." In Charleston Harbor, meanwhile, to safeguard his fleet from further attacks, Dahlgren ordered outrigged nets attached to all monitors during the night.

The *David* had failed to sink the *New Ironsides*. But its success in damaging the Union vessel boosted Confederate morale. And it was that success that caused Confederate officers to listen to the *David*'s commanding officer, James H. Tomb, when he told them of a recent incident involving the *Hunley*. The incident, a barely avoided accident of uncertain date, had occurred as the *David* was towing the *Hunley* past Fort Sumter, from the Inner to the Outer Harbor. According to Tomb, during a lull in the towing operation, the rope attached to the *Hunley*'s torpedo became entangled with the *David*'s propeller, and the bomb—suddenly, for some reason, sinking— "came near blowing up both boats before we got it clear of the bottom, where it had drifted."

The *David*'s Captain Tomb had already complained to Flag Officer John Tucker about the *Hunley*'s torpedo. On "three or four" occasions, Tomb later recalled, Tucker had issued such orders. And from the first of those orders and onward, Tomb had warned Tucker that the submarine boat's torpedo delivery system—essentially a bomb trailed perilously through the water at the end of a long rope—posed more danger to the *Hunley* than to enemy ships. All along, the *Hunley*'s plan was to dive under its prey, thus allowing its bomb to float upward and detonate after striking the enemy vessel's hull. As an alternative, Tomb had repeatedly advocated that the *Hunley* be outfitted, like the *David*, with a spar torpedo.

Prior to the close call that almost destroyed both the *Hunley* and the *David*, those warnings from Tomb had failed to nudge

Called the *Fish Boat* during its successful tests in Mobile, Alabama, where it was built, the submarine boat became known as the *H. L. Hunley* after its transfer to Charleston. Conrad Wise Chapman's contemporary painting depicts the sub atop a dock on Shem Creek, in Mount Pleasant, South Carolina. (The Museum of the Confederacy)

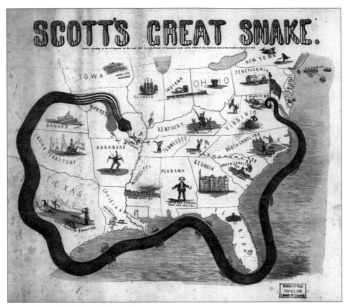

General Winfield Scott's strategy for Union victory, lampooned as the Anaconda Plan, called for an economic strangulation of the Confederacy through, among other actions, a naval blockade of its ports. Southern leaders reacted by embracing underdog tactics and technologies, including the *H. L. Hunley.* (Library of Congress)

Though President Lincoln (*left*), like most leaders of his generation, presumably questioned the morality of "torpedoes"—stationary mines, in modern parlance—and underwater warfare, he welcomed the French inventor Brutus de Villeroi's 1861 offer to build a submarine boat for the U.S. Navy. President Jefferson Davis (*center*) had an interest in underwater warfare dating back to his days as war secretary for President James Buchanan. Confederate Navy Secretary Stephen Mallory (*right*) possessed a similar enthusiasm that reached back to his days as a U.S. senator. (All images: Library of Congress)

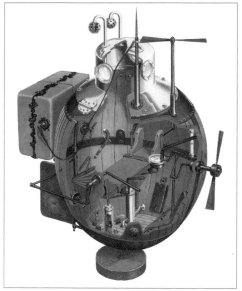

The *H. L. Hunley*'s sponsors were hardly the first to attempt to build a submarine boat capable of sinking an enemy ship. During the American Revolution, the Yankee patriot David Bushnell designed and built the *Turtle*, a one-man pear-shaped wooden submarine craft. (John Batchelor)

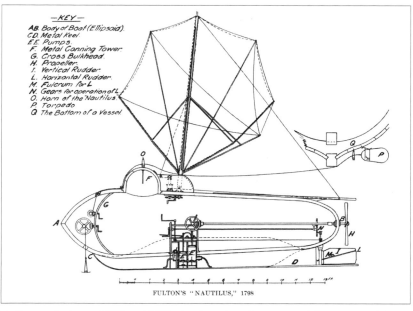

—KEY—

AB. Body of Boat (Ellipsoid).
CD. Metal Keel.
EE. Pumps.
F. Metal Conning Tower.
G. Cross Bulkhead.
H. Propeller.
J. Vertical Rudder.
L. Horizontal Rudder.
M. Fulcrum for L.
N. Gears for operation of L.
O. Horn of the Nautilus.
P. Torpedo.
Q. The Bottom of a Vessel.

FULTON'S "NAUTILUS," 1798

In France, between 1798 and 1800, the American inventor and, later, steamship entrepreneur Robert Fulton designed and built the *Nautilus* and tried unsuccessfully to sell it to Napoleon. Fulton's *Nautilus* became the namesake for the fictional Captain Nemo's craft in Jules Verne's 1870 novel *Twenty Thousand Leagues Under the Sea*. (From *Robert Fulton and the Submarine*, by William Barclay Parsons)

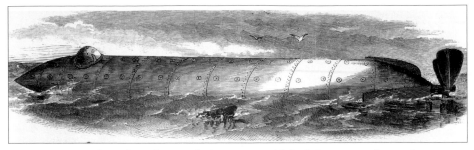

In 1861 *Frank Leslie's Illustrated Newspaper* published this image of an underwater craft built by de Villeroi, a vessel that soon became the prototype for the *Alligator*, the U.S. Navy's first submarine, completed in 1862. (U.S. Navy Historical Center)

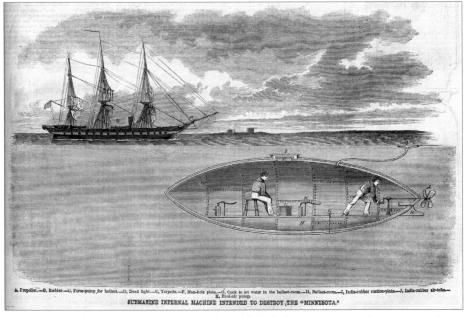

A, Propeller.—B, Rudder.—C, Force-pump for ballast.—D, Dead light.—E, Torpedo.—F, Man-hole plate.—G, Cock to let water in the ballast-room.—H, Ballast-room.—I, India-rubber suction-plate.—J, India-rubber air-tube.—K, Foul-air pump.
SUBMARINE INFERNAL MACHINE INTENDED TO DESTROY THE "MINNESOTA."

In November 1861, *Harper's Weekly* published this engraving of an unnamed Rebel submarine craft built at Richmond's Tredegar Iron Works. (Hargrett Rare Book and Manuscript Library, University of Georgia)

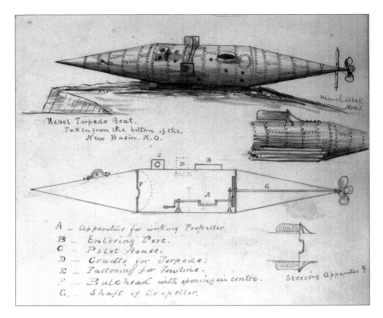

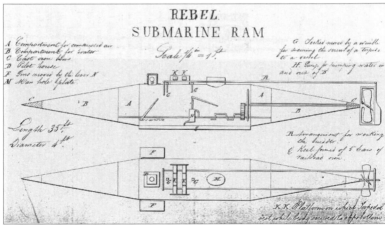

REBEL
SUBMARINE RAM

Built in New Orleans, the CSS *Pioneer* was scuttled in 1862 by Hunley and his fellow builders on the eve of the U.S. Navy's capture of that city. Both sketches here were made after the Federal occupation forces salvaged the boat in 1863. The image at top appears in a sketchbook of contemporary drawings by the artist David M. Stauffer. The bottom depiction, from a report on the boat conducted by U.S. Navy engineers, is considered accurate, save for one detail: the engineers apparently mistook an air chamber used to create buoyancy for one that provided breathing air for the crew. So far as can be known, however, the crew survived exclusively on ambient air inside its crew chamber, not compressed air. (Stauffer sketchbook image from Gilder Lehrman Institute of American History; U.S. Navy image from National Archives)

Two views of Horace Lawson Hunley: a daguerreotype of unknown origin (*left*) and a contemporary but unsigned portrait still in family hands (*right*). (Daguerreotype: Louisiana State Museum; painting: Wilson J. Gaidry III)

The sugar planter Robert Ruffin Barrow was Horace Hunley's brother-in-law and mentor. More than two decades older than Hunley, Barrow opposed secession and numbered among the antebellum South's wealthiest men. (Louisiana State Museum)

Beautiful with a lively intelligence, Volumnia was adored by her brother Horace, who often purchased books to further her self-education. In 1850, Volumnia married Robert Ruffin Barrow, twenty-seven years her senior. (Special Collections, Tulane University)

Sprawling over a full city block, the New Orleans Custom House faced—still faces—Canal Street, the major thoroughfare of antebellum New Orleans's business and political life. Within its walls, Horace Hunley was drawn into the web of intrigue that led to his resolve to build a submarine boat. (Hargrett Rare Book and Manuscript Library, University of Georgia)

James McClintock likely served as the principal designer for the *H. L. Hunley* and its two predecessor vessels—the CSS *Pioneer* and the *American Diver*. Along with his partner Baxter Watson, McClintock owned a machine shop at 31 Front Levee Street, just upriver from Canal Street. (Naval Historical Center)

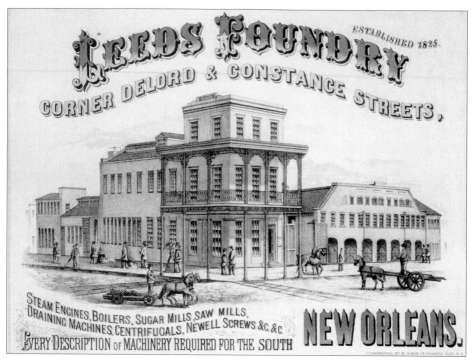

New Orleans's Leeds Foundry, at the corner of Constance and Delord streets, was the site of the construction of the CSS *Pioneer*. The foundry is shown here in a late-nineteenth-century advertisement. (The Historic New Orleans Collection)

After commanding the squadron that captured New Orleans in April 1862, U.S. Navy officer David Farragut was promoted to the rank of rear admiral. Anticipating that Union victory, Hunley and his partners had fled to Mobile, Alabama. (Library of Congress)

Soon after their arrival in Mobile, Hunley and his partners met the city's two chief Rebel military figures—Admiral Franklin Buchanan (*left*) of the Confederate Navy and General Dabney Maury (*right*) of the Confederate Army. While the older Buchanan proved to be an impediment to their work, Maury became an enthusiastic ally. (Library of Congress)

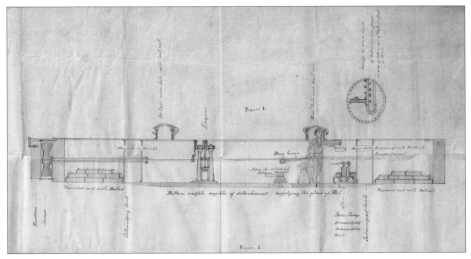

No images of the *American Diver* are known to exist. However, James McClintock's renderings of a submarine boat that he proposed to build for the British Navy in 1872, such as the one above, are often assumed to resemble the *American Diver*— or at least McClintock's original non-manually powered conception of that craft. (National Archives of the United Kingdom)

Impressed with reports from Mobile concerning a craft then called the *Fish Boat*, General Pierre Beauregard requested that the boat be transferred to his base of operations in Charleston, South Carolina. This 1861 portrait is by the artist Thomas C. Healy. (Loaned by the Louisianan Historical Society to the Louisiana State Museum)

Squadron commander of the Confederate Navy fleet based in Charleston, Captain John Randolph Tucker was overshadowed by Beauregard as Charleston's top military leader, but he matched the general in his support of the *H. L. Hunley*. (From *History of the Confederate Navy*, by J. Thomas Scharf)

Rear Admiral John Dahlgren—engineer, inventor, and commander of the South Atlantic Squadron—had a grudging intellectual respect for underwater warfare technologies. But like most military officers of his generation, he also disdained those who employed such weapons. (Library of Congress)

One of the few extant contemporary photographs of a locale associated with a key event in the history of the *H. L. Hunley*, this image of the Confederate Army's Fort Johnson was taken in 1865 after its evacuation by Confederate forces. During trials on August 29, 1863, the *Hunley* sank, killing five crewmen, near the dock in the background. (National Archives)

The USS *Housatonic* is shown here in its glory days. This illustration by R. G. Skerrett was completed in 1902, long after the ship's destruction. (Naval Historical Center)

Destruction of Housatonic by a rebel torpedo Feb 7.17 - 1864. Charleston

This unsigned contemporary drawing of the USS *Housatonic*'s destruction is sometimes attributed to the Civil War illustrator and journalist Arthur Waud. More likely, it was drawn by his brother and fellow artist William Waud. (Library of Congress)

A British-born mechanical engineer and a Confederate Army officer, Lieutenant William Alexander joined the submarine boat project in Mobile in 1862, then followed it to Charleston. After the war, he became a self-appointed keeper of the boat's flame, writing and speaking frequently on the subject. (Museum of Mobile)

In this fanciful 1908 illustration by the author and illustrator Cyril Field, the *Hunley* seems to jump Jet Ski–like out of the water—a nimbleness that would have been impossible for the actual boat, since it seldom attained speeds of more than four miles per hour. (*The Story of the Submarine from the Earliest Ages to the Present Day*, by Cyril Field)

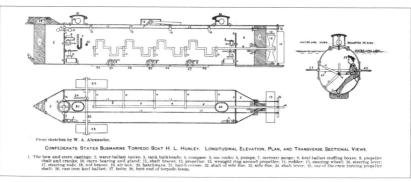

From sketches by W. A. Alexander.

CONFEDERATE STATES SUBMARINE TORPEDO BOAT H. L. HUNLEY. LONGITUDINAL ELEVATION, PLAN, AND TRANSVERSE SECTIONAL VIEWS.

1. The bow and stern castings; 2. water-ballast tanks; 3. tank bulkheads; 4, compass; 5, sea cocks; 6, pumps; 7, mercury gauge; 8, keel-ballast stuffing boxes; 9, propeller shaft and cranks; 10, stern bearing and gland; 11, shaft braces; 12, propeller; 13, wrought ring around propeller; 14, rudder; 15, steering wheel; 16, steering lever; 17, steering rods; 18, rod braces; 19, air box; 20, hatchways; 21, hatch covers; 22, shaft of side fins; 23, side fins; 24, shaft lever; 25, one of the crew turning propeller shaft; 26, cast-iron keel ballast; 27, bolts; 28, butt end of torpedo boom.

This circa 1900 schematic of the *H. L. Hunley* derives from drawings produced during that period by Alexander. While he helped keep the *Hunley* afloat in public memory, Alexander also introduced numerous errors into the historiography of the boat and its two predecessor vessels. In this drawing, for instance, he depicts the *Hunley* as having eight cranking stations—one more than it actually contained. (*Official Records of the Union and Confederate Navies in the War of the Rebellion*)

This mural by the artist John Augustus Walker imagines the construction of the *H. L. Hunley* in Mobile, Alabama. In 1936, as public interest in the boat revived, the federal Works Progress Administration commissioned Walker to paint a mural for Mobile's City Hall. The work was later moved to the Museum of Mobile. (Museum of Mobile)

On August 8, 2000, to the delight of thousands of onlookers ashore and in boats scattered about the harbor, the *H. L. Hunley*, after resting on the ocean floor for 136 years, once again broke the surface of Charleston's waters. (Friends of the *Hunley*)

The *H. L. Hunley* in its tank at Clemson University's Warren Lasch Conservation Center. (Friends of the *Hunley*)

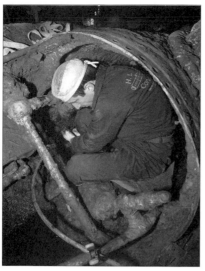

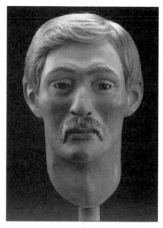

The conservator Philippe de Vivies drills out rivets from the *Hunley* in preparation for the removal of a hull plate. For modern researchers, excavating the wreck poses physical challenges. But for those men who, during the Civil War, labored about the *Hunley* when it was an operational craft, its darkened, perpetually damp crew chamber would have constituted an even greater ergonomic nightmare. (Friends of the *Hunley*)

Researchers at the Warren Lasch Conservation Center produced facial reconstructions of all eight members of the boat's final crew, like this one of the *Hunley*'s last commander, George Dixon. Based on human remains recovered from the wreck, the reconstructions were done manually in clay. Afterward, the clay representations were cast in plastic. (Friends of the *Hunley*)

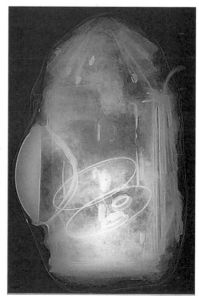

An X-ray of a lantern recovered from inside the *Hunley*. The lantern figures in a widely repeated legend concerning the submarine boat—the story that Captain Dixon flashed a blue light across the water to signal the *Hunley*'s destruction of a Union vessel. In the end, however, as potentially supporting physical evidence for that story, the recovered lantern may prove, at best, inconclusive. (Friends of the *Hunley*)

The Lasch Conservation Center's senior archaeologist Maria Jacobsen, inside the *H. L. Hunley*'s crew chamber on May 23, 2001, moments after finding Captain George Dixon's storied twenty-dollar gold coin. The bent coin's reverse side served as physical confirmation of a widely known legend. An until-then unrecorded inscription read: "Shiloh. April 6, 1862. My Life Preserver. G.E.D." (Friends of the *Hunley*)

Replete with horse-drawn caissons and Civil War reenactors, a funeral procession bearing the remains of the *Hunley*'s third and final crew leaves the Battery along Charleston's East Bay Street on April 17, 2004. Afterward, the remains of the eight crewmen were interred in Charleston's Magnolia Cemetery, which also holds the bodies of the men from the boat's first and second crews. (Friends of the *Hunley*)

any action by Tucker. The *Hunley*, as Tomb correctly recognized, was, after all, "not under the orders of the Navy." But after hearing of the two boats' shared brush with destruction, Flag Officer Tucker—ignoring all interservice rivalry—decided it was time to act. The army's Beauregard, after all, despite having ordered the *Hunley* to resume operations, shared Tucker's concerns about the boat's safety.

Finally, after the *David*'s successful assault on the *New Ironsides*, its commander, James Tomb, enjoyed no small amount of admiration from Beauregard, Tucker, and all other Confederate officers—army and navy alike—around Charleston. By contrast, the two disasters that had already befallen the *H. L. Hunley* loomed as cautionary lessons for Beauregard and other officers. And beyond that, during the *H. L. Hunley*'s four months in Charleston, it had failed to even attempt to place a single torpedo on the hull of a single Union ship. So, against that background, it came as no surprise when, complying with Tomb's request, Flag Officer Tucker ordered that the *David* suspend its towing of the *Hunley*.[7]

Moreover, Beauregard soon ordered the *Hunley* fitted with a spar torpedo. The general also later claimed that, mindful of the disasters that had befallen the craft's two earlier crews, he had simultaneously ordered that the *Hunley* be used "not as a submarine machine, but in the same manner as the David." The *David* and other boats modeled on its design were low-lying steam-powered ironclads designed to run with bow and stern just barely submerged. By adjusting interior ballast tanks, a *David*-class boat could, much like a modern submarine, cruise on the sea's surface, with only its smokestack and wheelhouse gliding above water.

The original *David* and its successor boats—all accorded

numbers rather than names—were built by the Southern Torpedo Company, a group of civilian entrepreneurs in Charleston.
And despite a fitful start, the original *David* soon won Beauregard's admiration—particularly after its October 5 attack on the
Union ironclad *New Ironsides*. And though the *David* had
failed to sink the *New Ironsides*, it would have been logical for
Beauregard and other Confederate officers in Charleston to
embrace the *David*—with its low freeboard design and spar
torpedo system—as an operational model for future operations
of the *Hunley*. But while Beauregard certainly sanctioned the
fitting-out of the submarine boat with a spar torpedo, evidence
that he simultaneously issued orders that the *Hunley* be used
"not as a submarine machine, but in the same manner as the
David" is less persuasive. That latter assertion, presented in a
postwar memoir by Beauregard, presents the general in a benign light—as a prudent commander, concerned with the overall safety of the boat's crew. But, alas, it finds no support in
contemporary documents. Moreover, raising still more doubts
about Beauregard's postwar claim, the *Hunley*, over the coming
weeks, openly continued its diving operations.[8]

After the *Hunley*'s averted accident that imperiled both it and
the *David*, work began to outfit the *Hunley* with a spar torpedo,
a task completed by early January. Extending less than a foot
from the boat's lower bow was a Y-shaped yoke of solid iron; attached to that was an iron pole—the spar—more than seventeen feet long. And at the tip of the spar was the torpedo—a
bomb, reputedly packed with ninety pounds of gunpowder,
and, at its tip, a barbed knifelike blade.

Debates persist over exactly how many pounds of gunpowder the torpedo contained and even how the bomb operated. A
1937 article by the U.S. Navy historian Lieutenant Harry Von

Kolnitz probably best expressed the consensus view of its design. "It consisted of a steel head which fitted as a thimble over the end of the . . . spar or pipe projecting from the bow," he wrote. "This was driven into the enemy's wooden hull by ramming and was retained there by saw-toothed corrugations when the fish boat backed off. As it slipped off the spar, [the enemy ship's hull] would keep with it the torpedo, which was a simple copper can of powder fitted with a trigger. This trigger was attached to a cord lanyard carried on a reel."

If all went as planned, as the spool played out, the rope would tighten, eventually throwing a trigger inside the torpedo that detonated its payload of gunpowder. Borrowing liberally from technologies recently developed by the whaling industry to adapt explosives for use with whale harpoons, the spar torpedo, as modified by military engineers, was designed to give torpedo boats ample time and space to move clear of any explosion.[9]

Inside the boat, meanwhile, to afford the crew members better illumination by which to conduct their various maneuvers, the workers overhauling the *Hunley* at Mount Pleasant also gave the boat's interior a thorough coating of white paint— the better to reflect the scant available light inside the crew chamber.[10]

After the death of the Hunley and Park crew, the *Hunley* was moved to a wharf at the town of Mount Pleasant. Situated on the harbor's east shore, just across the Cooper River from Charleston, Mount Pleasant enjoyed the virtue of being a less public setting. There, over the coming weeks, the *Hunley* underwent repairs and a thorough cleaning. And it was there, as the boat lay atop its Mount Pleasant dock, on Shem Creek, that the soldier-artist Conrad Wise Chapman produced a series of plein air sketches and at least one watercolor rendering of the *Hunley*—one of which, after the war, became the basis for an eventually well-known painting of the boat. In its foreground, that painting depicts two men, one standing and one seated, beside the craft's stern. Possibly for compositional reasons, the scale of the image is slightly skewed; the craft itself appears reduced in size in proportion to the two men depicted alongside it. Even so, the painting, as it turned out, would play a major role in accurately recording the boat's shape and features, if not its full size, for posterity.

During that same period, Dixon, in addition to other challenges confronting him, faced the daunting task of finding a new crew for his twice-cursed submarine boat. That chore was made no easier by General Beauregard's ongoing ambivalences about the *Hunley*. Up to then, during its time in Charleston, the *Hunley*, politically and militarily, had occupied an ambiguous administrative berth—subject to directives from both navy and army officials. But in the fall of 1863, the salvaged *Hunley*, by then regarded as an albatross by many military officials in Charleston, operated at the pleasure of a single officer, General Pierre G. T. Beauregard. Singularly among Confederate officers in Charleston, Beauregard could afford the potential risks to his stature posed by the submarine boat's continued operations. More broadly speaking, by the fall of 1863 the *H. L. Hunley* was, in every significant way, Confederate Army—not Navy—business.

Beauregard, weeks earlier, after much agonizing, had granted Dixon permission to resume operations aboard the *Hunley*. But he still nurtured concerns about the safety of the crew inside the boat. Those worries flared into full view after Dixon sought Beauregard's permission to board the CSS *Indian Chief,* still anchored in Charleston Harbor, to solicit volunteers for the *H. L. Hunley.*

The *Indian Chief* seemed a natural place for Dixon and William Alexander, the *Hunley*'s recently assigned second in command, to scout out a new crew for their boat. Over the past few months, members of the three-masted schooner's crew had watched in amazement as the *Hunley* made repeated dives beneath its bow. And, minutes later on each occasion—with one sadly conspicuous exception—they had gaped with still more amazement as the *Hunley* had subsequently resurfaced on their ship's opposite side. Beyond that, the *Indian Chief* was a receiving ship for the Confederate Navy—a vessel on which fresh recruits were based until more permanent assignments could be arranged. And that fact alone, the presence aboard the *Indian Chief* of scores of raw recruits, rendered the ship a promising place to hunt for *Hunley* recruits.

Beauregard was thinking along similar lines. After several refusals, he finally granted Dixon and Alexander permission to board the *Indian Chief* and seek enlistments among her crew. In granting that permission, however, Beauregard made one stipulation—that the two provide the prospective recruits with a candid account of the *Hunley*'s grim history. As Alexander later recalled, "He strictly enjoined upon us to give a full and clear explanation of the desperately hazardous nature of the service required."

Despite the full-disclosure requirement that Beauregard imposed upon Dixon and Alexander, the two soon gathered a new crew for the *Hunley*. Of the new enlistees, four came from the *Indian Chief*: James A. Wicks, Arnold Becker, Joseph F. Ridgaway, and Frank Collins. Rounding out the eight-man complement were two other volunteers, both apparently European-born, and whom we today know simply as Miller and Lumpkin.[11]

After the cleaning and repairs to the submarine boat were completed at the Shem Creek dock in Mount Pleasant, Dixon and his new crew prepared for their test runs of the boat. The crew would remain quartered at Mount Pleasant where the boat had been repaired; at some point in late December 1863 or January 1864—contemporary documents yield no precise date—the *Hunley* itself was transferred to Breach Inlet, a discreet and deep inlet facing the Atlantic near Battery Marshall, along Sullivan's Island's northeastern edge.

The Battery Marshall compound consisted of artillery pieces, earthen-walled bombproof quarters, and wooden pitched-roof buildings. Breach Inlet—formed by the gap between Sullivan's Island and a neighboring barrier island—was also where three tidal creeks emptied into the ocean. The coastal indentation teemed with strong tidal currents. More broadly, the area around Breach Inlet and Battery Marshall—largely devoid of civilians and civilian buildings—was controlled by Confederate military personnel, who in turn controlled who entered and left the vicinity. Thus, for once, the submarine boat project's seldom respected need for secrecy stood a fighting chance of being fulfilled.

As a military leader, Dixon, from the start, seemed to vindicate the faith that Beauregard invested in him. In Dixon, the general evidently believed he had found a captain for the *Hunley* possessed of greater military virtues than the three other men who, in succession, had recently been at the helm of the craft. In Dixon, Beauregard apparently hoped he had found a leader possessed of greater understanding of submarine boats than John Payne, more boldness than James McClintock, and more discretion than Horace Hunley.

At once Dixon commenced daily trials aboard the submarine boat. Methodically, he began nourishing his subordinates' confidence and skills. As they grew familiar and comfortable with the boat's operations, he soon welded the men into a disciplined crew. Those exercises, weather permitting, continued each day into mid-December. Then, on the fourteenth, the order which Dixon had long awaited finally came. Via a subordinate, General Beauregard instructed Dixon to "take command and direction of the submarine torpedo-boat H. L. Hunley and proceed to-night to the mouth of the harbor, or as far as capacity of the vessel will allow, and . . . sink or destroy any vessel of the enemy with which he can be in contact."[12]

Over the next few weeks, weather permitting, the *Hunley* each night ventured out on its nocturnal sorties—each time, however, failing to engage any enemy ships. Even more dispiriting was the fact that the *Hunley* had required assistance to achieve even those dismal results. Each evening the submarine boat was towed into the Outer Harbor by the *David*, the steam-powered ironclad. But, compounding Lieutenant Dixon's woes—pursuant to Flag Officer Tucker's earlier orders—that assistance soon ended.

Denied the towing assistance they once enjoyed, the crew of the *Hunley* fell back on their own physical exertions to cover the entire distance of their nocturnal sorties. In the weeks after the *Hunley*'s transfer to its Breach Inlet base, the men settled into a regimen in which each day, leaving their Mount Pleasant quarters on the mainland, they crossed a small footbridge over to Sullivan's Island, and from there continued their hike. As rendered by Alexander, the walk—attendant gunfire notwithstanding—sounds downright idyllic: "Leave Mount Pleasant about 1 p.m., walk seven miles to Battery Marshall on the beach (this exposed us to fire, but it was the best walking), take the boat out and practice the crew for two hours in the Back Bay."

Over the next few weeks, Dixon and his crew, now without the *David* to tow them, habituated themselves to the toils of providing all of their propulsion—labors that often resulted in speeds of no more than four miles per hour. By then it was winter, and the men would time their excursions so that they would venture out with the ebb tide and "come in, with the flood tide, a fair wind and dark moon."

For the men, frustration remained a constant companion. On January 31, 1864, Dixon wrote to his friend Henry Willey in Mobile to express his displeasure with the austere "soldiers rations" on which he and his men subsisted: no meat, just "corn meal and rice, for breakfast mush," and "dinner rice and cornbread for supper mush." Dixon likewise complained of the vagaries of weather and sea. "To catch the Atlantic Ocean smooth during the winter months is [a] considerable . . . undertaking and one that I never wish to undertake again. Especially when all parties [are] interested in sitting at home and wondering and criticizing all of my actions and saying why don't he do something. If I have not done anything 'God knows' it is not because I have not worked hard enough to do something."

Compounding Dixon's frustrations—and no doubt inducing nostalgia for his less stressful days as a riverboat engineer—was his knowledge that the enemy was well aware of the unique features of his boat, which had begun its life as a nominal secret but by now was hopelessly exposed. Writing to a friend, Dixon complained: "The fleet offshore have drawings of the submarine and of course they have taken all precautions that it is possible for Yankee ingenuity to invent, but I hope to flank them yet." William Alexander, later recalling that same period, expressed similar frustrations. "Often, after going out six or seven miles, we would have to return," he remembered. "Many times it taxed our utmost exertions to keep from drifting out to sea, daylight often breaking while we were yet in range."

In an estuarine setting much shallower than the open ocean, the men conducted diving experiments to test underwater endurance. As Alexander recounted, "It was agreed to by all hands to sink and let the boat rest on the bottom, in the Back Bay, off Battery Marshall, each man to make equal physical exertion in turning the propeller. It was also agreed that if any in the boat felt that he must come to the surface for air, and he gave the word 'up,' we would at once bring the boat to the surface."

On at least one occasion, however, male pride intruded upon the test of endurance. The *Hunley* had been on the bottom of the bay for some twenty-five minutes. Prior to the dive, Alexander recalled, "each man had determined that he would not be the first to say 'up!' Not a word was said, except the occasional, 'How is it,' between Dixon and myself, until it was as the voice of one man, the word 'up' came from all." Immediately, cranking commenced on the forward and aft pumps, and the boat soon resurfaced.

On still other occasions, when the *Hunley* would venture out into the night sea, the crew, upon surfacing, would raise but slightly the rear hatch and sit silently, and listen to the voices of Union sailors talking and singing in nearby picket boats—oblivious to the Confederates' presence.

At least since the *Hunley*'s transfer to Breach Inlet, the boat's sponsors had assumed that their craft's target would be a Union warship positioned well beyond Charleston's Inner Harbor. As Alexander recalled, "On account of chain booms having been put around the ironsides and the monitors in Charleston harbor, we had to turn our attention to the fleet outside. The nearest vessel, which we understood to be the United States frigate 'Wabash,' was about twelve miles off, and she was our objective from this time on."

Even so, Dixon and his second in command, William Alexander, remained ever open to other targets. So far as can be known, neither man possessed any prior familiarity with the waters of Charleston Harbor. But they also were determined to avoid any repetition of the sort of navigational errors that, in Mobile Harbor, had hampered operations, and ultimately led to the loss, of the *American Diver*. Thus, with a devotion not unlike that brought by novitiates to daily readings of their catechism, the two men methodically embarked upon their studies of the local waters.

Each afternoon, before venturing out onto the Atlantic inside the *Hunley*, the two men—drawing on the latest military intelligence of enemy ship movements—would lie on the beach and, compass in hand, plan their next sortie. As Alexander recalled those days, "Dixon and myself would . . . stretch out on the beach with compass between us and get the bearings of the nearest vessel as she took her position." Reliant upon magnetic forces, compasses of that era—before the invention of gyroscopic compasses—were notoriously unreliable inside iron boats. For that and other reasons, the officers tried to complete as many navigational chores as possible on dry land, in advance of that night's sortie.

Once the two had established the bearings of the evening's target, the torpedo was hoisted onto the *Hunley's* spar. And as darkness fell, the submarine boat would depart Breach Inlet on its nightly hunt. The crew, Alexander recalled, would "go out, steering for that vessel, proceed until the conditions of the men, sea, tide, wind, moon and daylight compelled our return to the dock." Afterward they would "unship the torpedo, put it under guard at Battery Marshall, walk back to quarters at Mount Pleasant and cook breakfast."[13]

During those days and nights, as the *Hunley's* crew searched in vain for their first prey, fate intervened to deal the men yet another demoralizing setback. For weeks, Captain Dixon had been resisting pleadings from other officers in his regiment— but apparently no hard orders from General Maury—seeking his return to Mobile and Alabama's Twenty-first Infantry Regiment. Writing on February 5 to Captain John F. Cothran of that regiment, Dixon insisted that "I am fastened to Charleston and its approaches until I can blow up some of their Yankee ships." However, on that same day, direct orders—instructions that could not be refused—reached William Alexander, summoning him back to Mobile to resume his work as an engineer. The orders, which led him back to the Park and Lyons shop, called for Alexander to direct, in Mobile, the construction of a rapid-fire repeating gun needed for the port's defense.

In his search for a new man to put at the aftmost crankshaft position and to operate the aft ballast tank and pump, Dixon eventually decided to move Joseph Ridgaway down the crew bench to Alexander's old aftmost position. Ridgaway, after all, was well qualified to assume the position of second in command beneath the rear conning tower. In his early thirties and a native of Maryland, Ridgaway had saltwater in his blood. His father had prospered as a merchant sea captain and eventually owned several ships. Young Joseph was just sixteen when he obtained his own seaman's credentials. And in August 1862 he had eagerly gone to Richmond to join the Confederate Navy. When, in the fall of 1863, he elected to join the crew of the *Hunley*, Ridgaway had been aboard the CSS *Indian Chief* since early that year.

To fill, in turn, the crew position vacated by Ridgaway, Dixon eventually won the services of a new volunteer—a young European-born sailor-soldier by the name of J. F. Carlsen. Earlier in the war, Carlsen had served aboard a Confederate privateer, the *Jeff Davis*; later he had joined a Confederate artillery unit based near Charleston, composed mainly of German immigrants, and it was that unit in which he was serving when he answered Dixon's call to join the *Hunley*.

That fall, as the *Hunley*, with its reconstructed crew, resumed its sea trials, yet another Federal ship, the USS *Housatonic*, replaced the USS *Wabash* as the submarine boat's target of choice. As much as anything, the *Housatonic*'s proximity to Breach Inlet had led to the change. Each evening, the 207-foot, steam-powered sloop of war could be seen swinging at anchor near Rattlesnake Shoal, about four miles from Breach Inlet.

The *Housatonic*'s proximity to Breach Inlet had led Dixon to designate it as the *Hunley*'s new target of choice. But when one is navigating a lumbering boat such as the *Hunley*, *proximity* can be a misleading term. Accounts of the *Hunley*'s speed vary: William Alexander recalled, "In comparatively smooth water and light current, our boat could make four miles per hour." But the craft's designer, James McClintock, complained that it generally made as little as two and one-half miles per hour. Given those two estimates and assuming—if only for the sake of argument—that the *Hunley* would face no pesky offshore currents, Dixon likely assumed that the four-mile sortie to Rattlesnake Shoal would require, minimally, more than an hour to complete.

Alas, however, such planning, at least initially, seemed destined to be doomed by the elements. And when February 1864 rolled around, the men at Breach Inlet, looking back over the past few weeks, could not say they'd seen much calm weather. Winds and storms had roiled Charleston Harbor for much of that period. During the lull, Dixon—increasingly self-conscious about the *Hunley*'s inactivity—informed the crew that they would sortie out on the next still evening. Upon locating a suitable target, they would attempt to ram their spar torpedo into the unsuspecting vessel. And afterward, according to later and widely disseminated assertions, the submarine boat's crew was to signal—with a light, possibly a blue light—to the Confederate garrison at Battery Marshall. According to that same legend, the soldiers at Battery Marshall were to answer the *Hunley*'s signal with their own show of light.[14]

On the evening of February 17, the *Hunley* ventured forth from its Breach Inlet dock. It was hardly an ideal night for an attack. Presumably, Dixon would have preferred to attack under a cover of total darkness. But a waxing moon—three days past its half-moon stage—precluded that option. Even so the waters were calm that night, and only a light wind stirred. And Dixon could not afford to wait. At Dixon's request, before the *Hunley* departed, Corporal Daniel W. McLaurin of the Twenty-third South Carolina Volunteers and another member of that regiment joined Dixon and other crew inside the *Hunley* to make some last-minute mechanical adjustments.

As McLaurin later recalled, "Another man and I went aboard and helped propel the boat for some time while the lieutenant [Dixon] and others adjusted the machinery and the rods that held the torpedo and got them to working satisfactorily." Afterward, at roughly 7:00 p.m.—accounts of the departure time vary—Dixon and the seven other men of the *H. L. Hunley* squeezed through the boat's two twenty-inch-wide hatchways.

By the light of a flickering candle he had lit, Dixon took his usual spot beneath the forward conning tower. The other seven men, crouching as they squeezed through the narrow, forty-two-inch-wide crew compartment, soon also found their way to their designated stations along the eighteen-foot port-side crew bench. There, each took his seat, hunched forward uncomfortably as his back and neck adjusted to the curvature of the hull's cramped chamber. Moments later, each of the seven men leaned still farther forward. In unison, they began turning the zigzagged crankshaft before them. As the men turned the long shaft, the iron chamber was filled with the sounds of the movements of the boat's various gears, the clanking of chains, and the fainter *whish*, from outside, of the screw propeller plowing the surrounding waters. Perhaps Dixon, meanwhile, raised his head for a moment into the forward conning tower. If so, through its four view-ports, perhaps he stole a glimpse of the by now moonlit winter evening. Then, angling the rudder-lever before him, he set a course toward the target on which he had settled earlier that day.[15]

11

A Tide Ripple on the Water

AT 8:00 P.M. ON FEBRUARY 17, 1864, slivers of moonlight dappled the chilled Atlantic waters off Charleston, South Carolina. Savoring the scene, Lieutenant John Crosby, USN, climbed to the quarterdeck of the USS *Housatonic* and commenced his supervision of that night's evening watch—the stretch between 8:00 p.m. and 12:00 a.m.

The *Housatonic*, a three-masted Federal sloop of war, belonged to the U.S. Navy's South Atlantic Blockading Squadron, a flotilla of some eighty vessels scattered offshore between Cape Henry, North Carolina, and Key West, Florida. And, as George Dixon and the crew of the *Hunley* had anticipated as they left Breach Inlet about an hour earlier and began their cruise, the *Housatonic* lay anchored tonight behind the sandbar that limns the entrance to Charleston's Inner Harbor.

The city itself, some eight miles to the northwest, could not be seen. However, in the same direction but three miles closer lay Fort Sumter, where this war had begun three years earlier—and, tonight, clearly visible from the *Housatonic*'s deck. An auxiliary steamer, a ship propelled by both wind and steam, the 1,240-ton *Housatonic* stretched 207 feet in length. At her beam, her deck reached thirty-eight feet. More salient, she bristled with a formidable arsenal of weaponry—a 100-pound Parrott rifle, three 30-pound Parrotts, one 11-inch Dahlgren smoothbore, and two 32-pound smoothbores.

During her one-and-a-half-year stint in Charleston Harbor, the *Housatonic*, like other vessels of the squadron, had experienced her share of Rebel engagements. Her guns had participated in the siege shelling that, by then, had reduced much of the city to rubble. She also had captured two blockade runners and caused several others attempting to enter the harbor to return to the open sea.[1]

Tonight, the *Housatonic* lay anchored snugly beyond the range of Fort Sumter and other Confederate batteries guarding Charleston's harbor. Bestowing a further measure of confidence upon the sailors aboard the *Housatonic*, a string of Confederate defeats had recently emboldened Union morale. Indeed, Charleston, along with Wilmington, North Carolina, constituted the Confederacy's only two remaining Atlantic ports open to blockade runners. For the men of the *Housatonic* and for the thousands of other blue-clad soldiers and sailors scattered across this conflict's vast theater, it seemed that their long-sought victory might be close at hand.

Based strictly on the Union's current military fortunes, in other words, that night's watch should have been relatively free of stress. Indeed, of all the assignments a Union Navy sailor might pull, surely blockade duty richly deserved its reputation as among the dullest, often consisting of months at anchor, with little to do except squint seaward toward the horizon and shoreward, often longingly, at whatever port the fleet was blockading. And, as Lieutenant Crosby and the *Housatonic*'s other watch officers could attest, what generally set one watch apart from another were weather and sea conditions—and that night, fortunately, despite the evening chill, both were agreeably tranquil, even pleasant.

Even so, a nervousness prevailed aboard the *Housatonic* that night. Officers and crew alike feared that Confederate torpedo boats lurked somewhere out there in those placid moonlight-flecked waters. Since last October's attack by the Confederate torpedo boat the *David*, on the *New Ironsides*, Union sailors blockading Charleston had lived with such fears. More recently—courtesy of a pair of Rebel informants from the CSS *Indian Chief*, who, weeks earlier, had found their way to the blockading squadron—Union officers and crews had learned that the Rebels even had a torpedo boat that could dive underwater.

One of the Confederate deserters, E. C. Belton, had worked as a mechanic in Mobile. He claimed to have witnessed the construction of the submarine boat and its subsequent trials in Mobile Bay. Mistakenly he referred to the boat that, since then, he said, had been transported by rail to Charleston, as the *American Diver*. Further conflating the identities of the *American Diver* and the *Hunley*, Belton, in addition to telling his interrogators that the boat now in Charleston had sunk twice in that city's harbor, also mistakenly reported that it had sunk once in Mobile, drowning members of an earlier crew. However, save for those errors, Belton and his fellow deserter George Shipp had managed to provide Admiral Dahlgren with a superbly accurate up-close description of the *Hunley*. Both had observed the craft, to the delight of ever larger crowds, making successful dives in Charleston Harbor. But, the two added, they had also witnessed the loss of the boat when it dived beneath the *Indian Chief* and then failed to resurface. Two weeks after the accident, they said, it was raised and eventually sent to nearby Mount Pleasant for repairs.

The deserters' account of the submarine boat included no

mention of the *Hunley*'s new spar torpedo. The two still assumed that the boat's strategy was to dive under its target, dragging a torpedo tied to a rope behind its stern. The natural buoyancy of the torpedo as it floated upward, eventually striking the targeted vessel's hull, would finish the job. As a consequence, Dahlgren's subsequent orders to his commanders—based on the defectors' testimony—reflected no awareness of the spar-mounted torpedo, the latest turn in the *Hunley*'s evolving modus operandi. "It is intended," Dahlgren wrote of the craft, "to go under the bottom of vessels and there operate."[2]

Acting on this latest intelligence and assuming that the boat would not be at Mount Pleasant for long, Dahlgren, from his squadron's flagship, the *Philadelphia*, issued orders on January 7 intended to protect the fleet blockading Charleston. He ordered more men posted to watches on all ships; he ordered guns trained on the water at all times; and—the better to keep enemy forces off balance—he ordered ships to frequently change their anchorages. To avoid accidentally firing on one another, he ordered the ships to anchor so that they were spaced far apart, beyond the range of each other's guns. To make it difficult for explosives to reach their hulls, he ordered chain netting hung from every vessel's sides—a precaution that the *Housatonic* that night of February 17 failed to take. To allow the vessels to slip their anchor cables at a moment's notice, and to get out of harm's way, he ordered all ships, at all times, to keep their coal bunkers full and their fires stoked. Specifically, during the night, when Confederate torpedo boats went on the hunt, Union commanders were under orders, even while anchored, to keep twenty-five pounds of steam in their engines' boilers from 6:00 p.m. to 6:00 a.m. They were, as a *Housatonic* engineer later recalled, "to keep everything ready for getting underway at a moment's warning, and to have the engine ready for backing"—for reversing the ship away from any Rebel torpedo.

And, finally, Dahlgren forbade his commanders—the *Housatonic*'s Charles Pickering among them—from dropping their anchors in the harbor's deeper waters. "By not leaving much space between the bottom of the vessel and the bottom of the channel it will be impossible for the diving torpedo to operate except on the sides and there will be less difficulty in raising a vessel if sunk."[3]

At 8:45 that evening, Lieutenant Crosby thought he spotted a suspicious object moving across the water, on the ship's starboard beam. "At first," he later recalled, "it looked to me like a porpoise, coming to the surface to blow." Whatever it was, the object of his curiosity appeared at that moment to be about seventy-five or a hundred yards from the *Housatonic*'s starboard beam.

Crosby alerted the ship's quartermaster, directed his attention to the spot he had been scrutinizing, and asked him if he noticed anything unusual. "He looked at it through his glass and said he saw nothing but a tide ripple on the water," recalled Crosby.

At that moment, Crosby realized that the object—whatever it was—was gliding "very fast" and straight toward the *Housatonic*. Assuming it to be an enemy craft, he ordered all crew members to battle stations. He also ordered the sloop's anchor chain slipped—disconnected—and for the ship's engine to be set into reverse.

As the distance between the sloop of war and the approaching object narrowed, the *Housatonic*'s executive officer, F. J. Higginson, was in his cabin below. But upon hearing the commotion above, he rushed up to the quarterdeck. "I then saw something resembling a plank moving toward the ship at the rate of 3 or 4 knots," he later recalled. The craft had the appearance of a "plank sharp at both ends; it was entirely a wash [*sic*] with the water, and a glimmer of light [showed] through the top of it, as though through a dead light."

Officers crowded along the *Housatonic*'s starboard rail were by then firing revolvers and muskets at the approaching craft. Captain Pickering later recalled blasting the boat with a load of buckshot from his double-barreled shotgun. Other sailors rushed to prepare one of the 32-pound guns to fire. But their efforts came too late, and they were never able to lower the gun's muzzle far enough to train it on the approaching craft.

By then, the Confederate vessel—assumed by the *Housatonic*'s men to be one of the *David*-class torpedo boats—had slightly shifted its course. And, by doing so, it had managed to attach a torpedo slightly forward of the Union ship's mizzenmast, the mast closest to the stern, whose interior included the ship's gunpowder-filled magazine.

For the men crowded along the *Housatonic*'s starboard rail, the Rebel craft then seemed to disappear as abruptly as it had appeared. Moments later, the night and the *Housatonic* exploded with a deafening blast. No one aboard later recalled seeing either flames or a column of water, only an inky black column of smoke rising toward the sky and shattered pieces of the deck, aft of the mizzenmast, flying through the moonlit night—some blown as high as that mizzenmast. Sailors below, those not killed instantly, soon found themselves fighting a torrent of cold Atlantic water rushing in through the gaping hole left by the blast.[4]

The attack on the *Housatonic* came at roughly 8:45 p.m. Thirty-five minutes later—at 9:20 p.m.—one of the *Housatonic*'s launches, after covering a little over a mile, reached the Union's 228-foot sloop of war *Canandaigua*. The *Canandaigua*'s commander took the men aboard, heard their story, then ordered flares shot into the air and lights flashed to signal the squadron's other vessels of the sinking. He also ordered his ship's chains slipped and for it to begin steaming toward the *Housatonic*. En route, ten minutes later, the *Canandaigua* encountered yet another launch from the sunken warship and rescued its passengers, among them Charles Pickering, the *Housatonic*'s commander.

At 9:35, the *Canandaigua* reached the *Housatonic*; and by 10:30 all of the *Canandaigua*'s launches, having been lowered into the water, had returned with all remaining survivors from the *Housatonic*. At least one of those *Housatonic* survivors, a black seaman named Robert Flemming, would later claim to have noticed, prior to his rescue, an unusual sight: "When the 'Canandaigua' got astern, and [was] lying athwart, of the 'Housatonic,' about four ships' lengths off, while I was in the fore-rigging, I saw a blue light on the water just ahead of the 'Canandaigua', and on the starboard quarter of the 'Housatonic.' "

In the end, only five sailors aboard the *Housatonic* died that night. All of the remaining crew members, 155 men, survived the sinking, most by scurrying up the ship's masts and into its rigging, and there waiting to be rescued. Even so, the ship itself, for all practical purposes, was a total loss. Heeling to port, the stern of the *Housatonic* had disappeared into the harbor's shallow waters in less than five minutes. Inaugurating a new era in naval warfare, the sloop of war had earned the unwelcome distinction of becoming the first ship in world history to be sunk by a submarine boat.[5]

12

We Can't Get at the Truth

ON THE EVENING of February 17, the same night that the *Housatonic*'s fractured stern sank to the floor of Charleston Harbor, the *Hunley*'s visual signal was—according to Lieutenant Colonel Olin Miller Dantzler—spotted at Battery Marshall, on Sullivan's Island. Upon spotting the signal, Dantzler also reported, the Battery Marshall garrison promptly, as planned, reciprocated by displaying its own light signal: "The signals agreed upon to be given in case the boat wished a light to be exposed at this post as a guide for its return were observed and answered."

But when the sun rose the following morning, and the *Hunley* had yet to return, few, if any, on Sullivan's Island perceived any cause for alarm. Had not this odd-duck boat ventured out before in the night, into the harbor's dark waters, and failed to return until hours after sunrise? As for the *Housatonic*'s demise, no Confederates in or around Charleston yet had any inkling of that. Yes, some had noticed, the previous evening, an unusual amount of back-and-forth signaling—flares and the like— among the ships of the blockading fleet. But no one around Charleston Harbor deduced that the commotion might have anything to do with the *Hunley*. Then again few around the city thought that the submarine boat might actually sink an enemy ship. By February 1864, after all, many, perhaps most, Charlestonians regarded the *H. L. Hunley* more as General Beauregard's folly than as a warship possessed of a realistic chance of destroying an enemy vessel.

Not until the following day, February 19—two days after the *H. L. Hunley* had left Breach Inlet—did a Confederate official, Lieutenant Colonel Dantzler, note the submarine boat's continued absence. In the same letter in which he reported the exchange of light signals, he also wrote, "I have the honor to report that the torpedo boat stationed at this post went out on the night of the 17th instant (Wednesday) and has not yet returned." Dantzler then concluded his report on an apologetic note: "An earlier report would have been made of this matter, but the officer of the day for yesterday was under the impression that the boat had returned, and so informed me."

That same day, General Roswell S. Ripley penned a letter to General Thomas Jordan, General Beauregard's chief of staff, speculating on the *Hunley's* fate: "Unless she has gone to Charleston, the boat has probably been lost or captured. I have no reason to believe that the crew would have deserted to the enemy. They were not however under my directions, and [I] fear it is more likely she has gone down judging from past experience of the machine."

For General Beauregard, who had invested so much personal prestige in the boat, the terrible truth of the *Hunley's* likely fate was becoming an open wound too obvious to deny. The following day, February 20, he issued a terse, one-sentence directive to subordinates that tacitly acknowledged the *Hunley's* presumed demise: "As soon as its fate shall have been ascertained, pay a proper tribute to the gallantry and patriotism of its crew and officers."

As for the Union commanders around Charleston Harbor,

they too, as if stunned, had been slow to react to their own loss. On February 19, two days after the attack on the *Housatonic*, Admiral John Dahlgren wrote to Navy Secretary Welles to report the loss of the ship. He also requested torpedoes for his fleet and suggested the construction of torpedo boats that could be deployed against Charleston. Still unaware of the identity or the precise type of boat that had sunk the *Housatonic*, he also suggested that the navy offer "a large reward of prize money for the capture or destruction of a 'David;' I should say not less than $20,000 or $30,000 for each. They are worth more than that to us."

On February 20, the USS *Canandaigua* returned to, and dropped anchor at, the *Housatonic*'s wreck site. Union naval officers inspecting the burnt hulk soon concluded that some of the ship's guns, but not much else, were salvageable. Afterward—lest the Confederates find anything else of value amid the remaining wreckage—sailors aboard launches from the *Canandaigua* began the grim business of destroying all remaining vestiges of possible value from the *Housatonic*.[1]

Within days of the *Housatonic*'s sinking and the *Hunley*'s failure to return, rumors began circulating around Charleston about the *Hunley*'s fate. Most residents, however, only slowly learned of the connection between the *Housatonic*'s destruction and the *Hunley*'s disappearance. On February 21, in a telegram to Richmond, General Beauregard jumped into the speculative fray: "A gunboat sunken off Battery Marshall. Supposed to have been done by Mobile torpedo boat, under Lieutenant George E. Dixon . . . Twenty-first Alabama Volunteers, which went out for that purpose, and which I regret to say has not been heard of since."

But if the *Hunley* was truly lost—destined never to return—

how to explain its demise? What had happened that night? Had it been destroyed by the same explosion that sank the *Housatonic*? Or had it, as some surmised, been sucked into the vortex created by the huge *Housatonic*'s plunge toward the harbor floor? Or had its hull or one or more of its conning towers been breached by lead from Captain Charles Pickering's double-barreled shotgun and other small-arms fire; and, if so, had the resultant leaks admitted enough water into the craft to send it to the bottom? Or, trusting a report from Battery Marshall, might one believe the *Hunley* survived long enough after sinking the *Housatonic* to have flashed a prearranged signal seeking guidance back to base? An officer there, after all, claimed that just such a signal had been "observed and answered."

But if the *Hunley* did survive the *Housatonic*'s sinking, what explained its failure to return? Perhaps, as some later surmised, after the *Hunley* that evening displayed "the signals agreed upon," some sort of collision—heretofore unreported—had taken place with the behemoth 228-foot sloop of war *Canandaigua*, the Union vessel that rescued the *Housatonic*'s survivors. And perhaps that collision—or some malfunction aboard the *Hunley*—had caused a leak that flooded the submarine or caused it otherwise to sink to the harbor floor while remaining dry inside. There, the crew—trapped inside by the surrounding water's overwhelming pressure and aware of their impending demise—would have suffered the slowest of all possible deaths.

Then again, assuming that something had gone wrong that night—during the attack on the *Housatonic* or still later—perhaps all of the men had managed to escape the *Hunley*. And perhaps some or all of them had drowned as they tried to swim the few miles to shore. Or maybe—in, from the Confederate perspective, the most optimistic of all imagined possibilities—some or all of those who escaped had made it to shore. And if so, was it not unfeasible to believe that any day now, those survivors would wander into Charleston, none the worse for wear?

Not until February 29—twelve days after the *Housatonic*'s sinking—did the *Charleston Mercury* report the identity of the vessel that the *Hunley* had destroyed. Days earlier, a Confederate picket boat had captured a Union picket boat that was operating near Fort Sumter. The Union prisoners, reported the *Mercury*, had informed Confederate interrogators that the USS *Housatonic* had been sunk by a Confederate boat operating in the Outer Harbor. Without mentioning the *Hunley* by name, the newspaper story praised the "glorious success" of the craft, "under the command of Lieut. DIXON." The *Mercury* concluded its report on a reassuring note. "We are glad to be able to assure our readers that the boat and crew are now safe."

Tellingly, however—and reflecting a public tendency to define the *Hunley* exclusively by its weaponry—the story referred to the craft simply as "the torpedo boat." In its emphasis on the craft's weaponry, the story thus ignored the quality that rendered the *Hunley* truly unique—its ability to dive beneath the water's surface. However, lest the reporter who penned that story be adjudged too harshly, yet another fact warrants mention: a local observer who, over those days, had gazed—from both Fort Sumter and Sullivan's Island—upon the Union Navy's forlorn wreck later recalled that its masts could be clearly seen, from each of those places, jutting above the waterline. Thus, he concluded, "It seems to me that it would have been impossible for any submarine to have got under the 'Housatonic' in that shallow water."[2]

Beauregard and other Confederate officers well understood that any officially sanctioned disclosure of the *Hunley*'s demise would undercut whatever boost to civilian and military morale had been won from the public's awareness of the *Housatonic*'s destruction. This, after all, was the same Beauregard who, during the Battle of Shiloh, upon learning of the death of General Albert Sydney Johnston, the commanding general in that engagement, had ordered his officers to keep that news from their men.

To preserve Confederate morale, Beauregard and his subordinate officers were thus in no hurry to tamp down the rampant rumors that kept the *Hunley* afloat—and in some versions even defiantly active. And local newspapers, taking their cue from the military commanders, likewise, when not offering naively sanguine reports on the boat's fate, otherwise presented a stony silence on the topic.

Reflecting the public's frustration with the dearth of authentic knowledge concerning the *Hunley*, Charlestonian Susan Middleton, in a March 4 letter to her sister, complained, "We can't get at the truth of the Fish boat story." She then repeated two widely divergent explanations then making the rounds concerning the vessel's status: "Some say she has never returned while the general belief is that she came ashore safe somewhere near Georgetown"—a South Carolina town some fifty miles northeast of Charleston. Of that latter possibility, Middleton added, "She is said to have sunk two vessels besides the 'Housatonic'—one a transport loaded with troops—this time she did not dive but attacked the enemy on the surface of the water." Middleton ended her speculation on an optimistic note: "Torpedoes have been sent to her at Georgetown to start on another expedition."

But, of course, there would be no new expedition. And slowly Charlestonians and the rest of the Confederacy acclimated themselves to the grim conclusion that something had gone badly wrong for the *Hunley* and its crew on the night it sank the *Housatonic*. From Mobile on April 28, a saddened

General Dabney Maury wrote Captain M. Martin Gray, the head of Charleston's torpedo operations, to inquire about the fate of George Dixon and the rest of the *Hunley*'s crew. Gray answered promptly, but said that he knew few specifics of the operation or its outcome—only that the submarine boat had managed to sink the *Housatonic* on the night of February 17. "Since that time no information has been received of either the boat or crew," Gray lamented. Likely reflecting an opinion widespread among Confederate brass, the Charleston officer then closed his dispatch with a speculative gambit. "I am of the opinion," he wrote, "that the torpedoes being placed at the bow of the boat[,] she went into the hole made in the *Housatonic* by [the] explosion of torpedoes and did not have sufficient power to back out, [and] consequently sunk with her."

The *Hunley*'s apparent fate was hardly the only bad news weighing upon Charleston that year. The city itself gradually succumbed to ongoing depredations by Union forces. Indicative of the once elegant municipality's declining grace, General William Sherman, in December 1864—having just concluded his "March to the Sea" by his capture of Savannah, Georgia— wrote General Ulysses S. Grant to explain his decision to sidestep Charleston and head directly to Columbia, South Carolina. "Charleston is now a mere desolated wreck, and is hardly worth the time it would take to starve it out," he wrote. The endgame for Charleston's resistance came in February 1865. Early that month, Admiral Dahlgren's fleet, in joint operations with the forces of U.S. Army general Quincy Gillmore, made a series of amphibious landings in locales close to Charleston—James Island and Bull's Bay, South Carolina.

Beauregard, meanwhile, finally accepting his powerlessness to stave off the inevitable, ordered all Confederate forces in and around the city to evacuate. And on the evening of February 17–18, 1865—one year to the day after the *Hunley's* destruction of the *Housatonic*—the city's long resistance to Union forces finally crumbled. Union forces entered the next morning. Two months later, on April 9, General Robert E. Lee surrendered his Army of Northern Virginia to General Grant. The war, for all practical purposes, was over.[3]

Back in Louisiana, meanwhile—three months later, on July 3, 1865—William Pitt Kellogg, the newly appointed U.S. customs collector in postwar New Orleans, had the pleasure of informing the U.S. treasury secretary that a subordinate had located the American flag that, until January 1861, had flown over the Custom House. Kellogg's predecessor, the Vermont-born Francis Hanson Hatch—likely indulging a native sentiment—had "secreted" the flag away rather than destroying it. Upon discovering the flag, Kellogg ordered its immediate restoration to its former location. And so, the next morning—July Fourth—the same Old Glory that had been hauled down four years earlier fluttered once again over Canal Street.[4]

PART IV

AMERICA

1865–2004

13

Skeletons at the Wheel

No one can gainsay the courage of the twenty-one men among the three successive crews who lost their lives aboard the *H. L. Hunley*. Moreover, few can fathom the wellspring of courage that would have been required to set out aboard a boat of such new and unproven capabilities. Formidable bravery would have been required to join the submarine boat's first crew. But to enlist in the second and third crews—with an ever darkening shadow falling across the boat's operations—would have required a courage of incomprehensible magnitude, one that, transcending all belief systems, evokes what F. Scott Fitzgerald called "a willingness of the heart."

And no one can challenge the fact that Horace Hunley did eventually attain the goal he set for himself—to become one of the prime movers in creating the first underwater craft in world history to sink an enemy ship.[1]

However, from other perspectives, commercial and military, the *Hunley*'s final triumph proved a Pyrrhic victory. As commercial ventures, the *Pioneer, American Diver*, and *Hunley* never won any of the various bounties—private and governmental—that so enticed their investors. Indeed, no record exists of the *Hunley*'s owners even seeking any bounties for the sinking of the *Housatonic*. Nor, so far as it is known, were the owners ever financially compensated for the Confederate military's August 1863 confiscation of their boat. Nor did any of the three underwater vessels built by Hunley and his partners ever become prototypes for a class of submarine boats that might have made the partners rich—and, in the process, vanquished the Union's blockade of the Confederacy and thus turned the tide of war for the South. And, finally, in fate's cruelest turn, the *Hunley*'s moment of glory ended in more deaths aboard the submarine boat than among the enemy sailors aboard the *Housatonic*.

For those involved in promoting the *Hunley*—or others whose lives were, by sheer chance, touched by the project—their postwar years offered a variety of fates. Horace Hunley, of course, had died in October 1863—two months shy of his fortieth birthday and four months before his eponymous boat secured its long-sought but Pyrrhic triumph. Horace's beloved sister, Volumnia Barrow, two years his junior, spent her few remaining years grieving over her brother's death. Compounding her woes, the happiness she had enjoyed with her husband soon, for reasons now unknown, evaporated. In June 1866 she and Robert were granted a legal separation, with Volumnia retaining custody of their two children. With the Barrows' fortune lost in the war, Volumnia became mired in lawsuits against her husband, seeking personal properties—furniture, jewelry, and the like—allegedly taken from her.

She also sought, and won, title to Residence and two other Barrow plantations in Terrebonne Parish. Volumnia died of an unknown cause at age forty-three on November 7, 1868, almost five years to the day after her brother's funeral.

To the end, however, she treasured her memories of her beloved brother, Horace. Indeed, the gold studs from his Confederate uniform, sent to her in 1863 from Charleston by Gardner Smith, survived Volumnia. Today they rest in a box in Tulane University's Howard Tilton Library—one of numerous boxes, at Horace's alma mater, which contain the accumulated records and mementos of Louisiana's storied Barrows.[2]

In 1858, after conducting an inventory of his employer's estate, Robert Ruffin Barrow's steward had estimated the planter's total worth at $2,150,000. That figure had prompted the steward to comment wryly of Barrow's prospects, "he is in very good circumstances and with economy he has enough to last him & his family for several years to come." But Barrow had no power to prevent the coming of the war that he feared would—and eventually did—prove ruinous for his and the South's other planter fortunes. After Volumnia's death in 1868, the couple's two children, Robert, Jr., and Roberta, sued their father to claim property willed to them by their mother. Throughout those postwar years, the once wealthy planter lived in New Orleans, in increasingly reduced circumstances. In 1873 he was declared destitute. Death from cholera came to the septuagenarian on July 10, 1875, seven years after his wife's death.[3]

Among Horace Hunley's friends and associates, those of a more urban bent prospered after the war. With fewer ties to Dixie's sugar and cotton agriculture, these men—a type epitomized by the men of Canal Street—proved to be the more agile in reinventing themselves amid the postbellum South's altered circumstances. Among those, Hunley's Custom House mentor, Francis Hatch—one of those Canal Street men who had robustly embraced Confederate nationalism—became president of the New Orleans branch of a life insurance company. And in his retirement the Vermont native spent his years in what, in the words of an obituary writer at the New Orleans *Picayune*, sounds like nothing if not the most splendid of idylls: "Of late years Mr. Hatch has traveled much, accompanied by his accomplished daughter, and when in Louisiana has resided quietly at his pleasant and hospitable house in Jefferson parish, on the right bank of the river." It was there that Hatch died, at the age of seventy, on July 19, 1884.[4]

The New Orleans *Daily Delta* co-owner and lawyer Henry J. Leovy—Hunley's college classmate, best friend, and ultimately the executor of his estate—proved to the end a stubborn advocate for Hunley's life work and the Confederacy. Upon Hunley's death, Leovy inherited Hunley's $400 share in the *H. L. Hunley*. On March 5, 1864, two weeks after the *Hunley-Housatonic* encounter, Leovy—identifying himself "as one of the owners of the torpedo boat 'H. L. Hunley' "—dispatched a letter to Beauregard, inquiring about the fate of the submarine boat's crew and if the rumors he had heard were true that it was the *Hunley* that had sunk the *Housatonic*. A Beauregard subordinate answered Leovy's letter on March 10; he confirmed that, indeed, the *H. L. Hunley*, commanded by Dixon, had sunk the *Housatonic*. "But I regret to say," he added, "that nothing since has been heard either of Lieutenant Dixon or the torpedo boat."

Two years earlier, in 1862—following the closing of the *Daily Delta* by Union forces in New Orleans—Leovy had joined the Confederate Army at the rank of captain. That same year, just prior to the Union capture of New Orleans, he accepted a post in Richmond, where his duties included investigating allegations of disloyalty among Confederate citizens in southwestern Virginia.

During the war's ragged endgame, Leovy numbered among those diehards who—in April 1865, on the eve of the Federal capture of Richmond—set out on the lam with President Davis and his cabinet. A vainglorious excursion, the trip ended weeks later with Davis's arrest by Federal soldiers in south Georgia. After the party split up, Leovy accompanied his friend Confederate secretary of state Judah Benjamin to Florida, where he assisted Benjamin in fleeing the country. In the postwar years, Leovy prospered after resuming his New Orleans law practice. In October 1902, upon suddenly feeling unwell while mingling with friends on Canal Street, he went home and died the following day.[5]

Baxter Watson had co-owned the Front Levee Street machine shop in New Orleans inside which Hunley became a habitué after forming, with Watson and McClintock, the partnership that eventually produced the CSS *Pioneer*. After the three partners fled New Orleans in spring 1862, Watson, according to his own assertion, remained an investor in and supporter of the two successor vessels. And like Leovy, to the war's end he remained true to the partners' vision of submarine warfare. In October 1864, eight months after the *Hunley*'s sinking of the *Housatonic*, Watson wrote to President Davis. "Being the inventor of the Sub-marine boat that destroyed the Yankee vessel 'Housatonic,' " he boldly introduced himself, then went on to request government funds for the construction of yet another such boat. "I have exhausted all the capital I had in building and experimenting with that one [the *Hunley*] which was lost in Charleston," he lamented.

In the months since the *Hunley*'s disappearance, Watson wrote, he had been pondering the craft's failure to return. "That boat," he wrote Davis, "was a complete success as far as the boat was concerned, but was a comparative failure from miissmanagement [*sic*] by those who had her under [their] controll [*sic*]."

But, Watson acknowledged, shortcomings in design had also played a role in the *Hunley*'s bedeviled fate. Unlike others, however, who had indulged such lamentations, he focused on the costs that the boat's crankshaft imposed on the crew—or, more specifically, the limited supply of air available to them during their exertions inside the boat's cramped iron chamber.

To remedy that shortcoming, Watson aspired to pick up where James McClintock had left off. He would realize Mc-Clintock's goal of equipping a submarine boat with an engine not dependent upon human muscle for its propulsion. To the Confederate president, Watson asserted that "without Electro-Magnetism as a motive power, the air in the boat will not sustain so many men long enough for the time required, or if it did, the labour necessary for the successful operation of the boat is more than they could possibly endure."

Of the electromagnetic motor for this new submarine boat that he proposed to build, Watson wrote, "I can procure an engine of this description by going to New York or Washington city." Cost, however, posed an obvious impediment. The price of the engine would be five thousand U.S. dollars—"more than I can raise," he complained. By then—by October 1864—the clock was inexorably ticking away on what by then seemed to be the Confederacy's final months, a perception hardly lost on businessmen in the South. "Moneyed men," Watson complained, "are afraid to invest lest the war is over before they could realize their profits."

To entice these reluctant investors—to allow them to hedge their bets on a risky venture—Watson offered Davis a proposal. "I think I can raise the money amongst my fellow mechanics if the government will give them the privilege of buying cotton and sending it out to a foreign port." The resultant profits from those sales, Watson wrote, would then be used to purchase the needed engine. Whatever response, if any, Davis offered to Watson's letter remains unknown.[6]

After being relieved of his command of the *Hunley*, James McClintock, the boat's principal designer, left Charleston and returned to Mobile. After the war, by then married with children, he opened a dredging business.

A chance introduction to Britain's consul in Mobile led, in the fall of 1872, to a trip by McClintock to Halifax, Nova Scotia. There, aboard the HMS *Royal Alfred*, he met with two British Navy officers in hopes of selling them on a new submarine boat he hoped to persuade the British to build. McClintock dazzled the two officers with tales of the *Pioneer*, the *American Diver*, and the *Hunley*. But, he added, because hindsight had instructed him in the shortcomings of those three vessels, he was now prepared to design a vastly superior submarine craft. To the two officers, the American seemed, though self-taught, highly intelligent and well versed in the latest scientific advances. Both also came to believe that, had it not been for a want of available materials during the war, McClintock's boats would have enjoyed greater success.

An inventor's passion still drove McClintock. But so did a contempt for the United States. "He hates his countrymen, Americans, and hopes some day to be a British subject," one of the two officers wrote to a superior back in London. But the Royal Navy ultimately declined McClintock's offer—and he did not live to become a British subject. In 1879, at the age of fifty, while demonstrating, in Boston harbor, a new contact mine he had designed and built, he was killed when the bomb detonated prematurely.[7]

Little is known of the postwar activities of John K. Scott, who had worked with Hunley at the New Orleans Custom House and later served as captain of both the *Pioneer* and the *American Diver*. In March 1874, however, the New Orleans *Picayune* included Scott's name in a listing of recent deaths. The note was brief: "Drowned March 1st, Capt. JOHN K. SCOTT, age 43 years[,] near Shreveport."[8]

William Alexander eventually completed the rapid-fire repeating gun that he was summoned back to Mobile to build. That summons had forced him to relinquish his spot aboard the *Hunley*, a serendipitous intervention that likely saved his life. After the war, he stayed in Mobile and lived long enough into the twentieth century to see his name listed in the local city directory as an electrical engineer. And during his later years—through articles and lectures—he became the *Hunley's* chief memorializer. He died on May 13, 1914.[9]

General Dabney Maury, who had supported the submarine partners during their turn in Mobile, returned to Virginia after the war and established an academy devoted to instruction in mathematics and classical literature. Like Alexander, he also retained an interest in history. In 1868 he organized the Southern Historical Society. He died in 1900.[10]

The submarine boat partners' other—though less supportive—military interlocutor in Mobile, Admiral Franklin Buchanan, was wounded and taken prisoner later in the war. Both misfortunes befell Buchanan in August 1864, during the Battle of Mobile Bay, while Buchanan was fighting the Union fleet under the command of—by then, following his July 1862 promotion—Rear Admiral David Farragut. After the war, Buchanan returned to his native Maryland, where he died in 1874. Three U.S. Navy destroyers and the superintendent's quarters at the U.S. Naval Academy were eventually named in his honor.[11]

Serving under Buchanan during the Battle of Mobile Bay was yet another Confederate naval officer, Lieutenant John Payne, who had had a brush with the *Hunley*—or, as it was then still known when he commanded it, the *Fish Boat*. Five of the crew's eight men had died on August 29, 1863, when an accident sent the *Fish Boat* to the bottom of Charleston Harbor. But Payne had numbered among the survivors and was later transferred to Mobile Bay. There, during Rear Admiral Farragut's invasion, Payne served as executive officer aboard the

CSS *Gaines*. During the battle, Farragut's flagship, the USS *Hartford*, struck the *Gaines* and forced it to run aground. But Payne survived. And after the war, the Alabama native settled in Mobile. There he worked for a company that sold iron, coal, and tin. He also worked, apparently briefly, as a policeman. But Payne's postwar life was short. In 1876, at the age of thirty-seven, he died after an unspecified illness of fourteen days.[12]

Of all the major figures who propelled the *Hunley*'s bedeviled history, not one remains at once more obscure and more celebrated than the boat's final commander, George E. Dixon. Recent speculation places Dixon's origins in the Midwest. But aside from his career as an engineer aboard a riverboat, his migration to Mobile, and his service at Shiloh and aboard the *Hunley*, little is known of his life. He left behind no will nor heirs.

After Dixon's death in 1864, his friend Henry Willey, who owned the Mobile boardinghouse where Dixon had recuperated from his wound at Shiloh—the same Willey to whom Dixon had written to complain about the "soldiers rations" at Mount Pleasant—became executor of Dixon's estate. And Willey, in turn—to liquidate costs associated with the estate's administration—successfully petitioned Mobile's probate court in February 1866 for permission to sell off the worldly possessions that Dixon left behind. Those items included various Masonic books, a flannel coat, a leather valise, a leather trunk, and Dixon's Confederate Army officer's uniform. Bearing witness to the distinct dandyism and presumed wealth of the otherwise obscure Dixon, the inventory also included nine linen shirts, a leghorn hat, a diamond pin, and three pairs of cashmere pants.[13]

After the war General Beauregard returned to Louisiana and worked for two rail lines as both an engineer and a corporate officer. During those years, he also flirted with but ultimately declined invitations to command the armies of Romania (1866) and Egypt (1870). As a Southern Democrat, Beauregard continued to believe in the inherent inferiority of black people. But, to end Republican rule in the state, he also became a pragmatic advocate for the civil rights of freed slaves. During the postwar years he also served Louisiana's state government in various roles. Among those positions—as if in penance for the roll-the-dice Canal Street ways by which he and his friends had lived and prospered—was a turn as a supervisor for the Louisiana State Lottery.[14]

In the postwar years, Admiral John A. B. Dahlgren, the final commander of the South Atlantic Blockading Squadron, returned to his former command at the U.S. Navy Yard. There he served until his death in 1870. Dahlgren spent much of his time during those final years attempting to disprove allegations against his son, Ulrich, who had died during a cavalry raid against Richmond, Virginia. It was alleged that the raid—the so-called Dahlgren affair—issued from a conspiracy to assassinate President Jefferson Davis. The accusations against young Ulrich derived from papers found in his pocket at the time of his death; his father would spend his remaining years arguing that the incriminating documents were forgeries.[15]

Like Dahlgren, the *Housatonic*'s commander, Charles Pickering, continued his naval service after the war. A U.S. Navy court of inquiry was convened in February and March of 1864 to investigate the *Housatonic*'s sinking. After eight days of testimony from crewmen and officers, the tribunal determined that her commander, subordinate officers, and crew had all behaved honorably before and after the attack on their ship. Reflecting that finding, Pickering was eventually awarded command of the USS *Vanderbilt*, a navy ship larger than the *Housatonic*.[16] The former flagship of rail baron Cornelius Vanderbilt's North Atlantic Mail and Steamship line, the 331-foot vessel had been converted into a fifteen-gun Union warship in 1862. Under Pickering's command, the *Vanderbilt* hunted for Confederate blockade runners off Halifax, Nova Scotia, a popular transit point for southbound Rebel commerce. And, in December 1864, she participated in the Union's first, albeit unsuccessful, amphibious assault on Fort Fisher, a Confederate redoubt on North Carolina's Cape Fear River. Pickering retired from the navy in 1867 and died in 1900.[17]

Three boats were built in succession between 1861 and 1863 by the submarine boat project's ever-changing lineup of partners. The first craft, the CSS *Pioneer*, was scuttled in New Orleans's New Basin Canal in the spring of 1862, on the eve of Flag Officer Farragut's capture of the city. During the subsequent Union occupation, Federal soldiers, in fall 1863, raised the boat from the canal. Four years later, on February 15, 1868, the *Pioneer*—once flagship to Horace Hunley's fondest dreams—suffered the ignominious fate of being sold as scrap iron at public auction by U.S. officials. Reported the New Orleans *Picayune* wistfully, "It was built as an experiment, and was never fully perfected, and is only valuable now for the machinery and iron which is in and about it." Fortunately, however, for posterity, before the *Pioneer* was sold for iron, U.S. Navy engineers studied the craft, recorded its dimensions and features, and preserved their findings in a drawing soon sent to Washington.

The partners lost their second boat, the *American Diver*, during its trials in winter 1863 in Mobile Bay. Presumably it still lies somewhere on the bottom of that estuary, where it remains the elusive quarry of shipwreck hunters.[18]

Due to its historical notoriety and the circumstances of its disappearance, the partners' third and final creation, the *Fish Boat*, later renamed the *H. L. Hunley*, retained—and still retains—a hold on America's popular imagination. Indeed, through the rest of the nineteenth and well into the twentieth century, the Confederate boat and its crew became naturalized as an *American* mystery. As such, the *Hunley*, its men, and the ongoing questions surrounding their demise won entry into the same national pantheon of gone-missing historical mysteries as Civil War–era author Ambrose Bierce, aviator Amelia Earhart, New York's Judge Crater, airplane hijacker Dan "D. B." Cooper, and labor leader Jimmy Hoffa.

Before the U.S. Navy even knew the name—or the underwater capabilities—of the craft that had sunk the *Housatonic*, its divers conducted the first search for the *Hunley*. In November 1864, as the Civil War was staggering through its final months, the U.S. Navy assigned a team of divers to investigate the feasibility of salvaging individual items from the wreck of the *Housatonic*. The team determined some of the ship's armaments to be recoverable, and they were later retrieved. But the divers also found time to search the same seabed area for the Union ship's assailant. By then, speculation was already astir that the same action that had destroyed the *Housatonic* had also sent the Confederate craft to the harbor floor. But alas, the divers found no Confederate vessel: "I have also caused the bottom to be dragged for an area of 500 yards around the wreck [of the *Housatonic*], finding nothing of the torpedo boat," W. L. Churchill, who supervised the investigation, reported to Admiral Dahlgren on November 27.[19]

The *Hunley* mystery persisted. Over the coming decades, rumors, half-truths, and outright falsehoods filled the gap created by the absence of hard information on the boat's disappearance and the whereabouts of its wreck. It was supposed, after all, that, unless divers had simply overlooked the *Hunley* in the murky waters near the *Housatonic*'s wreck site, the Confederate boat would be found somewhere northwest of where the *Housatonic* had gone down. That supposition assumed that, had the *Hunley* survived its attack on the *Housatonic*, Dixon would certainly have navigated the boat to one of two destinations: back to Breach Inlet or toward Charleston's Inner Harbor—both of which lay northwest of the *Housatonic*'s grave.

Exploiting public curiosity, the Charleston *Daily Courier*, in 1870, perpetuating an apparent hoax, reported that, after weeks of searching by divers in submarine armor, the *Hunley* had finally been located: "Death at the Bottom of the Deep. Discovery of Buried Torpedo Boat off Charleston—Nine Skeletons at the Wheel," a ghoulish headline proclaimed. The story, credited to the *Houston Telegraph*, reported that the divers had discovered the *Hunley* while visiting the wreck of the *Housatonic*: "They have found the little torpedo vessel lying by her huge victim, and within her are the bones of the most devoted and daring men who ever went to war." In all likelihood, the erroneous report originated from divers engaged in a survey of the harbor's floor, preparatory to the planned demolition of Civil War–era wrecks then still clogging the port. But nothing came of the claimed discovery. Nor did anything come from other searches and rumors of that decade.[20]

In 1885 the *Hunley* again became grist for public conversation after a former British naval officer, Augustus Charles Hobart-Hampden, published an article in *Blackwood's Edinburgh Magazine*. Hobart, by then a prolific author, was best known by his nom de plume, Hobart Pacha (or Pasha). The moniker derived from his recent commission to the rank of admiral in the Ottoman Empire's navy. But what gave Pacha credibility in the South was his command, during the American Civil War, of a blockade runner off North Carolina's coast. In his 1885 *Blackwood's* article, Pacha claimed to have met and

spoken with a young Southern naval commander toward the
war's end in a Charleston coffeehouse on two successive
evenings. In their first conversation, Pacha recalled, "He told
me that that night he was going to sink a Northern man-of-war
which was blockading the port, and invited me to see him off."

Pacha claimed to have accepted the invitation. He recalled
seeing, that evening, a craft "about forty feet long, shaped like a
cigar, on the bow of which was placed a torpedo." Then it departed: "He moved off into the darkness at no great speed—say
at about five miles per hour." The following evening in the same
coffeehouse, Pacha recalled, "I found my friend sitting quietly
smoking his pipe. He told me he had succeeded in making a
hole in the frigate which he attacked." But Pacha added, "On
the concussion made by firing the torpedo, the water had
rushed in through the hatches of his boat, and she had sunk to
the bottom. All his men were drowned."

The young officer, his boat, and the vessel he claimed to
have attacked all went unnamed in Pacha's article. And the
number of crewmen the described boat carried, in addition to
its commander, was four—not seven, as was the *Hunley*'s complement, excluding its captain. That aside, most of the story's
details comported with what Charlestonians knew about the
Hunley; and the tale allegedly recounted by the young Confederate officer squared with widespread suspicions of the
Hunley's final moments. Thus, upon reading the piece, many
Charlestonians optimistically rushed to the conclusion that the
unnamed officer in the story *had* to be the *Hunley*'s final commander, George E. Dixon.

But over the years ahead, as Charlestonians contemplated
other details of the article, it dawned on many that too many
discrepancies undermined Pacha's tale and the known facts of
the *Hunley-Housatonic* encounter. And slowly they concluded
that the man Pacha met could not have been Dixon. More

likely, the writer had conversed with the commander of one of the *David*-class torpedo boats—a four-man craft consistent with the one described in Pacha's story—that had operated in the harbor.

Pacha was hardly the first to confuse *David*-class torpedo boats with the *Hunley*. No less a Civil War hero than Admiral David Dixon Porter of the U.S. Navy had made the same error seven years earlier, in an article penned for the *North American Review*. "On the night of February 17, 1864," he wrote, "a 'David' attacked the sloop-of-war Housatonic, lying at anchor outside Charleston Harbor." And, as if that wasn't a sufficient indignity for public memory of the *Hunley*, Porter's article also offered a withering summing-up: "The 'Davids' were rather crude affairs, and drowned their own people oftener than those they were in pursuit of." A similar blurring of the two boats occurred in the 1904 novel *A Little Traitor to the South*. The book's author, the historian and adventure writer Cyrus Townsend Brady, obviously had the *Hunley* in mind as his novel's subject. But while George Dixon and company crewed the depicted boat, Brady called the craft the "David."[21]

From a broader perspective, however, the confusion between the two boats reflected an undeniable trend: public memory of the *Hunley* had been fading for years. After all, those closest to the submarine boat project—Horace Hunley, George E. Dixon, James McClintock, and others—had all perished aboard the *Hunley* or died shortly after the Civil War.

And as the postwar decades lumbered by, other individuals with direct knowledge of the *Hunley*, one by one, went to their graves. By the turn of the century, the memories of the handful of still living veterans who'd had any connection with the *Hunley* had grown unreliable. As a consequence, the veterans who bothered to publish recollections of their *Hunley* experiences produced works that often differed on key points. Most significant, they even offered conflicting accounts of the number of times that the *Hunley* had sunk. One report in circulation—doubling the actual number of sinkings—asserted that the boat had dropped to the ocean's sandy bottom an astonishing six times.

Beyond that, interest in the *Hunley* and its predecessor boats was waning, even in New Orleans, Mobile, and Charleston. In 1902, William Alexander—by then a gray-haired, bearded man in his mid-sixties—was still living in Mobile and employed as an engineer. That year, however, he became irked by press accounts of new developments in submarine technologies, reports that failed to acknowledge the *Hunley*—and, when they did, repeated bogus facts. Like many Southerners, then and now, Alexander also perceived a regional bias against the South in the outright omission of the *Hunley* in historical texts or, when it was mentioned, in the belittling of its significance to the advancement of naval technologies.

Possibly, Alexander also suffered from a tinge of survivor's guilt. After all, had he not been unexpectedly summoned back to Mobile for army work, he likely would have been aboard the *Hunley* on its final cruise. Alexander thus decided it was time to remind the public of earlier underwater ventures—and to set the record straight about the *Hunley*. In a lengthy article he wrote for the New Orleans *Picayune*, Alexander provided readers with a full, if flawed, account of the story of the *Hunley* and its two predecessor vessels. That same year, he also published recollections in other periodicals of his submarine years, and spoke widely on the subject before veterans' and historical organizations.

Unfortunately, an irony attended the timing of Alexander's efforts to redress the failing memories of other *Hunley* memorializers: by the turn of the century—four decades after the events he was describing—even Alexander's memory was faltering. "At this late date, it is hard for me to recall names and dates, how often I have regretted not keeping a regular diary," a fading Alexander lamented in an 1888 letter. Indeed, many of the details he thought he knew about the three boats were—we now know—incorrect. But most of his recollections were accurate, and Alexander also managed, at least for a while, to revive public interest in the submarine boat on which he had expended so much passion all those years ago.

Even so, Alexander's efforts could not forever forestall the public's waning interest in the *Hunley*, a trend illustrated by an oversight just six years after Alexander's *Picayune* article. In 1908, U.S. Army engineers in Charleston, concerned about ongoing dangers posed to harbor navigation by Civil War wrecks, sent divers down to the *Housatonic*'s wreck to determine its precise location. A subsequent local newspaper report of the search made no mention of the *Hunley* nor of the historical significance of the *Housatonic*'s demise.

Finally—in a sadly ironic turn—Alexander's own obituary in the *Mobile Register*, in May 1914, while duly noting his activities as a Civil War memoirist, also managed to mangle both the name of his boat and the type of ship it sank: the death notice referred to the "H. J. Huntley" as having destroyed "the famous monitor Housatonic."[22]

14

Discovery, Recovery, Excavation

THE FICKLENESS OF HISTORICAL MEMORY notwithstanding, as the nineteenth century gave way to the twentieth, public curiosity about the *H. L. Hunley* persisted. And, as the twentieth century marched onward, increasingly advanced submarine boats—by then known simply as submarines—repeatedly proved their mettle as engines of war. In the process, long-standing taboos against underwater warfare faded, and regional animosities from the Civil War abated. And those developments at once vindicated the *Hunley* partners' vision of marine warfare and stimulated public curiosity about the first submarine to sink an enemy ship.

Reflecting revived public interest in the Rebel boat, the federal Works Progress Administration, in 1936, commissioned the artist John Augustus Walker to paint a mural for Mobile's city hall—a mural later moved to the Museum of Mobile—that featured a fanciful, multicolored, Thomas Hart Benton–like representation of the *Hunley*'s construction in that city. Three years later, the Confederate artist Conrad Wise Chapman's 1863 portrait of the boat numbered among 290 paintings selected by the Metropolitan Museum for inclusion in an art show mounted in conjunction with New York's 1939 World's

Fair. In a celebratory story on the exhibit, *Time* magazine noted the presence of Chapman's work and quoted the exhibition catalog's catty comment on the painting's subject: "She could be submerged, but had a nasty trick of plunging to the bottom and drowning the men within." In time, the underwater boat—by then a staple of books, articles, and illustrations—even found its way into the new medium of television. In 1963, with America's Civil War centennial commemorations at full steam, an episode of the CBS weekly historical drama *The Great Adventure*—with Jackie Cooper starring as George Dixon—presented the submarine and its story. Four years later, a technical college in Charleston commissioned a model of the *Hunley*, based on Chapman's painting. And that life-size model was later acquired by the Charleston Museum.[1]

In Charleston Harbor, meanwhile, local divers never entirely abandoned their hunt for the Civil War–era submarine. Successive generations of marine explorers continued to prowl the harbor's floor looking for the boat. And so, finally, on May 3, 1995—after fifteen years of off-and-on searching—a team of divers, sponsored by the adventure novelist Clive Cussler, located and recorded coordinates for the *Hunley's* wreck site. Confounding expectations, the three divers, investigating an anomaly—a "target" detected using their towed marine magnetometer—found the wreck in Charleston's Outer Harbor, at a depth of twenty-six feet, about a thousand feet east, almost due east—seaward, that is—of the *Housatonic*.

For the two nautical archaeologists, Harry Pecorelli III and Wes Hall, who made the initial descent, the anomaly, buried in three feet of sand and other sediment, seemed at first to be some discarded boiler from another Civil War–era vessel. But, employing an underwater dredge to excavate the sediment above the object, they soon exposed the unmistakable shape, long familiar to them, of one of a certain submarine boat's two conning towers—as it turned out the forward tower. Both divers realized what they had found. "It's the *Hunley*," Hall told his partner a few minutes later, as they popped back to the water's surface. "That's it. That's all it can be."

The two divers—joined by their expedition leader and fellow archaeologist and diver Ralph Wilbanks—returned later that day to remove more of the sediment covering the wreck and to otherwise savor their triumph. That and subsequent dives suggested that the *Hunley*—though listing to starboard at a forty-five-degree angle—seemed generally intact. Tidal currents, storms, and other oceanic phenomena tend to jostle submerged objects, and can diminish—even, in some cases, render meaningless—the value of a wreck's position in ascertaining what transpired during its final moments as an operational vessel. But the divers could not help but notice that the *Hunley*'s bow pointed almost exactly toward Sullivan's Island, as if headed back toward its base.

A grapefruit-sized hole pierced the *Hunley*'s forward conning tower. A two-by-three-foot hole perforated the aft ballast tank area on the starboard side; and a dinner plate–sized hole breached the forward ballast tank area on that same side. A paper-thin yet cementlike layer of what marine archaeologists call concretion, formed from organic and inorganic materials, covered the craft. And beneath that rock-hard concretion lay the iron boat itself, subject to almost a century and a half of active marine corrosion. Otherwise, all things considered, the submarine craft seemed in remarkably good condition. It was later discovered that even the glass in all but one of its eighteen glass ports—twelve deadlights and six view ports—remained unbroken.

Over the coming days, Cussler and his diving team accomplished what Horace Hunley and his partners had never been able to do: they kept the submarine boat's location a closely guarded secret. But—lest their finding of the wreck be subject to later skepticism—Cussler asked the divers to return to the underwater site armed with an underwater camera and video-tape the wreck.[2]

In the years before and after Cussler's divers located the *Hunley*, a slew of nonprofit organizations, state and Federal government agencies, and two branches of the U.S. military, the navy and the coast guard, had been drawn into the search for the missing submarine boat and into the subsequent protection of its wreck site. High upon that list of government agencies was the *Hunley* Commission. Established by the state of South Carolina soon after Cussler's divers had located the wreck, the agency was charged with overseeing the recovery, excavation, and conservation of the boat. Other participants included the National Park Service, the South Carolina Institute of Archaeology and Anthropology, the Sons of Confederate Veterans, and Clive Cussler's National Underwater and Marine Agency—the novelist's nonprofit organization established to hunt for historically significant shipwrecks.

But in May 1995, as word that the *Hunley* had been located spread across the United States, the inevitable question of the boat's ownership came to the fore. Cussler and his nonprofit organization never asserted any claim of ownership to the craft. He was content merely to add the *H. L. Hunley* to the list of shipwrecks he had located. Meanwhile, questions concerning the boat's ownership soon acquired a historically familiar dynamic: reviving an issue of the Civil War, the struggle over the wreck quickly became one of Federal powers versus states' rights.

Countering robust assertions by Federal lawyers that the boat legally belonged to Uncle Sam came equally vigorous claims to ownership from the states of South Carolina and Alabama. The lawyers representing Alabama based their claim, soon abandoned, on the *Hunley*'s origins in Mobile. Unfortunately, however, for both South Carolina and Alabama, the ensuing legal battle over the *Hunley* seldom strayed from a long-established legal principle—that the Federal government holds title to all property of the former Confederate government. Indeed, in a vain attempt to sidestep that point of law, South Carolina's lawyers—in one of the more inventive propositions to emerge during the legal tug-of-war—briefly argued that, despite the fact that many, wrongly, attach the prefix *CSS*—Confederate States Ship—to the *Hunley*'s name, the boat was, in fact, never Confederate government property.

It was built, they argued, as a privateer, a private ship, and though eventually seized by the Confederacy, it had afterward been returned to its original private owners. Thus, at the time of its sinking, the *Hunley* was private—not Confederate government—property. Thus, South Carolina's lawyers argued, Uncle Sam enjoyed no right of title to the wreck.

As lawyers representing the state of South Carolina and the Federal government jostled over who legally owned the *Hunley*, the novelist Cussler was ever aware that the boat's wreck site constituted a rich field for looters. Thus, after his divers conducted their preliminary investigations of the wreck and videotaped it, they took care to rebury it. And until the legal questions about ownership were resolved and what Cussler adjudged to be competent plans for recovering and conserving the ship were developed, he and his divers would decline to disclose the geographical coordinates of the wreck's location. For good measure—to further thwart would-be shipwreck pirates—Cussler told a Charleston press conference that the *Hunley* had

been found in water eighteen feet deep—a figure eight feet shy
of the site's true depth.[3]

A compromise struck in late 1995 ended the dispute—an
agreement reputedly driven by South Carolina's longtime U.S.
senator, Strom Thurmond, then in his nineties. Three decades
earlier, Thurmond had sought to have a U.S. Navy nuclear submarine named after Horace Hunley. But instead he was forced
to settle for a sub tender, launched in 1961, bearing the Hunley
moniker. This time around, Thurmond reputedly told navy
officials that until the matter of this *Hunley*—the original
Hunley—was resolved, the Senate Armed Services Committee,
which he chaired, would be disinclined to consider various defense projects sought by the navy.

The 1995 agreement ending the Federal-state negotiations
awarded the Federal government title to the *Hunley* but accorded permanent possession of it to the state of South Carolina. The compromise stipulated that the boat would be on
permanent loan to South Carolina, provided the state government prove its ability to recover, excavate, and conserve the
Hunley in a manner consistent with the Federal government's
highest standards regulating such endeavors. Cussler played no
role in the Federal-state negotiations. But once the pact was in
place, he expressed satisfaction with it, then informed state and
Federal officials of the coordinates of the wreck site.

That same year, 1995, South Carolina's legislature—led by
Glenn McConnell, an ably energetic Republican state senator,
and since childhood a *Hunley* devotee—established the *Hunley*
Commission to assume responsibility for the wreck. In turn, the
Hunley Commission, chaired by McConnell, soon created yet
another group, Friends of the *Hunley*, a nonprofit organization
devoted to raising funds for the boat's recovery, excavation, and
conservation.

Twice in 1863, General Beauregard had called on Charleston's Smith and Broadfoot diving team to salvage the *Hunley*. And almost a century and a half later, those determined, once more, to recover the submarine boat turned yet again to the private sector. In this case, however, they hired an organization that, in size and technological sophistication, dramatically surpassed its predecessor in *Hunley* recovery operations. In addition to its work for the offshore oil and gas industry, Oceaneering International, Inc., based in Houston, Texas, had performed high-profile marine salvage work for various governmental agencies. Among its feats, the company had located and recovered wreckage from TWA's Flight 800, which, in 1996, exploded over Long Island Sound. And in 1999, it found and recovered the space capsule from U.S. astronaut Gus Grissom's 1961 Liberty Seven mission. After its lone passenger barely escaped, the capsule had sunk into the Atlantic, northeast of the Bahamas. When Oceaneering found the spacecraft, it was resting on the ocean floor at a depth of three miles.

The recovery plan developed by Oceaneering International, in collaboration with other parties, called for divers to find, if they could, and remove the submarine boat's spar. Divers would also conduct a thorough survey of the wreck site and remove all smaller debris associated with the submarine boat. Afterward, two giant eighteen-foot piles—hollow steel tubes, open-ended at their bottoms—were to be sunk into the sediments around the wreck site, each about twelve feet off the *Hunley*'s bow or stern. Vacuum pumps attached to each would then begin sucking sand and water through the top of each tube. By the end of the process, the piles would be sunk more than twelve feet into the ocean floor.

Once the piles were firmly in place, a concave metal truss— essentially a large metal cage—would be lowered to the seabed. Fifty-five feet long and ten feet wide, the truss would rest atop the two piles and tidily enclose the *Hunley*. The idea was for the metal truss to serve as a lifting cradle and as a support for the wreck during its later excavation.

In recovering the *Hunley*, Oceaneering International's divers and their colleagues faced a challenge that Smith and Broadfoot had not confronted. These latter-day salvagers would have to devise a recovery method that not only brought the boat back to the surface but did so in a manner that preserved the craft and its contents as subjects for later archaeological excavation. To avoid disturbing the artifact-rich sediments that filled the wreck's interior, the *Hunley* was to be placed in the truss and raised in a manner that maintained the position in which the boat was found at its wreck site—a position listing to starboard at a forty-five-degree angle. Modern parlance associates the phrase *location location location* with real estate agents. But those words could also serve as a credo for archaeologists, much of whose work entails sifting through the detritus of bygone eras and meticulously recording what they found and where. And for them, the precise location of where an artifact is found—where on a survey site's established grid system and at what level of the site's accumulated strata—can tell as much, often more, than the object itself.

After the recovery truss had been lowered but before the lift could take place, divers would run a series of two-feet-wide straps beneath the *Hunley*'s underside. The ends of the straps would then be bolted to the truss. To cushion the *Hunley* during the recovery—to avoid damaging the wreck—the straps were to consist of bags that would eventually be filled with a soft polyurethane foam. The foam, after about twenty minutes, would become rock hard, thus creating a castlike support along the length of the submarine boat.

Once all was in place, the assemblage—the truss, the

Hunley, and the straps beneath it—would be lifted by a large crane aboard a transport barge. And after the assemblage was lifted out of the water, it—the truss, with the submarine boat strapped snuggly inside—would then be lowered to the deck of another barge. Then the entire assemblage would be taken ashore to a conservation laboratory newly established by the *Hunley* Commission.

The laboratory—eventually named the Warren Lasch Conservation Center, after the Friends of the *Hunley's* first director—would be housed in a large former warehouse on a decommissioned U.S. Navy base, in the municipality of North Charleston. To lead the laboratory's work, the *Hunley* Commission hired a three-person team of seasoned nautical research scientists—archaeologist Robert Neyland, on loan from the U.S. Navy's Naval Historical Center in Washington; archaeologist Maria Jacobsen, a native of Denmark, from Texas A&M's Institute of Nautical Archaeology; and conservator Paul Mardikian, a native of France, from Paris's Sorbonne University Conservation Program. Together the three claimed almost a half century of underwater excavation experience, on vessels ancient to modern. The Lasch Center, in turn, hired and otherwise consulted with other scientific and archaeological specialists. It was also understood that, during the excavation and until a permanent museum for the *Hunley* could be built, the Lasch Center would find a way to accommodate visitors who longed to see the submarine boat.[4]

On August 8, 2000, as thousands of onlookers ashore and in vessels scattered about the harbor watched and cheered, the *H. L. Hunley*, for the first time in 136 years, broke the surface of Charleston's waters. After the boat was lowered to the barge's deck—lest the abrupt exposure to fresh air cause it to rapidly dry out and thus accelerate its deterioration—hoses kept it sprayed with steady streams of water. Three hours later, after traveling a distance of fifteen miles, the *Hunley*—still strapped to its truss—arrived at a dock at its new home in North Charleston. A shipyard crane mounted on rolling tracks lifted the boat from the barge, then took it through giant doors into the Warren Lasch Conservation Center. Welders cut off the protruding end pieces of the truss, on which it had rested on the ocean floor. Then the boat was lifted by yet another crane mounted in the lab's ceiling. By the day's end, the *Hunley* was resting in a large tank, 55 feet by 18 feet by 9 feet, at the Lasch Center.[5]

To reduce the growth of fungi and algae and to retard further corrosion of the craft, the 60,800 gallons of fresh water that each day was pumped into the Lasch Center tank was kept at fifty degrees Fahrenheit (ten degrees Celsius) and monitored closely for acidity, temperature, and other factors.

Initial pre-excavation studies conducted at the Lasch Center in fall 2001 confirmed the positive reports by the divers in 1995 of the *Hunley*'s condition. By the winter of 2001, the actual excavation had commenced. Each morning the holding tank's water would be lowered to allow the researchers access to the boat's upper sections. The craft's two conning tower entrances were much too narrow to provide day-to-day access for the researchers to the crew chamber. Thus, from the earliest days of the excavation, the researchers understood that they would have to create their own openings into the boat's hull.

After carefully removing the four upper plates—as well as the approximately four hundred rivets that had held them in place—the researchers made their way into the crew chamber. To access the fore and aft ballast areas, they removed another smaller plate at each end of the craft. Holding each of the two plates in place were another fifty rivets that had to be carefully removed and stored away. Once inside the craft, the researchers began removing the tons of sediment that filled the chamber. In time, as the excavation proceeded, the researchers also brought video scopes, X-ray machines, computers, and other modern technologies to their ratiocination of the *Hunley*.

And eventually—in March 2001—as the researchers knew it would, the day came when they began uncovering the remains of the crew: skeletal materials, all totaled, 1,600 bones (including skulls in, given the circumstances, pristine condition), fragments of clothing, personal objects of individual crewmen, and traces of adipocere—sometimes called "grave wax"—a waxy substance that may once have been brain tissue.

In 1863 Horace Hunley himself—concerned that men aboard his boat might, if captured, face severe treatment by an enemy outraged over the South's use of a submarine boat—had requisitioned Confederate Army uniforms for the men who were to crew his craft. But the *Hunley*'s final crew had had no such protector. Not surprisingly, therefore, the fragments of clothing recovered by the Lasch Center researchers bore an unpredictable ragtag quality—a combination of army, navy, and civilian attire. One of the men, likely Wicks, apparently even packed a peacoat from an earlier tour of duty with Uncle Sam's fleet—a coat from which three buttons, all stamped U.S. NAVY, were recovered. Personal objects recovered ranged from canteens and a wallet to four smoking pipes and two pocketknives.

By the end of 2002, the remains of all eight crew members had been recovered—an achievement that, if nothing else, solved one question that had hovered over the *Hunley* since at least 1885. That was the year of the article by Hobart Pacha in *Blackwood's Edinburgh Magazine*. Pacha had implied that Dixon had lived to boast in a Charleston coffeehouse of his experiences on that fateful night. Thus, with the removal of the remains of the eighth crewman, the Lasch Center researchers could finally and definitively refute the article's author: No, Admiral Pacha, none of the men—not one—had escaped the *Hunley!*[6]

The remains recovered from the *Hunley* were thoroughly studied. DNA and isotope samples were taken and meticulous photographs made, though, out of respect to the dead sailors, not publicly released. Moreover, research into written texts— military records, family Bibles, and the like—conducted independently of the forensic studies of the remains identified, to varying degrees, names and biographical backgrounds for all eight crew members.

Even so, positive matchups between the eight known names and the eight sets of remains recovered from the boat remain an elusive goal. In many ways, the approach taken by the Lasch Center's investigation of the *Hunley*'s wreck has more in common with the techniques of forensic detectives investigating a crime scene than the procedures used by historians and other bookish types. Historians seek to reconstruct the past primarily by deciphering the written flotsam of bygone eras. The Lasch Center researchers, by contrast, spend most of their days poring over nonverbal physical evidence, painstakingly recording precisely where each artifact was found; they then use the methods and disciplines of forensic sciences to examine each item, and ultimately, to retrieve the *Hunley*'s story. "This is basically just a large forensic scene," said the archaeologist Maria Jacobsen during a series of interviews.

To identify the eight crew members, the Lasch Center researchers began their work by assigning repeated letters in alphabetical sequence to each set of remains. The letters were assigned according to the relative position, forward to aft, of each set of remains in the submarine boat. The remains found in the most forward position of the boat thus became AA, the second set became BB, the third CC, and so on—all the way back to HH, in the craft's aftmost position.

Only after a DNA sample from a set of remains is matched with one from a relative with a direct linkage to a crew member do forensic archaeologists bestow the term *positively identified.* The *Hunley* project requires researchers to work with severely degraded DNA samples. They are therefore restricted to the study of mitochondrial DNA, a DNA type that is preserved better than other forms. The work thus can prove difficult. In investigating the crew of the *Hunley,* genealogist Linda Abrams, working with the Lasch Center, has located living collateral descendants for two crew members—Frank Collins and Joseph F. Ridgaway—and living direct descendants for James A. Wicks. But among those three, living maternally linked relatives have been located only for Ridgaway. Thus, strictly speaking, of the eight men in the boat's final crew, only Joseph Ridgaway's remains have been accorded the status of positively identified.

Fortunately, however, DNA sampling is not the only scientific tool available to forensic archaeologists. Insights into human remains may also be won through the study of stable isotopes. Isotopes are forms of the same element with different numbers of neutrons in their nuclei. Foods in different regions of the globe have different proportions of certain stable isotopes. When food is ingested, these isotopes become—and through a life remain—deposited in teeth. Thus, by looking at the stable isotope composition in the men's teeth, which they developed when young, the researchers can determine if the men were born in the United States or, say, Europe.

Osteological examinations, the study of skeletal remains,

combined with archaeological and genealogical investigations, have revealed the likely ages of *Hunley* crew members—from the youngest (Becker, approximately twenty years old) to the oldest (likely either Wicks, forty-four when he died, or the still unknown FF, whose estimated age was forty to forty-five); and from the shortest (Becker again, at five feet five) to the tallest (six-foot-tall Frank Collins). The studies likewise have revealed which men were pipe smokers—all but Dixon, Becker, and Carlsen. But even Dixon might turn out to have indulged the habit. The researchers have yet to analyze stains, likely from nicotine, on his teeth. But already they've tentatively concluded that if Dixon was indeed a smoker, he probably was not a pipe smoker. The researchers are also seeking to determine which of the men led the most strenuous lives, and which showed signs of past wounds or accidents. Dixon's remains, for instance, reveal signs of his souvenirs from the Battle of Shiloh—a healed gunshot wound and traces of lead fragments in the bone of his upper left thigh.

Of the three presumed crew members of the *Hunley* for whom living relatives have been located, only Wicks (five feet ten inches tall, a heavy smoker, and in his mid-thirties at the time of his death) seems to have been married and had children—four girls. Born in North Carolina, he joined the U.S. Navy in 1850 and served aboard the USS *Congress*. His ship was sunk in March 1862 by the ironclad CSS *Virginia*—formerly the USS *Merrimack*. The following month he deserted the Union Navy and joined the Confederate Navy. He was soon assigned to the *Indian Chief*, based in Charleston Harbor. From there he enlisted in the *Hunley*'s final crew.

Most members, probably five, of the *Hunley*'s final crew seem to have been young and likely unmarried—a probability that complicates efforts to locate living relatives of those men. Nonetheless, the researchers ascertained information on those five men similar—if less precise and comprehensive—to that garnered on the lives of the other three crewmen. Combined, the accumulated data yields a fascinating if sketchy group portrait of the entire crew: Captain Dixon and J. F. Carlsen had served in the Confederate Army. Five of the other men had served in the Confederate Navy. Surprisingly, however, only two of the eight men—Wicks and Collins—seem to have been native Southerners. Dixon, according to forensic expert Doug Owsley of the Smithsonian Institution, was "most likely from the Midwest." Ridgaway hailed from Maryland, a border state. Equally surprising, half the crew did not even hail from North America. Lumpkin, Carlsen, Miller, and Becker were likely born in Europe.[7]

On April 17, 2004, a stately funeral procession—replete with horse-drawn caissons and Civil War reenactors—bore the remains of the *Hunley*'s third and final crew through downtown Charleston. Afterward the remains of the eight men were interred in the same Charleston graveyard, Magnolia Cemetery, that held the bodies of the men from the same boat's first and second crews.

Horace Hunley and the other seven men of the second crew lost aboard the boat had been laid to rest in Magnolia Cemetery, in October 1863, immediately after their bodies were recovered from the submarine boat—after it had been raised, for the second time, from the harbor floor. The five men of the first group to die inside the craft perished in August 1863. Their bodies were soon recovered from the boat after it was raised the first time from the harbor floor; and they were originally buried in Charleston's Seaman's Burial Ground. Since that burial, however, that cemetery had fallen victim to neglect and was eventually lost amid the sprawl of twentieth-century urbanization. But in 1999 the remains of those men were discovered and ultimately—following their own solemn funeral procession—relocated to Magnolia Cemetery. There, in an expanded *Hunley* plot, they joined the remains of Horace Hunley and the other members of the boat's second crew. Thus, with the interment, in April 2004, of the remains of the third group of men to die aboard the *Hunley*, the dead among all three crews had been united in that same sylvan precinct.[8]

Beyond finding and removing the crewmen's remains from the submarine boat, the Lasch Center researchers also discovered heretofore unknown aspects of the *Hunley* and corrected past misconceptions about the craft. Equally important, the researchers were, at last, able to offer the world definitive measurements of the boat's length (forty feet) and beam (forty-two inches). Past accounts of the *Hunley*'s length had ranged from thirty to forty feet. It was the sort of descriptive imprecision that still mars accounts of the *American Diver* and, to a lesser extent, the CSS *Pioneer*.

Ironically, perhaps, many of the long-standing misconceptions surrounding the *Hunley* came from earlier accounts of the boat written by those who had had firsthand experience with it. Many errors arose from the fact that by the time that most of those men got around to writing of their experiences, their memories for details were fading. Most of the *Hunley*'s memoirists, after all, wrote about the boat decades after the Civil War. And all of them—including Alexander—who focused on the *Hunley* erred in recounting key facts. For instance, while Alexander accurately described the *Hunley*'s propulsion, navigation, and diving systems, he erred on many key details— including the boat's length (his version was but thirty feet long, ten feet shy of its actual length) and the number of men it carried. (Alexander recalled nine crewmen. The recovered *Hunley* has eight crew stations—seven cranking stations and one commander's station.)

To be fair, however, Alexander had correctly depicted the essential workings of the *Hunley's* mechanical systems. And his writings did include his oft-stated caveat that, after forty years, his memory of specifics had dimmed; and, lacking Civil War–era sketches of the boat's design, he could only guess at details. Thus, consequent to the new post-recovery revelations about the *Hunley*, naval historians have thoroughly revised their past understanding of the craft.

Happily for those starved for hard facts about the *Hunley*, the wreck's recovery and subsequent examination allowed researchers to correctly record the boat's precise dimensions. But that access also provided other collateral measurements—such as the distance between the two hatches (sixteen feet) and the length of the crew bench (eighteen feet). Significantly, the close-up examination of the wreck allowed researchers to correct errors and omissions perpetuated by past accounts and visual depictions of the boat. For instance, all past depictions of the *Hunley*—save one—portrayed its hull as awkwardly boxy in appearance, with a bow and stern inelegantly conical in shape. As it turned out, only Conrad Wise Chapman's painting of the craft—an image once dismissed as fanciful—had managed to capture the *Hunley's* true sleekness.

In retrospect, however, it's difficult to imagine why such skepticism had surrounded the young artist's depiction of the boat. After all, alone among the *Hunley's* myriad memorializers, only Chapman had produced a depiction of the boat based on firsthand, on-the-scene observation. His oil painting of the submarine boat, completed after the war, was based on a series of

plein air sketches he executed in late 1863, as it was undergoing
repairs and sitting atop its Shem Creek dock at Mount Pleasant.

Consistent with the elegant craft depicted by Chapman, the
actual *Hunley*, the one recovered in 2000, turned out to be far
more hydrodynamic than previously imagined—more, as James
McClintock had put it, "elliptical" in its cross-section profile.
Moreover, the cast iron caps that formed the craft's bow and
stern proved to be less prosaically conical (like traffic cones)
and more elegantly tapered. Viewed down its length, with the
observer facing either the stern or the bow, the boat—depending upon one's imagination—resembled either a hatchet blade
turned on its side, narrowing to a one-inch width, or a porpoise,
or a whale.

Even the origins and composition of the real-life *Hunley*'s
hull might yet prove to be inconsistent with past understand-
ings. It seems clear to the Lasch Center researchers that the
Hunley's iron bow and stern "caps," with their unique shapes,
were cast specifically for use on this craft. But the plates of the
hull's main section were long believed to have had a prior life.
William Alexander, for instance, recalled that the craft had been
constructed with sections cut from an old boiler. Thus far,
dense marine concretions still cover most of the surfaces of the
forty-two wrought iron plates from which the craft's hull was
constructed. Only along the seams of the already removed
plates—where the concretion was removed in order to take out
the rivets holding those plates in place—has the actual iron of
the hull been exposed. And until the concretions now covering
those cast iron plates are removed, and metallurgical studies
are conducted on the iron itself, the precise origins of the
Hunley's main hull section will remain an open question.

Those other continuing mysteries notwithstanding, new revelations have been won at the Lasch Center. For instance, researchers learned that the rivets piercing the section plates and

bow and stern caps were attached to a heretofore unknown skeletal frame that gave the boat added structural stability. Yet another Lasch Center discovery: to improve the boat's hydrodynamic prowess, the *Hunley's* builders had hammered those rivets until they were flush with the hull's surface.

Beyond matters concerning dimensions, shape, and construction, the wreck's recovery and excavation allowed researchers to correct erroneous information about other specific features of the boat—all perpetuated by past chroniclers presumably from firsthand knowledge of the *Hunley*. For instance, the boat's spar—which was found and recovered prior to the rest of the *Hunley*—was revealed to be made of iron and mounted on the bottom of the bow. Most past accounts had asserted that the spar was made of wood and mounted atop, not below, the boat's bow—technical errors that, as recently as 1999, had found their way into a made-for-TV movie about the *Hunley*.

In another error, one of omission, William Alexander's sketches had failed to show the boat's eighteen glass ports. Prior to the *Hunley's* recovery, most descriptions of the craft had implicitly assumed that its commander had been forced to steer the boat essentially blind.

Still other surprises for the archaeologists related to the *Hunley's* propulsion and navigation systems. Alexander's sketches had failed to indicate the presence of the differential gear box that James R. McClintock had designed into the boat's propulsion system. The differential gear box, which multiplied and regularized the force of the crew's cranking, had also allowed McClintock to mount the boat's crankshaft and its crew bench—approximately a foot in width—to the port side, while centering the propeller on the *Hunley's* stern.

Alexander had also, erroneously, shown the crankshaft running straight down the boat's middle, which had led past historians—unaware of the differential gears—to assume that the crankshaft connected directly to the propeller. Likewise erroneously in his sketches, he had also shown the *Hunley's* commander controlling the boat's rudder with a steering wheel. Instead, the archaeologists soon realized, the commander controlled the *Hunley's* rudder with a joysticklike lever.

Still other empirical discoveries raised as many questions as they answered, an outcome that likewise applies to many of the artifacts recovered from the muck that once filled the crew compartment. Those relics include a dog tag worn around the neck of a *Hunley* crewman but inscribed with the name of a Union soldier, and a bottle containing the vestiges of some as yet undetermined medicine or liquor. A gold ring, a diamond brooch, and a gold watch—all three later determined to be the property of George Dixon—were also recovered. Still other recovered items seemed to comport with oft-told stories about the boat—including a recently excavated lantern, presumably that with which Dixon allegedly flashed, or intended to flash, the boat's now storied blue light.[9]

Then there was the twenty-dollar gold piece that the archaeologist Maria Jacobsen, in May 2001, found inside the crew compartment. Jacobsen and her colleagues needed no explanation of the artifact she had found that day. From the start, they were aware of the coin's existence—it had long ago entered the realm of *Hunley* legend—and all along they had been cautiously hopeful of finding it.

At the Battle of Shiloh, George Dixon had been struck by a musket ball in his upper left thigh. But the coin had deflected the projectile, thus lessening the extent of his wound. Without the coin, Dixon may have lost his leg or even bled to death from the severing of a femoral artery.

On the day archaeologist Jacobsen found the coin—139 years after the Battle of Shiloh—she noticed that it bore a warp from the musket ball's point of impact, below Lady Liberty's head and the piece's 1860 mint mark. Once again, history—in this case, the Battle of Shiloh—had found voice in a silent material artifact. Yet the artifact had yet another fillip in store for the researchers: an inscription on the coin's reverse side—an inscription heretofore unrecorded—commemorated the significance of the twenty-dollar piece to Dixon: "Shiloh. April 6, 1862. My Life Preserver. G E D."

Subsequent research, however, dealt less kindly with yet another story, more recently attached, to the coin. According to an anecdote included in a 1995 *Hunley* book—and soon repeated in other books and articles—the coin had been given to Dixon as a last-minute gift, as he headed off to war, by his fiancée, a young woman named Queenie Bennett, of Mobile. After Shiloh—as a memento of her affection for him and because the coin had turned out to be a good luck piece for him—he was said to have carried it in his pocket wherever he went.

From the story's inception, however, it lacked a sound provenance in contemporary documents—including the now published letters of fellow soldier James M. Williams, with whom Dixon served at Shiloh. The two became close friends. Williams's letters home to his wife teem with caring references to Dixon; one, for instance, recounts how a gold coin had saved Dixon's life at Shiloh. And after Dixon was granted leave from the Twenty-first Alabama Infantry to return to Mobile to recuperate, Williams's letters to his wife abound with entreaties for her to be sure to look in on his dear friend. Eventually, the couple even named their first-born son after George Dixon.

By the late 1990s, the story of Dixon and his alleged Mobile sweetheart, Queenie Bennett, had become for many *Hunley* devotees their equivalent of such storied star-crossed lovers as Romeo and Juliet, and Abelard and Héloïse. The couple, it was said, had planned to marry when peace returned, and the ornate diamond brooch and the gold ring that he carried aboard the *Hunley* were gifts that he had planned to give to his betrothed. But tragically, their fond hopes were dashed by Dixon's sad ending.

But—unlike that of Dixon's gold coin—the George and Queenie story always hung from the thinnest of evidentiary threads. Suspiciously, for example, James Williams's war-front letters contain no references to Bennett. That Bennett was a real person, and that she lived in Mobile, have been established. Indeed, in 1871 she married. And her two daughters later claimed that, after their mother's death in 1883, they had allowed a Mobile newspaper to publish an article that included two letters that Dixon had written to Queenie during the war.

But that article and the alleged letters have never surfaced. Nor have any other contemporary documents linking her and Dixon. Indeed, the earliest known, and possibly the originating, source recounting the tale of a gift by a Mobile sweetheart to Dixon of a twenty-dollar gold coin seems to have been a newspaper article that appeared in the *Mobile Daily Item* in 1910, decades after Bennett's death in 1883. But even that article fails to mention the name of the alleged girlfriend. Beyond that, there is the matter of the gap in age between the actual Queenie and her supposed betrothed. To wit, she would have been but thirteen years old when the war broke out, and Dixon about a decade her senior. And for that matter, how would a girl of that age, from a family of modest means, even have, much less afford to give away, a twenty-dollar gold coin?

By 2002, devotees of the George and Queenie story were pinning their hopes on a possible matchup between the Lasch Center's computer-assisted re-creation of Dixon's face, based on skeletal remains, and a by now widely published studio photograph of an unidentified young man, a photo found amid Bennett's belongings after her death. Cherishers of the George and

Queenie story held out hope that the Lasch Center's studies would vindicate their faith that the unidentified young man in the photograph was Dixon.

Alas, however, a study soon conducted for the Lasch Center of the photograph—or more precisely, the tintype—concluded that the image likely was taken *after* the Civil War. Key elements in the man's wardrobe and the studio furniture in the image belonged to a later era. The story suffered yet another blow in 2002 when Lasch Center researchers, working with forensic anthropologists at the University of Tennessee, oversaw a photo superimposition study that compared specific "landmarks" on the face of the tintype's mystery man with the same features on Dixon's cranium. In the end, the study revealed no matchup. Nor did the investigators find a resemblance between Dixon and another unknown young man depicted in a second photograph presented to the Lasch Center by Bennett's descendants. In its provenance, the ballad of George and Queenie had reached a denouement as sad, in its own way, as the love affair it presumed to tell. Still, no one would deny the tale's intrinsic appeal—an allure that conjures the lament uttered by the chastened romantic who concludes Ernest Hemingway's *The Sun Also Rises*: "Isn't it pretty to think so?"[10]

15

The Signals Agreed Upon

SINCE THE FINDING of the wreck of the *Hunley* in 1995 and its recovery five years later, many mysteries concerning the boat have been resolved or nudged closer to resolution. In other cases, however, the closing of old questions has only opened newer mysteries. For instance, when divers finally found the submarine boat, its location—east of the *Housatonic*'s site— confounded long-standing expectations that the Confederate wreck would lie somewhere west of that Federal ship. More specifically the wreck's location raised the question of why Dixon—if his craft did remain operational after sinking the *Housatonic*—would have headed the *Hunley* out to sea, in a direction away from land.

As they conducted their excavation of the wreck, the Lasch Center scientists found it, for the most part, remarkably intact and free of signs of major damage from either explosion or small-arms fire or, for that matter, from a collision with the *Canandaigua* or any other large ship. But then again, as the archaeologist Maria Jacobsen acknowledged, "We have no idea what kind of damage we may find on the surface of the plates once the concretion is removed."

The Lasch Center researchers have determined that the two

holes, respectively, in the forward and aft ballast tank areas were made *after* the boat sank. But that still leaves unanswered the question of what caused the broken view port and the soft-ball-sized hole that pierces the forward conning tower. And those damages, their small size notwithstanding, have raised their own set of questions.

Were they caused by small-arms fire from the *Housatonic*? Or did the view port's glass shatter years after the *Hunley* sank to its grave? Or did that broken view port, as well as the hole in the conning tower, play some role in the boat's demise? More pertinently, did those breaches allow a torrent of water to fill the crew chamber, eventually sending all eight men to their graves? And what of those reports over the years that the *Hunley* had failed to survive its sinking of the *Housatonic*? Had the submarine boat—as Captain M. Martin Gray suggested in his April 1864 letter to General Maury—likely been swept into a vortex created as that larger ship sank to the harbor floor? Or did the *Hunley*, as others believed, survive for several hours after it sank the *Housatonic*?

Thus far—at least partially, because the researchers have yet to study the hull itself—their archaeological investigation has yielded no conclusive evidence for any particular side in those debates. Indeed, the strongest evidence that the *Hunley*, at least for a while, survived its attack on the *Housatonic*, continues to be, on the face of it, the testimony of the *Housatonic* crewman Robert Flemming. Days after the assault, the sailor testified to the U.S. Navy court of inquiry that was investigating the *Housatonic*'s sinking that shortly after his ship was attacked, he saw a peculiar sight. At the time, Flemming was positioned in the *Housatonic*'s fore-rigging, waiting for the approaching Union ship that would soon rescue him. Recalling that moment, he told the court of inquiry, "I saw a blue light on the water just ahead of the 'Canandaigua', and on the starboard quarter of the 'Housatonic.' "

Unlike the Confederates ashore at Breach Inlet that same night—who, according to Lieutenant Colonel Olin Miller Dantzler, witnessed a signal beacon from the *Hunley*—Flemming would have had no motivation to fabricate testimony. Beyond that, an incident that occurred earlier on the evening of the sinking establishes Flemming's credibility as a witness. Stationed as a lookout on the ship's starboard bow, Flemming, at 8:25 p.m., had noticed a suspicious object approaching the *Housatonic*. The sailor, an African American, immediately directed the attention of his immediate superior to the object. But he was rebuffed by the officer. "He told me it was a log," Flemming recalled. "I then told him this was not floating with the tide like a log would do but moving across the tide."

Attesting to Flemming's confidence in his observational prowess—as well as his boldness as an African American seaman aboard a ship dominated by white officers and crew—he refused to relent. Rebuffed by his immediate superior, Flemming then asked his counterpart lookout on the ship's port bow to have a look at the approaching object. Upon seeing the portside lookout crossing the deck, the officer who, moments before, had dismissed Flemming's concerns, decided to take a second look. As Flemming recalled, "He looked at the object through his glasses and then"—realizing that the approaching object was no log—"ran aft" to warn the ship's senior officers gathered on the quarterdeck.

But did Flemming see the blue light with which Dixon allegedly had agreed to signal his comrades back at Breach Inlet? Lending support to those who believe that he did was the "bull's-eye" lantern that Lasch Center archaeologists, in 2001, recovered from the *Hunley*. Through its bulbous glass lens, the bull's-eye lantern, a type popular during that era, gave off light only after a door on its side was opened.

However, subsequent to the discovery of the lantern came

yet another revelation—one that, while not destroying, at least raised still more questions concerning claims that the *Hunley* flashed a blue light that night. In their examination of the recovered bull's-eye lantern, the Lasch Center researchers found no evidence that its clear glass lens was ever colored. As archaeologist Jacobsen put it, "Any blue it would have given off would have had to have come from the lantern's fuel source."

Then what *did* seaman Flemming see that night? Did he spot a signal light, blue or otherwise, originating from the lantern later recovered from the *Hunley*? Or did he instead spot an inadvertent flash of light emanating from that lantern or perhaps a candle inside the crew chamber of the still-sealed submarine boat? After all, if Flemming did truly see a signal, is it not reasonable to assume that he would have said so more explicitly? Might he, perhaps, have also described a man holding aloft, and swinging, a lantern glowing with a blue light? And, beyond that, if the light from the *Hunley* that Flemming testified to seeing was truly a signal and it was answered from ashore, would not he, being high in the *Housatonic*'s rigging, have been in a better position to see that reciprocated beacon from ashore than the Confederates in their low-lying submarine boat?

Unfortunately, Flemming's testimony offers no other words on the matter. His navy interrogators pressed no further on the topic. Their task, after all, was to determine what role, if any, crew negligence or malfeasance had played in the *Housatonic*'s demise, not whether the Confederate boat that had attacked that Union vessel had displayed any particular signal.

So—again—did Flemming actually spot the *Hunley*'s storied blue light? Or did he merely spot a flash of light from the boat's interior? As it turns out, all of the boat's twelve deadlights possessed covers that could be closed to prevent the emission of light. And, after the boat was recovered in 2000, researchers found those covers closed on all of the deadlights. However, the view ports—six in all—on the two conning towers lacked such covers. And that circumstance opens the possibility that Flemming could have indeed spotted, as the *Hunley* trailed away from its victim, light emanating from Dixon's lantern or his candle—light that could have escaped through one of the four view ports in the *Hunley*'s forward conning tower.

And what of the claim made by Lieutenant Colonel Dantzler that "the signals agreed upon" were "answered" by the garrison at Breach Inlet's Battery Marshall? To that question, archaeologist Jacobsen counterposes some of her own: "The question is, what light did the people on land see? A light from a bull's-eye lantern, shone from the surface of the ocean at a distance of some four miles from the coast? Or did they perhaps spot the signaling between the Union ships communicating the loss of the *Housatonic* and [signaling] the movement of the Union fleet."

Flemming's account of the blue light he claimed to have witnessed is vague. But so too are the few located contemporary references in Confederate sources that suggest the intended purpose of the alleged exchange of lights between the *Hunley* and Battery Marshall. Even so, for its believers, that blue light burns with mythic powers. Indeed, not since F. Scott Fitzgerald's fictional Jay Gatsby—the "Great Gatsby"—obsessed over the green light at the end of the elusive Daisy Buchanan's Long Island Sound dock has colored light, projecting over a body of open water, glowed with such intensity. By now—amid the legends crowding around the submarine boat—the *Hunley*'s alleged beacon occupies a central place in the boat's mythology. The Friends of the *Hunley* organization even entitles its newsletter the *Blue Light*. More to the point, the assumption that the celebrated craft, on the night of its triumph over the *Housatonic*, survived long enough to show that blue light has become a matter of faith among *Hunley* devotees.

Alas, does a sinking truly "count" if, in the process, your own boat also goes to the bottom? The rules of U.S. Major League Baseball stipulate that for a defensive player's caught ball to be scored as an out, that player must "hold the ball long enough to prove that he has complete control of the ball and that his release of the ball is voluntary and intentional." Modern *Hunley* devotees yearn to believe that the object of their affections experienced a similar moment of equipoise on that moonlit evening of February 17–18, 1864—a state of grace that, however fleeting, allowed the men to savor their long-sought moment of triumph. And, in the absence of other revelations, the blue light offers the faithful precisely such reassurance.

Still more vexing, the handful of references to the beacon found in contemporary documents tend to differ on the signals' purpose—and even as to whether the light or lights were observed by witnesses ashore. In a memoir published in 1866 by Charleston newspaper journalist and editor Jacob Cardozo, he described an exchange that purportedly took place before the *Hunley* ventured out on the night it sank the *Housatonic*: "The officer in command told Lieutenant Colonel Dantzler when they bid each other good-by, that if he came off safe he would show two blue lights." But Cardozo added, "The lights never appeared." It also should be noted that Cardozo made no claim to have personally witnessed the conversation he purported to record. Nor did he have any known links to the *Hunley*. Even so, it remains reasonable to assume that Cardozo's assertion that the lights "never appeared" reflected, if nothing else, a grim consensus that, by 1866, had settled over post–Civil War Charleston.

Equally significant, Cardozo's allusion to the blue lights included no reference to any planned reciprocal beacon from Confederate forces ashore. The passage implied that the *Hunley*'s alleged signal was intended to play a singular role—to alert comrades ashore of the submarine boat's successful destruction of an enemy ship. By contrast, in the letter that Lieutenant Colonel Dantzler wrote from Battery Marshall two days after the *Hunley*'s attack upon the *Housatonic*, he indicated quite another, more practical, purpose for the exchange of lights—and without reference to any particular color. "The signals agreed upon to be given in case the boat wished a light to be exposed at this post as a guide for its return were observed and answered."

So did the *Hunley* flash its alleged blue light that night? And even if the signal wasn't sent, what would have been its intended purpose had it been displayed? Was the light intended to mark a military triumph, or to elicit a reciprocal signal from ashore needed to guide a vulnerable boat back to base?

Lasch Center archaeologist Jacobsen suspects the latter. Moreover, she doubts that Dixon ever intended to hoist the *Hunley*'s blue light, or any other beacon, in the heavily trafficked zone where it had attacked the *Housatonic*. "That would have been crazy," she says. "In that area, crowded with all manner of Union vessels—from ironclads to picket boats—it would have been foolish for Dixon to draw attention to their location by stopping the boat to unlock the hatch—and then stand there in the conning tower, waving such a light. If anything, they would have been trying to hightail it out of that area as fast as they could manage." Beyond that, Jacobsen adds, "All of the Union ships out there were armed and much faster than the *Hunley*. And they had a heck of an incentive to find the enemy vessel that had just destroyed the *Housatonic*."

Some assume that the alleged blue light of the *Hunley* and the supposed reciprocal signal shown by Confederate soldiers at Breach Inlet were beacons intended to guide the boat back to land. Jacobsen, however, suspects that any such navigational signals, if actually arranged and given, would have had a more specific purpose. "The crew would have had no need for a signal to guide them back to land," she says. If simply finding a landfall was the objective of the *Hunley*'s crew, she adds, they could have simply headed in any northern to northwestern direction—toward land but not toward the harbor's mouth. "Any other direction would have been problematic for them—into the open ocean or toward the enemy."

According to Jacobsen, if any lights were intentionally exchanged that night, they would have been displayed much closer to land. And they would have been flashed for the sole purpose of getting the *Hunley* back to Breach Inlet. More specifically, in approaching the inlet, the *Hunley*'s crew would have had to find their way to, and through, a channel that cut through the broad sandbar that, then and now, fronts the inlet. While the sandbar is evident on a contemporary chart of Breach Inlet, that same chart fails to indicate any channel—an omission that Jacobsen attributes to a lack of interest by surveyors and mapmakers in depicting what was, to them, an insignificant coastal feature. "Around 1900 is when you get the first charts of that area that clearly show where the channel runs across the sandbar."

According to Jacobsen, the channel off Breach Inlet—depicted on charts since the early twentieth century and still present today—has, over the decades, shifted in its course. "But having said that, we also know that Dixon's team was coming in and out of the inlet, and they had to cross the sandbar somehow without getting stuck and swamped in the breakers." And to accomplish that, they would have needed a channel. And to enter that channel, "They would have had to come at Breach Inlet at a very specific angle. Hence, I believe, they may have needed a signal guide. And, frankly, there is nothing to say that they did not request this every time they went out and came back late."[1]

But had the crew remained inside the *Hunley* after that attack? Or did they soon leave the craft? Between March 2001 and the end of that year, as one by one, the remains—biological and sartorial—of each of the eight crewmen were located and removed from the crew compartment, that question too was put to rest. Yes, they—all eight of them—had remained aboard. But how then had they died? More specifically, did they die after a torrent of water—perhaps from the broken view port and the hole in the forward conning tower—rushed into the crew compartment?

Some *Hunley* devotees conjecture that the submarine survived its sinking of the *Housatonic*—only to become trapped on the harbor floor hours later. Some who hold that view theorize that the men may have died from anoxia, a condition that results when oxygen is not delivered to the body's organs, tissues, and blood. Or perhaps they died from toxic levels of carbon dioxide produced by their own bodies during their exertions. By both of those slow death scenarios, the men would have eventually blacked out, then died. Like the crew of the Russian submarine *Kursk*, the men of the *Hunley* would have been aware of their impending death, and the experience would have been much like falling asleep. (As if balancing some grim ledger book of Davy Jones's locker, the *Kursk* sank on August 12, 2000, four days after the *Hunley*'s final recovery.)

At first glance, both slow death theories concerning the *Hunley* seem consistent with the location of its crew's remains when they were recovered from the boat. As the researchers recovered the crewmen's remains, they concluded that each man seemed to have died at his assigned station. Of what further investigations will reveal, one can only conjecture.

Will researchers find evidence that suggests a grisly scene in the crew's last moments—one similar to that apparently confronted by General Beauregard and William Alexander, when, in November 1863, the *Hunley* was opened to reveal the bloated corpses of its second crew? After all, the remains of those men too were found near their respective stations. Or will the investigators conclude that the crew's final moments betrayed no signs of panic—no signs of struggle, no futile Pompeii-like dash toward the exits?

Archaeologist Jacobsen—while noting that she and her colleagues located the remains of each of the eight men at his respective crew station—also warns that that configuration offers no conclusive indication of how the men died. Nor does it indicate whether they died slowly or suddenly—from, say, a rush of water into the crew chamber. Nor, for that matter, does it exclude the possibility that they perished amid circumstances that entailed both sudden and gradual actions. Perhaps, she speculates, the men became unconscious as the result of a concussion from an explosion and then, much later, drowned. "They were in a small, very confined space, and there wasn't much room to move around in. The evidence here, thus far, is inconclusive. And, so far, it's equally strong for either a slow death or an abrupt one."[2]

There is also, of course, the matter of the *Hunley*'s resting place, at a site *east* of the wreck of the *Housatonic*—a direction away from land and farther into the Atlantic Ocean. How does one even begin to explain that conundrum? One explanation for the *Hunley*'s presumed eastward course supposes that Dixon, after sinking the *Housatonic*, became disoriented. Navigating with limited vision inside an iron boat equipped with a notoriously unreliable compass, he simply became confused about his coordinates and direction of travel.

Yet another explanation for the *Hunley*'s position east of the *Housatonic* assumes that Dixon knew exactly where he was that night. In the night's confusion, as the *Canandaigua* steamed toward the *Housatonic* to rescue survivors, the *Hunley*'s crew possibly assumed that another Union ship was hunting for them. Amid the bustle, Dixon—aware of his crew's fatigue—might have decided it prudent to head east, the last direction that his pursuers would suspect. And once east of the *Housatonic*, he dived to the ocean floor to await the incoming tide to take his boat back to shore.

Observational tidal data for the Charleston area on February 17, 1864, does not exist. But, according to a later reconstruction of Charleston's tides for that date, calculated by the U.S. Coast and Geodetic Survey, that evening's flood tide would have commenced at 10:50 p.m.—almost exactly two hours after the *Hunley*'s assault on the *Housatonic*. And Dixon, no doubt, would have consulted the tide table for that evening. During earlier cruises, after all, he had demonstrated a predilection for navigating with the tides—for hitchhiking a ride back to base on incoming currents. Moreover, he and his crew had a demonstrated willingness to clock time on the ocean's bottom. Only a month earlier, displaying an impressive familiarity with their boat's abilities, they had managed to raise it from a sandy bottom and cruise home.[3]

Of course, even if one holds the view that the crew deliberately dived to the ocean floor and, once there, died a dry death from either anoxia or carbon dioxide poisoning, that hardly explains why Dixon and the men would have *stayed* on the ocean floor. Why—assuming for the sake of argument that the crew chamber did not then flood—did the men remain on the sandy bottom?

Perhaps, fatigued, they simply fell asleep. Or, then again, perhaps they never intended to dive to the bottom. Perhaps the crew had unintentionally filled their ballast tanks with a sufficient volume of water to squander the boat's buoyancy. And upon reaching the ocean floor, they were unable—for whatever reason—to expel enough water to resurface.

Then again—unless, or until, dramatic new revelations come to light—perhaps Captain M. Martin Gray, in his April 1864 letter to General Dabney Maury, offers the likeliest imagining of the boat's final moments—that the *Hunley* "went into the hole made in the *Housatonic* by [the] explosion of torpedoes and did not have sufficient power to back out, [and] consequently sunk with her." If nothing else, whatever its other shortcomings, Gray's theory, among all of those offered, certainly best squares with that venerable, complexity-shedding principle known as Ockham's razor.

That principle—propounded by the fourteenth-century English philosopher William of Ockham—affirms that, all things being equal, the simplest solution tends to be the most plausible one. And by the pitiless, slicing reductionism of Ockham's razor, General Gray's version of the *Hunley*'s demise—that it sank along with, or soon after its encounter with, the *Housatonic*—would seem to beat all competing theories. Swept into a vortex created as the *Housatonic* went down, or otherwise structurally compromised by the explosion of the Union ship's magazine or the small-arms fire its crew directed into the *Hunley*—or even by the explosion from the submarine boat's own torpedo, the *Hunley* simply sank before its crew had time to ponder what options, if any, were available to save their lives. If that indeed was the case, tidal actions, storms, later dredging operations, the angle of the *Hunley*'s own path to the ocean's bottom, and any number of other circumstances could easily account for the fact that the submarine boat's wreck, in 1995, was found to lie a thousand feet east of the *Housatonic*—not really so great a distance to stray in the course of 136 years.[4]

Meanwhile, research on the *Hunley* and the origins of its crew continues. Specialists in metallurgy, chemistry, forensic analysis, and other fields continue to probe the submarine boat for its secrets. As of this writing, DNA samples and skeletal remains of crew members continue to be analyzed and used to produce visual reproductions of the men's faces and three-dimensional images designed to settle the lingering mysteries surrounding their and their boat's final hours and minutes. Likewise, the hunt for living relatives goes on.

All the while, *Hunley* Internet sites and discussion groups crackle with the latest news, gossip, and conspiracy theories seeking to explain its demise. Sellers on eBay hawk the latest illustrations and models of the boat, purported relics from its wreck, and even *Hunley* mouse pads (the latter, however, not presented as relics from the vessel).

Around Charleston, admirers venerate the *Hunley*. From near and far, Civil War buffs make pilgrimages to gaze upon the celebrated wreck. Seeking to benefit from that veneration, the Friends of the *Hunley*'s website, with apparently unintended ghoulishness, entreats prospective donors with the invitation "BE A PART OF THE HUNLEY'S FOURTH CREW."

Boosters, meanwhile, savor an affiliation, implemented in 2005, between the Lasch Center and South Carolina's Clemson University. That new arrangement entails the eventual construction of a glossy new museum that is envisioned as the centerpiece of a new eighty-acre Clemson campus in North Charleston, devoted to research and instruction in "restoration industries and environmentally sustainable technologies." Opponents of the deal—and there are many—view it as yet another means of spending public money on what they view as a wasteful shrine to the Confederacy.

Indeed, in February 2007 *Reader's Digest*, traditionally no bastion of political correctness, in a story on government waste, singled out the *Hunley* project as a prime case of just such misbehavior. To finance various *Hunley*-related projects, the *Digest* predicted, "South Carolina taxpayers will eventually shell out a whopping $80 million." The *Digest* story drew heavily on a withering May 2006 investigative series on *Hunley*-related state public spending, published in *The State*, the daily newspaper of Columbia, South Carolina, the state's capitol. Much of the series targeted Senator Glenn McConnell, whose political star, in recent years, had steadily ascended. In 2001, when the Republicans gained control of South Carolina's state senate, McConnell, at the age of fifty-three, had become that body's youngest president pro tempore.

The *State* series accused McConnell and his allies of essentially hijacking the reins of state government and, with little or no oversight by appropriate agencies, of diverting vast public funds to *Hunley* projects. The stories cited specific examples of alleged wrongdoing and questioned "how in a poor state, with billions needed for worn-out school buses, run-down schools, unsafe bridges and roads, and job creation, a powerful politician can set his own priorities and steer tens of millions toward a pet project." The series also accused McConnell and his allies of a lack of transparency in their *Hunley*-related spending of public money. "It's a stealth strategy," John Crangle, director of the South Carolina arm of the national group Common Cause, was quoted as saying. "The whole scheme involves rivers of underground money flowing to the Hunley from many sources, and the obvious intent is to not let people know."

In response, McConnell soon answered with his own article in *The State*. Dismissing the series as a "tsunami of errors," he disputed the financial figures cited in the stories and asserted that all his actions with regard to *Hunley*-related projects were proper and aboveboard. "I'm proud of the Hunley project," he wrote. "During my two decades of public service, I can't think of any other historical project that has accomplished so much in such a short period of time with so few demands for public funding."

African Americans as of 2006 comprised 29 percent of South Carolina's population. How then to explain the success of this conservative Sons of Confederate Veterans member in steering substantial public funds toward projects that conserve but also arguably celebrate a Confederate ship? Perhaps the answer lies in a McConnell personal attribute readily acknowledged by supporters and detractors alike—his mastery of the essential quid pro quo dynamics of working politics. McConnell's dealings with his African American colleagues in the state legislature have exemplified that talent. For instance, the state senator has routinely supported projects favored by members of that body's Black Caucus. Over the years, McConnell has supported, among other such initiatives, bills to create an African American history monument on the grounds of the state capitol and a stipulation that historically black colleges get three to five million dollars annually from funds raised by the state's lottery. As Black Caucus member Senator Darrel Jackson described the relationship to *The State*, "It's like, 'Let him do his thing.' He's passionate about it—it's not worth the scars." Beyond that, Jackson told the newspaper, "It was mutually understood we would respect each other's passions and not try to derail them."[5]

In the meantime, politics aside, as the various historical investigations into the *Hunley*'s fate move ever onward, new discoveries will be made, old stories refuted, new questions asked, and fresh theories offered. For instance, one new theory focuses on the recent discovery that the boat's forward hatch cover, in the hours before or after the *Hunley*'s final dive, may have been left, intentionally or inadvertently, in an unlocked position. That assertion, if true, raises myriad other questions—including the dark possibility that the *Hunley* may have been sabotaged by Dixon or another crew member, or more plausibly by someone else who wished the Confederates harm and had access to the craft.

Then there was the matter of George Dixon's gold pocket watch. The timepiece, recovered from the wreck, seemed to offer researchers the enticing possibility of establishing, once and for all, a definitive time line of the events of that fateful night. Speculation about the watch focused on its hands, frozen at 8:23.

But was that a.m. or p.m.? There was no way of knowing. Another complication arose from the fact that time in that pre-standardization era was set locally and derived from solar observation. So did Dixon during his sortie against a Union ship have his watch set to Charleston time or to Union blockading squadron time—which ran twenty-six minutes ahead of Charleston time? And, for that matter, could the investigators be sure that the watch had been set accurately by either standard? Beyond that, how could they even know if 8:23—a.m. or p.m.—represented a defining moment in the *Hunley*'s life and death? Did it mark some cataclysmic event, or did the watch simply run down and stop, independently of the crew's demise? In 2007, a study by the National Association of Watch and Clock Collectors cast still more doubt over the significance of the clock hands' position. Humidity inside the submarine boat, the study concluded, may have caused the watch to run slow.

Still other evidence—albeit of less dramatic import—

suggests that this boat may have been even more advanced than researchers previously imagined. As a case in point, newly discovered evidence suggests that the *Hunley* perhaps carried an electrical battery to detonate its spar torpedo.

Amid the public clamor for quick answers to the complex questions that still surround the submarine boat, *Hunley* Commission chairman Glenn McConnell, in the fall of 2006, offered a dizzying prediction: "Between the science of archaeology and the science of conservation in that laboratory, they will solve the ultimate mystery. I think it's reasonable to say we're probably within a year of solving that."

But McConnell's otherwise laudable optimism overlooked the methodical, painstaking ways of scientists. It also misunderstood the nature of historical mysteries. More often than not, those addressing such mysteries experience a frustration similar to those known by alpinists as they climb long-sought summits. Just as mountaineers think they have reached the top, they realize that they are standing upon a "false peak"—an elevation from which rises yet another, still higher elevation.

Like all great mysteries, historical and otherwise, inevitably the *Hunley* will, perhaps must, keep many secrets—including, alas, those that might explain how, amid the ragged vagaries of a desperate war, its builders managed to design and assemble such a sublimely elegant craft. Moreover, as the work at the Lasch Center went forward, it soon became clear that the secrets the submarine boat did divulge would come but slowly. Indeed, it was as if the old boat, in its informational obstinacy, was echoing an injunction from a character created long ago by the novelist André Gide. "Please do not understand me too quickly."[6]

Epilogue: Legacy

In 1871, months before his death the following year, the naval scientist and engineer Matthew Fontaine Maury, looking back on a lifetime of devotion to nautical matters, reflected that, despite the qualified successes of the *Hunley* and other underwater vessels, it seemed to him that submarine travel and warfare had stalled in their development. "Attempts to construct such boats have been made over and over again," he wrote to an increasingly desperate James McClintock, then seeking support for his effort to enlist the British Navy in a new submarine boat venture. "The idea is an old one and I am not aware of any attempt which has been so near success, as that of your boat which destroyed the 'Housatonic.' It is true, she with her gallant crew perished with their victim, but that I conceive, need not have been a necessary part of the performance.

"Nevertheless," Maury added pessimistically, "there are so many difficulties in the way of navigating and managing a boat under water that I think nothing short of actual & practical demonstration will convince me that it can be done."

As late as—or, perhaps more to the point, as recently as—1910, *Harper's Weekly*, looking back wistfully at the *Hunley*, concluded that "though theoretically it could accomplish wonders," effective underwater war boats remained the stuff of fantasy: "the submarine of to-day has yet to demonstrate its merits as a fighting craft."

From an early twenty-first-century perspective, it's difficult to accept the proposition that humankind ever truly doubted the practicality of underwater travel and warfare. But that was indeed the case. After the *Hunley's* demise in 1864, the world, over the next five decades, witnessed the development of larger, more sophisticated submarines—powered by steam, diesel, and electrical energy. The new subs were armed with mobile gas- and later propeller-driven torpedoes that were capable of speeding toward their targets with ever increasing accuracy and force.

Even so, it would not be until World War I—September 5, 1914, to be precise, a half century after the *Hunley's* triumph and just four months after William Alexander's death—that the world again witnessed a successful attack by an underwater boat against an enemy vessel. That afternoon, off Scotland's Firth of Forth, the German submarine *U-21* dispatched a torpedo into the forward magazine of the British cruiser *Pathfinder*, killing 256 men—a staggering loss, and 251 more casualties than the *Hunley* had inflicted.

During the American Civil War, torpedoes and torpedo boats did produce substantial defensive and tactical—if not offensive and strategic—results for the Confederacy. Ship-to-ship battles were rare during that conflict. But Confederate torpedoes— albeit, most of them, fixed mines, rather than explosives launched from ships—struck forty-three Union vessels, of which twenty-nine sank. By contrast, during the entire war, Union torpedoes were responsible for the sinking of but one Rebel ship, the *Albemarle*.

As for the *Hunley*'s sinking of the *Housatonic*, that Confederate triumph, late in the war, had little if any impact—tactical or psychological—on the war's outcome. In retrospect, however, that sinking did inaugurate a new era in naval warfare—one that looms as one of the more ominous developments of the entire Civil War. Fifty years later, during World War I, the German Navy outraged the world by deploying submarines and torpedoes against enemy ships. And those vessels and armaments were vastly deadlier than anything ever imagined by Horace Hunley and his partners.

Compounding world outrage, the Germans—borrowing yet another Confederate tactic, the time-honored practice of commerce raiding—used those same subs to target zones in which civilian vessels, including passenger ships, sailed. In Confederate commerce raiding, the passengers and crew of captured ships were taken aboard a raider before its "prize" was destroyed or "bonded"—released after the vessel's captain promised to pay the Confederacy some stipulated amount of money after the war. By contrast, the German version of commerce raiding—borrowing a page from Horace Hunley's original intentions, going back to the CSS *Pioneer*—used subs rather than surface ships. Grimly, it was also a vision of warfare that, by necessity, precluded the taking of prisoners. Those souls not killed by the initial blast or through drowning could only hope to find their way to a lifeboat and then pray for the best.

The German Navy's approach to naval warfare during World War I not only upended conventional notions of military honor. It also erased traditional distinctions between noncombatants and soldiers. Indeed, it was as if the doctrine of total war propounded by the Union general William Tecumseh Sherman had been brought to the high seas—albeit in a far more lethal form than its terrestrial counterpart. This newer version of total war entailed the actual killing of civilians rather than merely the destruction of their property; and it represented an era that, at least partially, had begun in February 1864 with the *Hunley*'s destruction of the *Housatonic* in Charleston Harbor. In the end, it was a development that Leonardo da Vinci—declining to publish his plans for a submarine boat—had long ago feared. It welcomed to the world's waters "men who would practice assassinations at the bottom of the sea."[1]

APPENDIX
NOTES
BIBLIOGRAPHY
ACKNOWLEDGMENTS
INDEX

Appendix
The *Hunley*'s Three Crews
and Deaths Aboard the USS *Housatonic*

FIRST CREW
Lieutenant John A. Payne
Michael Cane
Nicholas Davis
Frank Doyle
Lieutenant Charles Hasker
John Kelly
William Robinson
Absolum Williams
All of the first crew except for Payne, Hasker, and Robinson were lost on August 29, 1863, during a training exercise in Charleston Harbor.[1]

SECOND CREW
Horace Lawson Hunley
Henry Beard
Robert Brookbank
John Marshall
Charles McHugh
Thomas W. Park
Joseph Patterson
Charles L. Sprague
All of the second crew were lost on October 15, 1863, during a training exercise in Charleston Harbor.

THIRD CREW
Lieutenant George E. Dixon
Arnold Becker

J. F. Carlsen
Frank Collins
"Lumpkin"
"Miller"
Joseph F. Ridgaway
James A. Wicks
The third crew disappeared with the *Hunley* on the night of February 17–18, 1864.

DEATHS ABOARD THE USS *HOUSATONIC*
Edward C. Hazeltine
Charles O. Muzzey
Theodore Parker
John Walsh
John Williams
The *Housatonic* was sunk off Charleston on February 17, 1864.

Notes

Preface: Of Boats, Books, Barnacles, and Archives

1. For claim by Watson to having played central role in the *Hunley's* development, see Watson to Jefferson Davis, October 10, 1864, File 434-W-1864, NARA Microfilm Publication M437, Letters Received by the Confederate Secretary of War, RG 109, War Department Collection of Confederate Records, NA; for similar claim by McClintock, see statement by McClintock, n.d., in Records of October 1872 Interview by Royal Navy Officers with James McClintock, in Admiralty Records, National Archives of the United Kingdom; for similar claims made on behalf of Hunley, see account of craft's history, ostensibly provided by crew member Charles Hasker, in Fort, "First Submarine," *Confederate Veteran* 26:459; for similar claim on behalf of Hunley as "the Submarine's designer," see Duncan, *Captain and Submarine*, 85. For Grant on Confederate press, see Grant, *Personal Memoirs*, 296.

Prologue: Canal Street
1. For profiles of Hatch, see Jewell, *Crescent City*, no pagination (henceforth n.p.); and two different Hatch obituaries, both on page 6, in New Orleans *Picayune*, July 20, 1884. For politics and customs collectors, see Summers, *Plundering Generation*, 62–63, 266.
2. For background on New Orleans Custom House, see *Harper's Weekly*, February 16, 1861, 11; King, *Great South*, 66; and Arthur, *Custom House*, 37–42. For Beauregard's Custom House work, see Williams, *Beauregard*, 39–40.
3. For background on ports, see Albion, *New York Port*, 15; see also ibid., appendixes I–XIV, 389–406. For Hatch's expedition plans and enlistment of Hunley therein, see Hatch to [Walker], June 1861, in Duncan, *Captain and Submarine*, 57.

1: A Man of Property, Intelligence and Probity
1. Peterson, *U.S. Lighthouse Service Tenders*, 5. For Hatch-Hunley gun-smuggling plan, see Hatch to [Walker], June 1861, in Duncan, *Captain and Submarine*, 57; L. P. Walker to Hatch (telegram), May 24, 1861, in *ORN*, Series 1, vol. 16, 820–21; and Duncan, *Captain and Submarine*, 57–58. For Fort Pickens reoccupation, see Haskin, *History of the First Regiment*, 130, 134. For blockade and blockade runners, see Wise, *Lifeline*, 56, 58; and Burton, *Charleston*, 84. For Hatch endorsement of Hunley, see Hatch to John Slidell, March 14, 1860 (typed copy of orig.), in Williams Collection, MPL.
2. L. P. Walker to Hatch (telegram), May 24, 1861, in *ORN*, Series 1, vol. 16, 820–21; Hatch to Walker, July 6, 1861, in *OR*, Series 4, vol. 1, 422–23; Hatch to Walker, July 12, 1861, in *OR*, Series 4, vol. 1, 467; Hatch to John Slidell, March 14, 1860 (typed copy of orig.), in Williams Collection, MPL; Hunley to Hatch, July 9, 1861 (typed copy of orig.), in ibid.; and Duncan, *Captain and Submarine*, 53–60.
3. For results of *Adela*'s Cuba trip, see Hunley to Hatch, July 9, 1861 (typed copy), in Williams Collection, MPL; Hatch to L. P. Walker, July 6, 1861, in *OR*, Series 4, vol. 1, 422–23; and Hatch to Walker, July 12, 1861, in *OR*, Series 4, vol. 1, 467. For Barrow, see Floyd, *Barrow Family*, 24–26. "Horrid fellows" quotation from Hunley to Robert Ruffin Barrow, August 9, 1860 (typescript of orig.), in Barrow Family Papers, Tulane University.
4. For births of Horace and Volumnia Hunley, see "Family Record" section of Hunley family Bible, 678, in James Peyton collection. For other background on Hunley family and Horace's law practice, see Duncan, *Captain and Submarine*, 13–16, 19–20, 53–54; see also 1850 U.S. Census, Horace Hunley entry in "Schedule 2, Slave Inhabitants in the 3rd Ward,

2nd Municipality in the County of Orleans" (Hunley's name could not be found in the 1860 U.S. Census). See also Gardner, *Gardner's New Orleans Directory for 1861*, 233. For Hunley's plantation, see ibid., 560; Champomier, *Sugar Crop, 1859–60*, 24; and Champomier, *Sugar Crop, 1861 62*, 24 "Castor oil" quote, Hunley to Robert Ruffin Barrow, August 9, 1860, in Barrow Family Papers, Tulane University. For Hunley as gentlemanly, see Gardner Smith to Volumnia Barrow, November 29, 1863, in Barrow Family Papers, Tulane University. For Hunley's Texas lands, see will of Horace Hunley, filed December 21, 1863, in St. Tammany Parish, Louisiana. For background on Leovy, see Hewitt and Bergeron, *Louisianans in the Civil War*, 81–83; *Biographical and Historical Memoirs of Louisiana*, 544; Leovy's obituary in New Orleans *Picayune*, October 4, 1902; and Walther, *Fire-Eaters*, 222.

5. For background on Leovy and his co-ownership of and editorial involvement with the *Daily Delta*, see his obituary in New Orleans *Picayune*, October 4, 1902; and Walther, *Fire-Eaters*, 222. See also Hewitt and Bergeron, *Louisianans in the Civil War*, 81–83; and *Biographical and Historical Memoirs of Louisiana*, 544.

6. For Hunley's debts to Barrow, see Hunley to Leovy, May 4, 1863, in papers associated with will of Horace Hunley, filed December 21, 1863, in St. Tammany Parish, Louisiana.

7. G. W. Pierce, "Historical and Statistical Collections of Louisiana—Terrebonne," *De Bow's Review* 11 (December 1851): 606. Barrow obit, from unspecified newspaper, quoted in Floyd, *Barrow Family*, 26. Louisiana Purchase quote, from Barrow, *On the political parties of the country*, 12.

8. For magazine profile of Robert Barrow, see Pierce, "Historical and Statistical Collections of Louisiana—Terrebonne," 606; for further background, see Floyd, *Barrow Family*, 24–26, 101, and plates 56, 57, 59; Scarborough, *Masters of the Big House*, 15, 181, 251, 430. For Barrow as Whig, see Becnel, *Barrow Family*, 71. For Barrow's canal project, see ibid., 41–98. For Horace Hunley's book purchases for Volumnia, see Horace Lawson Hunley Memorandum Book, Hunley Papers, Louisiana State Museum, 3. For Horace's vacation with Volumnia, see Volumnia Barrow to Robert Ruffin Barrow, August 9 and September 17, 1860, in Barrow Family Papers, Tulane University. For absence of familial ties between Robert Ruffin Barrow and Edmund Ruffin, historian William Scarborough, e-mail to author, April 21, 2007. For Barrow's antisecessionist views, see Barrow, *On the political parties of the country*, 11. Barrow's preference for Breckinridge in the 1860 race is extrapolated from quote in ibid.: "Mr. Breckinridge . . . has the proud consolation of having received the cordial support of all true National and Southern men." For Barrow's conviction that secession was a mistake, see Barrow to Hunley,

April 19, 1863, in Barrow Family Papers, Tulane University. For Barrow's fears about the collapse of sugar tariffs, see Barrow, *On the Political Parties of the Country*, 11; and Becnel, *Barrow Family*, 71.

9. For James De Bow's advocacy of Southern economic diversification, see *De Bow's Review* 7 (September 1849): 230–31. For background on De Bow, see Walther, *Fire-Eaters*, 195–227. For Whig opposition to and *Daily Delta* support for Narciso López, see Chaffin, *Fatal Glory*, 89, 95–97. For Hunley's 1858 resumption of his role as key Barrow business agent, see Hunley to F. W. Latham, March 20, 1858, in Barrow Family Papers, Tulane University. For Hunley's advice against newspaper investment, see Hunley to Barrow, December 28, 1860, in Hunley Papers, Louisiana State Museum. For Barrow as gambler, see Becnel, *Barrow Family*, 72. For Hunley's gambling advice, see Hunley to Barrow, November 12, 16, 1860 (typed copies of origs.) in Barrow Family Papers, Tulane University. For Hunley's bet against Dickinson, see Horace Lawson Hunley Memorandum Book, 26. For other ledger book entries referred to, see ibid., 1, 2, 3, 19, 21, 33, 39, 43, 45, 49.

2: The Inventive Faculty of the Country

1. For article containing "inventive faculty of the country" quote, see *Scientific American* 4 (May 4, 1861): 281. For briefer quoted article from same issue, disparaging underwater warfare technology, see ibid., 280. For discussion of origins of taboos against underwater warfare, see Roland, *Underwater Warfare*, 7, 28, 181. For "infernal machine" as term applied to explosives disguised as pieces of coal, see Taylor, *Running the Blockade*, 129.

2. For Smith article, see *Mobile Advertiser and Register*, June 26, 1861. For interest of Davis, Mallory, and other Confederate leaders in torpedo warfare, see Roland, *Underwater Warfare*, 156–59, 169. Anecdote from Maury's daughter from Perry, *Infernal Machines*, 8. Fulton anecdote from Philip, *Fulton*, 74. For *Albemarle* notoriety, see Perry, *Infernal Machines*, 4. For advocacy by Lincoln, Welles Fox, et al. of naval technological innovations, see Fowler, *Under Two Flags*, 81–84. For quoted *Harper's Weekly* story on *Cairo* and growing Union military awareness of dangers of torpedoes, see *Harper's Weekly*, February 7, 1863, 95. For numerical advantages of Union over Confederate fleet, see Chaffin, *Sea of Gray*, 12–13.

3. For claims by Watson and McClintock, respectively, to have been project's chief designer, see Watson to Jefferson Davis, October 10, 1864, File 434-W-1864, NARA Microfilm Publication M437, Letters Received by the Confederate Secretary of War, RG 109, War Department Collection

of Confederate Records, NA; and Statement by McClintock, n.d., in Records of October 1872 Interview by Royal Navy Officers with James McClintock, in Admiralty Records, National Archives of the United Kingdom; and McClintock to Matthew Maury (undated letter), folio numbers 9087–94, vol. 46, Matthew Fontaine Maury Papers, Library of Congress.

4. For background on McClintock's early years, see typed caption by *Hunley* researcher Eustace Williams beneath photocopied portrait of McClintock, in Williams Collection, MPL. Williams derived his information through correspondence with Henry C. Loughmiller of New York City, a grandson of McClintock. Also see Reports from Rear Admiral Edward Augustus Inglefield, RN, October 19, 1872; and from Vice Admiral Edward Gennys Fanshawe, RN, October 21, 1872, in Records of October 1872 Interview by Royal Navy Officers with James McClintock, National Archives of the United Kingdom. See also Hore, "Secret Journey," *Naval History* 16:32–36.

5. Robinson, *Privateers*, 21–23; Schell, "Submarine Weapons," *Alabama Review* 45:164.

3: Men Who Would Practice Assassinations at the Bottom of the Sea

1. For Alexander the Great legend, see Marx, *Underwater Exploration*, 30. For Leonardo diving inventions, see Leonardo, *Notebooks*, 96–97. For those of Bourne, Drebbel, Bushnell, and others, see Hutchinson, *Submarines*, 7–10. For Washington's assessment of Bushnell as "genius," see ibid., 10.

2. For submarine boats invented by Fulton and Bauer, see Hutchinson, *Submarines*, 10–11. For more extensive background on Fulton's work, see Philip, *Fulton*, 72–118. For more on Bauer, see Burgoyne, *Submarine Navigation*, 27–34. For Monturiol's underwater boats, see Stewart, *Dream*, 113, 151, 168, 187, 198, 217, 253, 282–83, 322.

3. For McClintock's claim of early unfamiliarity with work of Fulton et al., see statement by McClintock, n.d., in Records of October 1872 Interview by Royal Navy Officers with McClintock, in Admiralty Records, National Archives of the United Kingdom. For contemporary documents chronicling Brutus de Villeroi and his U.S. activities, see Philadelphia *Evening Bulletin*, May 17, 18, 1861; and *New York Herald*, May 17, 1861. See also Welles to Goldsborough, June 19, 1862, in *ORN*, Series 1, vol. 7, 488; and de Villeroi to Lincoln, September 4, 1861, in RG 45, Naval Records Collection of the Office of Naval Records and Library, Entry 36, Records of the Office of the Secretary of the Navy, Miscellaneous Letters Received, 1861, Volume XIII, page 121. For Lincoln's invention and his dealings

with inventors, see Donald, *Lincoln*, 156, 431, 432. For announcement of Lincoln's patent, see "List of Patents," in *Scientific American* 4 (June 2, 1849), 294. Cited monetary figures for *Alligator* deal are from Bolander, *Alligator*, 850. For general overview, drawing on contemporary documents, of de Villeroi's career and his dealings with the U.S. Navy, see Bolander, *Alligator*, 845–54; for general overview of Lincoln's attitudes toward weapons and technology, see Bruce, *Lincoln and the Tools of War*.

4. Hutchinson, *Submarines*, 13–14; Parrish, *Submarine*, 26–33. As of this writing, the *Intelligent Whale* is on display at the National Guard Militia Museum of New Jersey, at Sea Girt, N.J.

5. For *Shenandoah* incident, see Chaffin, *Sea of Gray*, 156–58. Pinkerton, apparently mistaking the date of Mrs. Baker's spy activities, asserts that she witnessed a test of the Confederate submarine in November 1861. Other documentation, however, suggests that the trials she witnessed took place earlier that fall. For background on Cheeney's Confederate submarine boat, see Wills, "*Hunley* in Historical Context," electronic access, n.p.; Pinkerton, *Spy*, 395–404; *The New York Herald*, October 15, 1861; Coski, *Capital Navy*, 116–21. For Shreveport boat building, see Report of Major A. M. Jackson, March 13, 1865, in *ORN*, Series 1, vol. 22, 103–105; Goldsborough to Captain William Smith, USS *Congress*, October 27, 1861, in *ORN*, Series 1, vol. 6, 363. For speculation concerning possible other submarine boats built in New Orleans, see Lambousy, *Monster*, 1–28.

6. For Union capture of New Orleans, see Welles to Farragut, January 20, 1862, in *ORN*, Series 1, vol. 18, 7–8; Hearn, *Farragut*, 55–67.

4: The CSS *Pioneer*

1. New Orleans population figures from 1860 U.S. Census; others from Albion, *New York Port*, 419, appendix XXVIII, statistics adapted from U.S. Census figures.

2. De Bow to William P. Miles, February 5, 1861, in Miles Papers, Southern Historical Collection, UNC, quoted in Walther, *Fire-Eaters*, 223; DuFour, *Night the War Was Lost*, 106–07; New Orleans *Daily Delta*, October 27, 1861; Robinson, *Privateers*, 35; Chaffin, *Fatal Glory*, 90–91.

3. O'Brien, "Hunley," *Gulf South Historical Review* 21:38; New Orleans *Daily Crescent*, May 9, 1861. For alleged other submarine boat activity, see Lambousy, *Monster*, 4, 5; Schell, "Submarine Weapons," *Alabama Review* 45:166–67; E. P. Dorr to Welles, June 25, 1861, in *ORN*, Series 1, vol. 22, 288–89.

4. New Orleans *Daily Delta*, August 17, 1861. For details on *Pioneer*, see

William H. Shock, fleet engineer West Gulf Blockading Squadron to Gustavus V. Fox, Assistant Sec. of the Navy and accompanying detailed sketch of craft, January 21, 1864, in January 1864, vol. 2, NARA Microfilm Publication M148, Letters Received by the Secretary of the Navy from Commissioned Officers Below the Rank of Commander ("Officers Letters") 1802–84, RG 45, Naval Records Collection of the Office of Naval Records and Library, NA; McClintock to Matthew Maury (undated letter), folio numbers 9087–94, vol. 46, Matthew Fontaine Maury Papers, Library of Congress. See also Baird, "Submarine Torpedo Boats," *Journal of the American Society of Naval Engineers* 14:845–47.

5. The naval engineer to whom McClintock spoke after the war and described the *Pioneer*'s shortcomings, including its tendency to slip off keel due to movement of crew members, was G. W. Baird. See Baird, "Submarine Torpedo Boats," *Journal of the American Society of Naval Engineers* 14:845–46. However, Baird's assertion, in ibid., 845, that the partners' New Orleans submarine boat employed a Bushnell-type torpedo "intended to be screwed to the bottom of the enemy's ship" seems incorrect—inconsistent with known facts drawn from contemporary documents of the craft's design. For further background on that craft, see McClintock to Matthew Maury (undated letter), folio numbers 9087–94, vol. 46, Matthew Fontaine Maury Papers, Library of Congress. For Scott's diving expertise, see Scott to N. & A. F. Tift, April 20, in *ORN*, Series 2, vol. 1, 556; Wills, "*Hunley* in Historical Context," electronic access, n.p.; Baird, "Submarine Torpedo Boats," 845–46; Records of October 1872 Interview by Royal Navy Officers with James McClintock, in Admiralty Records, National Archives of the United Kingdom; *New Orleans Daily Delta*, August 17, 1861; Robinson, *Privateers*, 166–67.

6. For Scott's application for a letter of marque, see Hatch to Benjamin, April 1, 1862, with two enclosures: notarized application from Scott and notarized statement by Hatch, in *ORN*, Series 2, vol. 1, 399–400. The register of the *Pioneer*'s commission is in *ORN*, Series 2, vol. 1, 401. See also Robert Barrow to Hunley, April 19, 1863, in Barrow Family Papers, Tulane University. For the *Pioneer*'s distinction as the only submarine vessel accorded a letter of marque, see Wills, "*Hunley* in Historical Context," electronic access, n.p. For report of deaths aboard the *Pioneer*, see Shock to Fox, January 21, 1864, in January 1864, vol. 2, NARA Microfilm Publication M148, Letters Received by the Secretary of the Navy from Commissioned Officers Below the Rank of Commander ("Officers Letters"), 1802–84, RG 45, Naval Records Collection of the Office of Naval Records and Library, NA; Floyd, *Barrow Family*, 26, also asserts, without mention of crew deaths, that the *Pioneer* "sank on one of its early trials,

and was raised, only to be immersed again to prevent its capture by Admiral Farragut."

7. For the partners' scuttling of the *Pioneer*, see Alexander, "Confederate Submarine Boat," *Gulf States Historical Magazine* 1:80, 81. For "Invincible Armada" quote, see Volumnia Barrow to Mrs. Young, October 16, 1863, in Duncan, *Captain and Submarine*, 42; for more on *Pioneer*, see Robinson, *Privateers*, 166–67.

5: The *American Diver*

1. For Hatch's presence in Mobile, see C. G. Memminger to Jefferson Davis, May 27, 1862, in *OR*, Series 4, vol. 1, 1130–31. Hunley's proposal for river defenses is presented in Hunley to unidentified addressee, April 30, 1862 (photocopy of orig.), in Hunley Papers, Historic Mobile Preservation Society. Mobile population figures from 1860 U.S. Census. English visitor quote from Russell, *My Diary North and South*, 137. For other background on Mobile, see Symonds, *Confederate Admiral*, 178–79; Hearn, *Mobile Bay*, 9, 10.

2. For Custom House under Union occupation, see Arthur, *Custom House*, 25–26. Sugar crop statistics from Prichard, "Louisiana Sugar Industry," 316–19; Volumnia Barrow to Robert Barrow, Jr., March 13, 1862 (typed copy of letter), in Barrow Family Papers, Tulane University. See also Duncan, *Captain and Submarine*, 44, 45 nn. 2, 3, 4.

3. For background on Dabney Maury, see Hearn, *Mobile Bay*, 9, 11–12. For Mobile's strategic posture during period, see ibid., 1–12. For quoted passages from Maury letter doubting "early attack" on Mobile and possible use of ironclads *Nashville* and *Tennessee* to recapture New Orleans, see Dabney Maury to General Samuel Cooper, June 22, 1863, in *OR*, Series 1, vol. 26, pt. 2, 74. For "running under the water" quote, see McClintock to Matthew F. Maury, undated letter, Matthew Maury Papers, Library of Congress. For dispatch of submarine boat partners to, and location of, Park and Lyons shop, see Alexander, "Confederate Submarine Boat," *Gulf States Historical Magazine* 1:80–81; and O'Brien, "Hunley," *Gulf South Historical Review* 21:31.

4. Duncan, *Captain and Submarine*, 62. For background on Alexander, see Alexander obituary in Mobile *Register*, May 14, 1914; and Alexander speech to Iberville Historical Society, December 15, 1903, 5–6, in Williams Collection, MPL.

5. Schell, "Submarine Weapons," *Alabama Review* 45:164, 169–70, 172–74; Wills, "*Hunley* in Historical Context," electronic access, n.p.; O'Brien, "Hunley," *Gulf South Historical Review* 21:31–48.

6. On the name *American Diver*, see testimony of deserter "Belton," Janu-

ary 7, 1864, in *ORN*, Series 1, vol. 15, 229. For background on McClintock and efforts in Mobile, see Reports from Rear Admiral E. A. Inglefield, RN, October 19, 1872, and from Vice Admiral E. G. Fanshawe, RN, October 21, 1872, in Records of October 1872 Interview by Royal Navy Officers with James McClintock, in Admiralty Records, National Archives of the United Kingdom. For J. G. Wire patent, see patent no. 127, registered December 8, 1862, in [Confederate] *Patents*, 8, 12. For other background on the boat, see McClintock to Maury, undated but apparently post–Civil War correspondence, in vol. 46, Maury Papers, Library of Congress; and Buchanan to Mallory, February 14, 1863, Buchanan Letterbook, UNC.

7. For background on Buchanan, see Symonds, *Confederate Admiral*, xv–xvi, 153, 156–72, 178–85, 189, 190, 202; and Luraghi, *Confederate Navy*, 322. For quoted remarks by Buchanan on need for public trial of *Tennessee*, see Buchanan to John K. Mitchell, March 13, 1864, Buchanan Letters, Virginia Historical Society.

8. Buchanan to John Shorter, December 22, 1862; Buchanan to Mallory, November 6, 1863—both from Buchanan Letterbook, UNC. For Buchanan's resistance to civilian initiatives in naval technology, see Symonds, *Confederate Admiral*, 187–88.

9. For official assistance rendered to *American Diver*, description of its torpedo modus operandi, and Buchanan's attitude toward the craft, see Buchanan to Mallory, February 14, 1863, in Buchanan Letterbook, UNC. For alleged failed attempt to attack a Union ship, see Alexander, "Confederate Submarine Boat," *Gulf States Historical Magazine* 1:82. For a tantalizing account of a failed attempt by a submarine boat in Mobile Bay to attack a Union ship, see testimony of confederate deserter James Carr, taken down by Commodore R. B. Hitchcock, in *ORN*, Series 1, vol. 19, 628–29. While certain details of the Confederate vessel described by Carr—identified as "an infernal machine, consisting of a submarine boat"—are consistent with features of the *American Diver* and he may indeed have witnessed one of that vessel's trial runs, other recounted details suggest he saw another Confederate craft. Discrepancies include his recollection of the date of the alleged incident, his description of the torpedo modus operandi of the observed vessel, and a reference to that craft as being under the command of "the Frenchman who invented it." In that same document, Carr's testimony also refers to "three or four" other submarine boats under construction at that time in Mobile—an assertion consistent with rumors then circulating around Mobile. For evidence supporting such claims, see Schell, "Submarine Weapons," *Alabama Review* 45:164–83; and O'Brien, "Hunley," *Gulf South Historical Review* 21:31, 43–44.

10. Buchanan to Mallory, February 14, 1863, Buchanan Letterbook, UNC; Buchanan to Mallory, March 3, 1863, Buchanan Letterbook, UNC.

6: The *Fish Boat*

1. The "at least $15,000" figure for money spent in building the *American Diver* is a rough estimate by the author and is based on the capital apparently raised to construct the partners' next craft, the *Fish Boat*, later known as the *H. L. Hunley*. However, in light of the added costs of the attempts to install electric and steam engines in the *American Diver*, it must be considered a conservative estimate. For *H. L. Hunley* costs, see also J. D. Breaman to his wife, Nelly, March 3, 1864, in *ORN*, Series 1, vol. 26, 188. For Hunley's debts to Barrow, see Hunley to Leovy, May 4, 1863, letter contained in papers associated with the will of Horace Hunley, filed December 21, 1863, in St. Tammany Parish, Louisiana.

2. Perry, *Infernal Machines*, 28–29, 42–44; H. N. Hill, "Texan Gave World First Submarine Boat," *San Antonio Express*, July 30, 1916. Report from ordnance commission, July 14, 1863, in *ORN*, Series 1, vol. 26, 189–90; J. D. Breaman to his wife, Nelly, March 3, 1864, in *ORN*, Series 1, vol. 26, 188. Hunley's $400 share in the *Fish Boat* is revealed in the will of H. L. Hunley, May 4, 1863, filed June 3, 1864, in St. Tammany Parish, Louisiana.

3. For newspaper coverage of loss of *Alligator*, see *The New York Times*, April 10, 1863, Savannah *Daily Morning News*, April 18, 1863, *The New York Herald*, April 15, 1863, and San Francisco *Daily Evening Bulletin*, April 18, 1863.

4. Hunley to Leovy, May 4, 1863, letter contained in papers associated with the will of Horace Hunley, filed December 21, 1863, in St. Tammany Parish, Louisiana; Volumnia Barrow to Robert Barrow, June 9, 1863 (typescript of original letter), in Barrow Family Papers, Tulane University. For "early biographer" quoted, see Duncan, *Captain and Submarine*, 63; for Hunley's business travails, see ibid., 84 n. 7.

5. The building that housed Mobile's Park and Lyons shop was destroyed by a fire in 1877. A later building—erected on that same site in 1884 and demolished in 1965—is often and erroneously presented in a widely published photograph as the structure that housed the shop. But the Seaman's Bethel Church, the actual, original building, still stands—albeit in a new location. It was moved from its original Church Street site to its present setting on the campus of the University of South Alabama, in Mobile, where it now houses university offices. The relocation of the church, prompted by architectural preservationists, took place during the 1960s, before its role in the construction of the *Fish Boat* had been

reestablished. For background on the building that housed the Park and Lyons foundry, see *Mobile Daily Register*, April 6, 14, 15, 24, 1884. For the role of the Seaman's Bethel Church in the construction of the *Fish Boat/Hunley*, see O'Brien, "Hunley," *Gulf South Historical Review* 21:31–48. For reference to "at least one other submarine boat" built in Mobile during war, see Charles H. Poolen to Gen. D. Leadbetter, January 5, 1862, in McMillan Collection, Museum of Mobile, in which Poolen reports that a "submarine apparatus" in the Mobile River "was boarded and sunk by some reprobate" the previous week.

6. Alexander, "True Stories of the Confederate Submarine Boats" (hereafter "Submarine Boats"), New Orleans *Picayune*, June 29, 1902; and Alexander, "Thrilling Chapter," *SHSP* 30:164–67. For promotion, reaching back to early nineteenth century, of barometer as device for measuring altitude and depth, see Chaffin, *Pathfinder*, 37–38. Details of *Fish Boat* from archaeologist Maria Jacobsen, various e-mails to author, 2006–2007.

7. For use of name *Fish Boat* by a contemporary, see Fort, "First Submarine," *Confederate Veteran* 26:459. For other background on this boat's names, see O'Brien, "Hunley," *Gulf South Historical Review* 21:18. For Horace Hunley's presence in Rome, Georgia, on July 23, 1863, see receipt signed by him on that date, cited in Duncan, *Captain and Submarine*, 63. For "saw her in all stages" quote, see examination of Confederate deserter E. C. Belton, January 7, 1864, in *ORN*, Series 1, vol. 15, 229. For recollection of "small boy"—B. B. Cox—of the boat's launch in Mobile, see his article in Mobile *Register*, November 1, 1914.

8. For the presence of Johnston and Slaughter at demonstration of *Fish Boat*, and latter's frequent visits to machine shop, see Johnston to Slaughter, September 28, 1872, and Slaughter to McClintock, October 1, 1872—both in Records of October 1872 Interview by Royal Navy Officers with James McClintock, in Admiralty Records, National Archives of the United Kingdom. For Buchanan's earlier assertion of *American Diver* as "impracticable," see Buchanan to Mallory, February 14, 1863, in Buchanan Letterbook, UNC. For Buchanan's subsequent evaluation of craft after witnessing July 1863 tests, see Buchanan to Tucker, August 1, 1863, in ibid. For Watson and Whitney's trip to Charleston, see Beauregard to Maury, August 5, 1863, page 16, Chapter II, Volume 45, Telegrams Sent, Department of South Carolina, Georgia, and Florida, 1863–64, RG 109, War Department Collection of Confederate Records, NA.

9. For Beauregard's visit to Bladon Springs and Mobile and his responsibilities after returning to Charleston, see Williams, *Beauregard*, 157–59, 175. For Hunley's introductory letter to Beauregard, see Hunley to Beauregard, September 19, 1863, in H. L. Hunley File, NARA Microfilm Publi-

cation M346, Confederate Papers Relating to Citizens or Business Firms, RG 109, War Department Collection of Confederate Records, NA.

10. Comparison of Union and Confederate armament in Charleston theater, from Fort Sumter National Monument historian Richard W. Hatcher III, e-mail, October 17, 2007, based on figures in Johnson, *Defense of Charleston*, and Wise, *Gate of Hell*—particularly appendix, "Roll of Battle," 221–54.

11. Beauregard to Maury, August 5, 1863, page 16, Chapter II, Volume 45, Telegrams Sent, Department of South Carolina, Georgia, and Florida, 1863–64, RG 109, War Department Collection of Confederate Records, NA. Gift to fiancée Ellen Shackleford, August 8, 1863, in George Washington Gift Papers, UNC.

7: The Consequences of Faltering in the Hour of Success

1. *Fish Boat's* likely arrival in Charleston "by Wednesday, August 12" deduced from various previously cited contemporary documents and from General Thomas Jordan's order, on that date—issued at General Beauregard's behest—to Chief Quarter-Master Hutson Lee, to provide Gus Whitney "such articles" as needed to prepare the boat for operations—Jordan to Lee, August 12, 1863, page 424, Chapter II, Volume 31, Letters Sent, Department of South Carolina, Georgia, and Florida, May–September 1863, RG 109, War Department Collection of Confederate Records, NA. For quoted Holmes diary passage, see Holmes, *Diary*, 302.

2. Grant, *Personal Memoirs*, 296; Ruffin, *Diary*, vol. 3, 182–83; Holmes, *Diary*, 302; Cohen, "Master Song," *Stranger Music*, 106.

3. [Jordan] to Trevezant, August 16, 1864, August 5, 1863, Entry 71, Letters Sent, Department of South Carolina, Georgia, and Florida, 1863–64, RG 109, War Department Collection of Confederate Records, NA. For various cited aspects of Beauregard's life, see Williams, *Beauregard*, 1–7, 36, 38–41, 166–96; and Arthur, *Custom House*, 37–42. For Hatch-Slidell connections, see first of two Hatch obituaries on page 5, New Orleans *Picayune*, May 20, 1884. For Chapman's assignment from Beauregard, see Bassham, *Chapman*, 128–29. For Beauregard as Charleston "demigod," see Chesnut, *Mary Chesnut's Civil War*, 32. For Beauregard's carte blanche offer to Whitney, see Jordan to Major Hutson Lee, August 12, 1863, page 424, Chapter II, Volume 31, Letters Sent, Department of South Carolina, Georgia, and Florida, May–September 1863, RG 109, War Department Collection of Confederate Records, NA. For John Fraser & Co. bounties, see Burton, *Charleston*, 216. For presence and activities of Breaman, Singer, and Whitney in Charleston, see J. D. Breaman to wife, Nelly, March 3, 1864, in *ORN*, Series 1, vol. 26, 188.

4. For Charleston as sieve, see Williams, *Beauregard*, 166–67. Charleston population figures from 1860 U.S. Census. Hunley to McClintock, August 15, 1863, Historical Manuscripts, Navy Department Library, Naval Historical Center. For general background on Civil War in Charleston, see Burton, *Charleston*; and Wise, *Gate of Hell*.

5. Hunley's request for uniforms to unnamed correspondent, August 21, 1863, in NARA Microfilm Publication M-347, reel 197, Unfiled Papers and Slips Belonging in Confederate Compiled Service Records, RG 109, NA. For Fulton's request, see Philip, *Fulton*, 73–75.

6. For praise of McClintock from British naval officer, see Report of Admiral Edward Fanshawe, October 21, 1872, in Records of October 1872 Interview by Royal Navy Officers with James McClintock, in Admiralty Records, National Archives of the United Kingdom. For test dives and McClintock's refusal of request to allow Confederate Navy officer aboard *Fish Boat*, see Theodore Honour to wife, Beckie, August 30, 1863, in Honour Papers, University of South Carolina. For Clingman's impatience with *Fish Boat*, see Clingman to Nance, August 23—two letters on same day—in *OR*, Series 1, vol. 28, pt. 1, 670. Descriptions of *Fish Boat*'s operations from archaeologist Maria Jacobsen, various e-mails to author, 2006–2007.

8: In Other Hands

1. S. G. Haynes to Gideon Welles, August 24, 1863, page 40, August 1863, Volume III, NARA Microfilm Publication M124, Miscellaneous Letters Received by the Secretary of the Navy, 1801–1884, Roll 453, August–September 1863, RG 45, Naval Records Collection of the Office of Naval Records and Library, NA. Caveat re alleged use of boiler iron in boat's construction from archaeologist Maria Jacobsen, various e-mails to author, 2006–2007.

2. For Dahlgren's threat to hang prisoners, see Perry, *Infernal Machines*, 84. For an excellent study of Dahlgren, see Schneller, *Quest for Glory*—in particular the book's discussions of the officer's attitudes and actions concerning underwater warfare, 235, 239, 251, 263–64, 267–69, 275–77, 314, 315–16, 349.

3. For $27,500 assessed value of *Fish Boat*, see letter from referees, November 9, 1863, in Smith and Broadfoot File, Confederate Papers Relating to Citizens or Business Firms, NARA Microfilm Publication M346, reel 946, RG 109, War Department Collection of Confederate Records, NA. For background on Payne, his crew, and the *Fish Boat*'s sinking in August 1863, see Stanton, "Submarines," *Confederate Veteran* 22: 398–99 (though Stanton misrecalls Hasker's surname as "Hooker"); for identification of Hasker, see Wills, "Hunley in Historical Context," electronic ac-

cess, n.p. For recommendation of Sprague as torpedo expert, see Jordan to Beauregard, August 26, 1863, Entry 71, Letters Sent, Department of South Carolina, Georgia, and Florida, 1863–64, RG 109, War Department Collection of Confederate Records, NA; for presence of Singer et al. in Charleston, see Thomas Jordan to RSR [Ripley], August 26, 1863, #144, August 1863, Entry 71, Letters Sent, Department of South Carolina, Georgia, and Florida, 1863–64, RG 109, War Department Collection of Confederate Records, NA. For other background on Singer et al., see Hill, "Texan Gave World." For Hasker's account of sinking, see Fort, "First Submarine," *Confederate Veteran* 26:459–60; for slightly different version of Hasker account, see Lake, *Submarine*, 38–39. Hasker put the depth of the harbor where the *Fish Boat* sank as forty-two feet. That figure, however, likely exaggerates the true depth. An earlier U.S. government–published chart, based on still earlier government surveys of the harbor, estimated the depth in that area as from twelve to twenty-five feet—see *Charleston Harbor and Its Approaches, Showing the Positions of the Rebel-Batteries*, U.S. Coast Survey, A. D. Bache, 1863. For McClintock assessment on cause of accident, see McClintock to Matthew Maury (undated letter), folio numbers 9087–94, vol. 46, Matthew Fontaine Maury Papers, Library of Congress. For partial list of survivors and those killed aboard *Fish Boat*, see "unfortunate Accident," Charleston *Daily Courier*, August 31, 1863. For identification of Robinson, his escape from *Fish Boat*, and how his "great strength took him out of the . . . terrible rush of water," see undated article from unidentified newspaper, but apparently authored by individual with close, firsthand knowledge of Confederate military matters in Charleston, in Smythe Letters, South Carolina Historical Society; for identification of Absolum Williams as casualty in accident, see reference to him as "Drowned in Submarine battery on 29th August 1863," in "Extract from Pay, Receipt and Muster Roll of CSS *Palmetto State*" for July–August 1863 [typescript of orig.], Williams Collection, MPL. For "sad accident" lament, see Augustine Smythe to aunt, August 30, 1863, Smythe Letters, South Carolina Historical Society.

4. Beauregard to Ripley, n.d., page 46, Chapter II, Volume 45, Telegrams Sent, Department of South Carolina, Georgia, and Florida, 1863–64, RG 109, War Department Collection of Confederate Records, NA. For account of boat "lying at an angle of about 35 degrees," see Alexander, "Submarine Boats," New Orleans *Picayune*, June 29, 1902. For September 1863 payment vouchers for raising of submarine boat; and October 1, 1863, payment voucher for removal of five bodies, see both in Smith and Broadfoot File, Confederate Papers Relating to Citizens or Business Firms, NARA Microfilm Publication M346, reel 946, RG 109, War Department Collection of Confederate Records, NA. For Ruffin's account of

corpses, see Ruffin, *Diary*, vol. 3, 177 (October 6, 1863). For Payne's reference to the need for "larger coffins," see Requisition of Payne to Joseph Poulah, September 22, 1863, Area File, Area 8, Confederate States Navy, NARA Microfilm Publication M625, Area File of the Naval Records Collection, 1775–1910, Roll 414, RG 45, Naval Records Collection of the Office of Naval Records and Library, NA.

5. Hunley to Beauregard, September 19, 1863, H. L. Hunley File, NARA Microfilm Publication M346, Confederate Papers Relating to Citizens or Business Firms, RG 109, War Department Collection of Confederate Records, NA; for Alexander on naming of *Hunley*, see Alexander to T. G. Holmes, April 6, 1888, in Smythe Papers, South Carolina Historical Society; for further background on naming, see O'Brien, "Hunley," *Gulf South Historical Review* 21:41–42. For Beauregard's orders to turn the boat over to Hunley and to have it "ready for service in two weeks," see Jordan to Ripley, September 22, 1863, #222, September 1863, Entry 71, Letters Sent, Department of South Carolina, Georgia, and Florida, 1863–64, RG 109, War Department Collection of Confederate Records, NA.

9: The *H. L. Hunley*

1. Hunley's alleged use of the stencil derives from an oral tradition passed down by descendants of Volumnia Hunley Barrow. The metal stencil purportedly used by Hunley, originally to create signage for his law offices and later his submarine boat, is now in a private collection of Hunley materials owned by descendant Wilson J. Gaidry, III. Source for anecdote, author's interviews with Wanda Gaidry, 2007–2008.

2. For Dixon's taking an "active part" in construction of boat, see Dabney Maury, "How the Confederacy Changed Naval Warfare," *SHSP* 22:80; for "successfully experimented" quote, see Alexander, "Confederate Submarine Boat," *Gulf States Historical Magazine* 1:85; for "taken a great interest in" quote, see Beauregard, "Torpedo Service," *SHSP* 5:153. While all three cited memoirists admired Dixon, only Maury and Alexander, because they were based in Mobile, had direct knowledge of Dixon's involvement in that port with the *Fish Boat*. The knowledge of Beauregard, based in Charleston, of those same activities would perforce have been mostly secondhand. Therefore, Maury and Alexander—who recount an involvement by Dixon with the submarine boat that went beyond the mere "great interest" recounted by Beauregard—would seem to be the more credible sources.

3. Speculation concerning Dixon's origins by Smithsonian Institution forensic scientist Doug Owsley, in Press Release, Friends of the *Hunley*,

April 12, 2004. See also *Mobile Daily Herald*, November 15, 1904. Register of wound suffered by Dixon, in Compiled Service Records of Confederate Soldiers Who Served in Organizations from the State of Alabama, RG 109, M-311, NA; Alexander, "Heroes of the *Hunley*," *Munsey's Magazine* 29:747–48. For gold coin story, see James Williams to Lizzie Williams, April 8, 1862, in Williams, *Terrible Field*, 53. For Dixon's promotion to lieutenant, see May 8, 1862, in Register for Dixon, George Dixon File, Compiled Service Records of Confederate Soldiers Who Served in Organizations from the State of Alabama, NARA Microfilm Publication M311, reel 285, RG 109, War Department Collection of Confederate Records, NA. For wardrobe of Dixon, see court order granted to petitioner Henry Willey, with inventory of Dixon's estate, February 22, 1866, Division of Records, Mobile Probate Court.

4. Alexander, "Heroes of the *Hunley*," *Munsey's Magazine* 29:747–48. Background on Thomas Park, e-mail from historian Jack O'Brien to author, July 19, 2007.

10: 'Tis More Dangerous to Those Who Use It Than to the Enemy

1. For evidence that orders to salvage the *Hunley* had been issued by October 18, 1863, see Smith and Broadfoot to W. Nance, October 18, 1863, in Smith and Broadfoot File, Confederate Papers Relating to Citizens or Business Firms, NARA Microfilm Publication M346, reel 946, RG 109, War Department Collection of Confederate Records, NA. Estimate of depth at which the sunken *Hunley* was found is based on chart, *Charleston Harbor and Its Approaches, Showing the positions of the Rebel-Batteries*, U.S. Coast Survey, A. D. Bache, 1863. Grant, *Memoirs*, 296. For story that raised Beauregard's ire, see Augusta *Constitutuional-ist*, October 18, 1863. For Beauregard's reacation, see Jordan to editor of Augusta *Constitutionalist*, October 19, 1863, page 161, Chapter II, Volume 32, Letters Sent, Department of South Carolina, Georgia, and Florida, September–December 1863, RG 109, War Department Collection of Confederate Records, NA. For Beauregard's travel decree regulating movement by Charlestonians, issued by his chief of staff, Jordan, see *Charleston Mercury*, October 17, 1863.

2. For the fee for raising the *Hunley*, see letter from referees, November 9, 1863; for the fee for removal of bodies from and cleaning of the craft, see payment voucher, November 9, 1863; for second-guessing of recovery figure, see "Report of Board of Survey," November 9, 1863—all three documents in Smith and Broadfoot File, Confederate Papers Relating to Citizens or Business Firms, NARA Microfilm Publication M346, reel 946, RG 109, War Department Collection of Confederate Records, NA.

Beauregard, "Torpedo Service," *SHSP* 5:153; Alexander, "Thrilling Chapter," *SHSP* 30:167–70 and ibid., "Submarine Boats," New Orleans *Picayune*, July 29, 1902. For account of Horaace Hunley's funeral, see *Charleston Mercury*, November 9, 1863. As of 2008, concretions still obscured the sections where one would expect to locate the keel-block bolts referred to by Alexander. Even if such bolts exist, Maria Jacobsen believes that, due to the task's arduous nature, the dropping of the keel-blocks would have required some additional (now undiscovered) mechanism. Interview with Jacobsen, 2008.

3. For personal effects found on Hunley, and his estate, see Hunley will, May 4, 1863, and inventory of estate's assets, June 3, 1864, in St. Tammany Parish courthouse, Covington, Louisiana; Robert Barrow to Hunley, April 19, 1863, in Barrow Family Papers, Tulane University. For Hunley's funeral, see *Charleston Mercury* and *Daily Courier*, both in November 9, 1863, editions; Gardner Smith to Volumnia Barrow, November 27, 1863, in Barrow Family Papers, Tulane University. Quoted inscription derives from the actual headstone on Hunley's grave. Rendition of inscription in Smith's letter includes slight variation.

4. For complete list of the eight men who died aboard *Hunley* on October 15, 1863, see Appendix; and "Melancholy Occurrence," in Charleston *Daily Courier*, October 16, 1863. For Simms's action, see *Lots Owners Book for Magnolia Cemetery*, entry for November 7, 1863: 2.

5. Dixon to Beauregard, November 12, 1863, in Register of Letters Received, October 1862–November 1864, Chapter II, Volume 34, page 77, Department of South Carolina, Georgia, and Florida, RG 109, War Department Collection of Confederate Records, NA.

6. For Jefferson Davis's visit to Charleston and other described events concerning Beauregard, see Williams, *Beauregard*, 198–204; for Beauregard dye anecdote, see Freemantle, *Three Months*, 193. For quoted correspondence, see Beauregard to Dixon, November 5, 1863, page 84, Chapter II, Volume 45, Letters and Telegrams Sent, Department of South Carolina, Georgia, and Florida, 1863–64, RG 109, War Department Collection of Confederate Records, NA; and Dixon to Jordan, November 14, 1863, D-125, Entry 72, Letters Received, Department of South Carolina, Georgia, and Florida, 1862–64, RG 109, War Department Collection of Confederate Records, NA. For requisition of Dixon, November 15, 1863, and various documents associated with his movements between Mobile and Charleston, see George Dixon File, Compiled Service Records of Confederate Soldiers Who Served in Organizations from the State of Alabama, NARA Microfilm Publication M311, reel 285, RG 109, War Department Collection of Confederate Records, NA.

7. Dahlgren to Welles, October 7, 1863, in *ORN*, Series 1, vol. 15, 13–15;

Schneller, *Quest for Glory*, 268; Tomb, "Submarine and Torpedo Boats," *Confederate Veteran* 22:168–69; Tomb, "Notes from papers of First Assistant Engineer Tomb," in *ORN*, Series 1, vol. 15, 334–35. For "three or four" quote from Tomb, see ibid., 334–35.

8. Beauregard, "Torpedo Service," *SHSP* 5:151–54; Konstam, *Confederate Submarines*, 33–36, 45.

9. Hill, "Texan Gave World," *San Antonio Express*, July 30, 1916; Kolnitz, "Confederate Submarine," *Proceedings of the U.S. Naval Institute* 63:1457. The ninety pounds of powder figure comes from Alexander and by his account applies to both the floating torpedo and the later spar-mounted torpedo: "Confederate Submarine Boats," New Orleans *Picayune*, June 29, 1902. It should, however, be noted that accounts of the amounts of gunpowder carried by the *Hunley* torpedo as well as descriptions of the length of the spar that carried that bomb vary widely. In the end, definitive figures for both remain unknown. The spar section later recovered from the *Hunley* is seventeen feet in length, but its extremity is missing. It also should be noted that chief U.S. Coast Guard historian Robert M. Browning plausibly argues that the *Hunley*'s spar carried a contact torpedo that required no lanyard to detonate its explosive: interview by author with Browning, August 6, 2007; and Browning, *Success*, 433–34 n. 24.

10. Dixon's "Special Requisition," November 15, 1863, includes a reference to "two paint brushes" (see George Dixon File, Compiled Service Records of Confederate Soldiers Who Served in Organizations from the State of Alabama, NARA Microfilm Publication M311, reel 285, RG 109, War Department Collection of Confederate Records, NA). Otherwise surveyed contemporary documents and later memoirs contain no references to the *Hunley*'s interior as having been painted white. The conclusive indication of that act, according to *Hunley* archaeologist Maria Jacobsen, derives from physical evidence recovered during the boat's excavation at the Warren Lasch Center—specifically particles of white paint found throughout the wreck's crew chamber. Author's interviews with Jacobsen, 2006–2007.

11. Background on Chapman and his depictions of the *Hunley* derive from Bassham, *Chapman*; and author's interviews, in 2008, with Suzanne Savery, director of collections at the Valentine Richmond History Center in Richmond, Virginia; and, in 2007, with Fort Sumter National Monument historian Richard W. Hatcher III. Beauregard, "Torpedo Service," *SHSP* 5:153–54; Alexander, "Thrilling Chapter," *SHSP* 30:170; Alexander, "Heroes of the *Hunley*," *Munsey's Magazine* 29:748. Crew background from interviews with *Hunley* archaeologist Maria Jacobsen, August 2007. Description of Mount Pleasant, Shem Creek, Battery Marshall, and Breach Inlet area during Civil War from author's interviews and e-mail exchanges

with Fort Sumter National Monument historian Richard W. Hatcher III, 2007.

12. Contemporary documents give no precise date for the *Hunley's* transfer from Mount Pleasant to Breach Inlet. But one may assume that the move had taken place by—at the latest—January 10, 1864. That assumption rests on a letter of introduction issued to Dixon on that date and directed to General W. S. Walker, whose military district included Breach Inlet. The letter—originating from the "commanding general," Beauregard— noted that Dixon "goes to your District for the purpose of monitoring the several positions of the enemy in front of you [on the Atlantic Ocean] with a view to operations (by water) against the enemy" [Jordan?], to Walker, January 10, 1864, Entry 71, Letters Sent, Department of South Carolina, Georgia, and Florida, 1863–64, RG 109, War Department Collection of Confederate Records, NA. However, other surveyed documents—too numerous to detail—suggest an earlier date, in December 1863, for the transfer. For Beauregard order to Dixon to "proceed tonight," see Beauregard order issued by Jmo [John M. Otey], December 14, 1863, in *OR*, Series 1, vol. 28, pt. II, 553. Background on crew from author's interviews with *Hunley* archaeologist Maria Jacobsen, 2006–2007. Descriptions of Civil War–era Mount Pleasant, Shem Creek, Battery Marshall, and Breach Inlet from interviews with Fort Sumter National Monument historian Richard W. Hatcher III, 2007.

13. Dixon to Willey, January 31, 1864 (typescript of orig.), in Hunley Papers, Historic Mobile Preservation Society. Alexander, "Confederate Submarine Boat," *Gulf States Historical Magazine* 1:87–88.

14. Alexander, "Confederate Submarine Boat," *Gulf States Historical Magazine* 1:89–90. For his work on guns, see Alexander Iberville Historical Society speech, December 15, 1903, 7 in Williams Collection, MPL. For the *Hunley's* speed, see McClintock to Matthew Maury (undated letter), folio numbers 9087–94, vol. 46, Matthew Maury Papers, Library of Congress; and Alexander, "Heroes of the *Hunley*," *Munsey's Magazine* 29:748; Dixon to Cothran, February 5, 1864, letter in *Mobile Daily Item*, November 15, 1904. Background on Ridgaway and Carlsen from Maria Jacobsen interviews, August 2002. For blue light et al., see Cardozo, *Reminiscences of Charleston*, 124–25, and Dantzler to John A. Wilson, February 19, 1864, in *ORN*, Series 1, vol. 15, 335.

15. McLaurin interviewed in article by unidentified author, "South Carolina Confederate Twins," *Confederate Veteran* 33:328.

11: A Tide Ripple on the Water

1. For accounts of sea and weather conditions on February 17, 1864, see Proceedings U.S. Navy Court of Inquiry on *Housatonic*, Records of Gen-

eral Courts-Martial and Courts of Inquiry of the Navy Department, NARA Microfilm Publication M273, reel 169, Records of the Office of the Judge Advocate General (Navy), RG 125, NA. For a description of the *Housatonic* and its weapons, see its statistical entry in *ORN*, Series 2, vol. 1, 104.

2. Belton and Shipp testimony, January 7 and 8, 1864, in *ORN*, Series 1, vol. 15, 227–33. "It is intended to go under the bottoms of vessels," in Dahlgren order of January 7, 1864, in *ORN*, Series 1, vol. 15, 226.

3. Dahlgren order of January 7, 1864, in *ORN*, Series 1, vol. 15, 226–27. For twenty-five pounds of steam order, see testimony of assistant engineer W. W. Holihan, in Proceedings U.S. Navy Court of Inquiry on *Housatonic*, Records of General Courts-Martial and Courts of Inquiry of the Navy Department, NARA Microfilm Publication M273, reel 169, Records of the Office of the Judge Advocate General (Navy), RG 125, n.p., NA.

4. For testimony of Crosby, see RG 45. Proceedings U.S. Navy Court of Inquiry on *Housatonic*, Records of General Courts-Martial and Courts of Inquiry of the Navy Department, NARA Microfilm Publication M273, reel 169, Records of the Office of the Judge Advocate General (Navy), RG 125, n.p., NA. For Higginson testimony, see ibid., n.p. For Pickering testimony, see ibid., n.p. For all other testimony and details of described activities aboard the *Housatonic* on the night of its sinking, see entire report.

5. For Flemming's testimony of "blue light," see Proceedings U.S. Navy Court of Inquiry on *Housatonic*, Records of General Courts-Martial and Courts of Inquiry of the Navy Department, NARA Microfilm Publication M273, reel 169, Records of the Office of the Judge Advocate General (Navy), RG 125, n.p., NA. For account of *Housatonic*'s position and tidal and weather conditions that evening, see Higginson and Pickering testimony, respectively, in ibid., n.p. For deaths aboard the *Housatonic*, see testimony of Assistant Surgeon William T. Plant, in ibid., n.p. See also report on sinking of *Housatonic* by Captain J. F. Green, commander of USS *Canandaigua*, to Dahlgren, February 18, 1864, in *ORN*, Series 1, vol. 15, 327–28; and Abstract of log of USS *Canandaigua*, February 17–22, 1864, in *ORN*, Series 1, vol. 15, 332.

12: We Can't Get at the Truth

1. Dantzler to Wilson, February 19, 1864, in *ORN*, Series 1, vol. 15, 335; Ripley to Jordan, February 19, 1864, in George Dixon File, Compiled Service Records of Confederate Soldiers Who Served in Organizations from the State of Alabama, NARA Microfilm Publication M311, reel 285,

RG 109, War Department Collection of Confederate Records, NA; Beauregard to unknown recipient, February 20, 1864, in *ORN*, Series 1, vol. 15, 336; Dahlgren to Welles, February 19, 1864, in *ORN*, Series 1, vol. 15, 329–30; Abstract of log of USS *Canandaigua*, February 17–22, 1864, in *ORN*, Series 1, vol. 15, 332; J. F. Green to Commodore S. C. Roway, in *ORN*, Series 1, vol. 15, 331; Beauregard to Gen. S. Cooper, February 21, 1864, in *ORN*, Series 1, vol. 15, 336.

2. Beauregard to Gen. S. Cooper, two telegrams, February 21 and 27, 1864, in *ORN*, Series 1, vol. 15, 336. *Charleston Mercury*, February 29, 1864. For quoted account by local observer of *Housatonic*, see H. W. Feilden to Augustine Smythe, June 25, 1914, in Feilden Papers, South Carolina Historical Society.

3. Susan Middleton to sister, March 4, 1864, in Middleton Family Papers, South Carolina Historical Society. Maury to Gray, April 28, 1864; Gray to Maury, April 29, 1864—both in *ORN*, Series 1, vol. 16, 427. Gray identified in Wise, *Gate of Hell*, 134. Sherman, *Memoirs*, 585. Burton, *Charleston*, 318; Schneller, *Quest for Glory*, 308–309; Williams, *Beauregard*, 140, 250–51.

4. Arthur, *Custom House*, 25–26; Kellogg to Hugh McColloch, July 3, 1865, quoted in ibid., 26.

13: Skeletons at the Wheel

1. Fitzgerald, "The Swimmers," in *Short Stories*, 512.

2. For Volumnia Barrow's final years, see Becnel, *Barrow Family*, 76–78. Horace Hunley's lock of hair and gold studs are contained in Box 21, Barrow Family Papers, Tulane University.

3. For background on Robert Barrow's final years, see Becnel, *Barrow Family*, 77–81; Duncan, *Captain and Submarine*, 51–52; Scarborough, *Masters*, 15; and Floyd, *Barrow Family*, 26, 101.

4. Two Hatch obituaries, both on page 6, New Orleans *Picayune*, July 20, 1884; and Hatch profile in Jewell, *Crescent City*, n.p.

5. Leovy to Beauregard, March 5, 1864, in George Dixon file, Compiled Service Records of Confederate Soldiers Who Served in Organizations from the State of Alabama, NARA Microfilm Publication M311, reel 285, RG 109, War Department Collection of Confederate Records, NA. H. W. Feilden to H. J. Leary [sic; Leovy], March 10, 1864, in *ORN*, Series 1, vol. 15, 337. For Leovy background, see entry in Hewitt and Bergeron, *Louisianans in the Civil War*, 81–83, and obituary in New Orleans *Picayune*, October 4, 1902.

6. For Watson's proposal for new submarine boat, see Watson to Jefferson Davis, October 10, 1864, File 434-W-1864, NARA Microfilm Publication

M437, Letters Received by the Confederate Secretary of War, RG 109, War Department Collection of Confederate Records, NA.

7. For background on McClintock's early years, see typed caption by *Hunley* researcher Eustace Williams beneath photocopied portrait of McClintock, in Williams Collection, MPL. Williams derived his information through correspondence with Henry C. Loughmiller of New York City, a grandson of McClintock. For other background on McClintock, see Alexander talk, December 15, 1903, to Iberville Historical Society, also in Williams Collection, MPL. For more on McClintock's dealings with British Navy, see Hore, "Secret Journey," *Naval History* 16:32–36. "Hates his countrymen" quote from Report from Rear Admiral E. A. Inglefield, RN, October 19, 1872, in Records of October 1872 Interview by Royal Navy Officers with James McClintock, in Admiralty Records, National Archives of the United Kingdom.

8. For Scott death notice, see New Orleans *Picayune*, March 13, 1874.

9. For Alexander's postwar career as engineer, see entries for him in *Mobile City Directory*, 1903, 1905, 1906 editions; see also Alexander obituary in *Mobile Register*, May 14, 1914.

10. Maury obituary, *The New York Times*, January 12, 1900.

11. Symonds, *Confederate Admiral*, 220–31.

12. For Payne in Battle of Mobile Bay, see Friend, *West Wind*, 210–11; and "Report of Lieutenant Payne," undated account of activities during Battle of Mobile Harbor, in *ORN*, Series 1, vol. 21, 593–94. For Payne's postwar life in Mobile, see John A. Payne entries in *Mobile City Directory*, 1867, 1869, 1870, 1871, 1872, 1873, 1874, 1875 editions; and "Physician's Certificate of Death" for Payne, dated February 25, 1876, in Mobile Death Certificates, MPL.

13. Speculation concerning Dixon's origins by Smithsonian Institution forensic scientist Doug Owsley, in Press Release, Friends of the *Hunley*, April 12, 2004; see also *Mobile Daily Item*, April 26, 1910. For Dixon probate records, see court order granted to petitioner Henry Willey, with inventory of Dixon's estate, February 22, 1866, Division of Records, Mobile Probate Court.

14. Williams, *Beauregard*, 257–329.

15. Schneller, *Quest for Glory*, 321–72.

16. For conclusions of official investigation, see Proceedings U.S. Navy Court of Inquiry on *Housatonic*, Records of General Courts-Martial and Courts of Inquiry of the Navy Department, NARA Microfilm Publication M273, reel 169, Records of the Office of the Judge Advocate General (Navy), RG 125, n.p., NA.

17. Callahan, *List*, 435; *Register of . . .* [U.S. Navy] *Officers* [to 1865], n.p.; *Dictionary of American Naval Fighting Ships*, electronic access.

18. For an account of the recovery of the *Pioneer* by Union occupation forces, a description of the craft, and accompanying drawing, see William H. Shock, fleet engineer West Gulf Blockading Squadron to Gustavus V. Fox, Assistant Sec. of the Navy, January 21, 1864, in January 1864, Volume 2, NARA Microfilm Publication M148, Letters Received by the Secretary of the Navy from Commissioned Officers Below the Rank of Commander ("Officers Letters"), 1802–84, RG 45, Naval Records Collection of the Office of Naval Records and Library, NA. For auction of *Pioneer*, see New Orleans *Picayune*, November 15, 1868—two different stories, respectively, in morning and evening editions that day.

19. .Churchill report, November 27, 1864, in *ORN*, Series 1, vol. 15, 334. For later correspondences, newspaper reports, and an account of *Housatonic* salvage activities, see Conlin, *Housatonic*, 36–40.

20. For "Skeletons at the Wheel" story, see *Charleston Daily Courier*, October 11, 1870. Persistent reports to the contrary, no hard evidence has surfaced—not in biographies of him, nor in his personal papers—that showman P. T. Barnum ever offered a reward for the *Hunley* or the location of its wreck site. Assertion based on author's search for such materials and November 2007 telephone interview with Kathy Maher, director and curator of Barnum Museum, Bridgeport, Connecticut.

21. Pacha, "Torpedo Scare," *Blackwood's Edinburgh Magazine* 137:745–46. Porter, "Torpedo Warfare," *North American Review* 127:231; Brady, *Little Traitor*.

22. Report of six sinkings alluded to and corrected in Stanton, "Submarines," *Confederate Veteran* 22:398. Alexander, "Submarine Boats," New Orleans *Picayune*, June 29, 1902. For Alexander's failing memory, see Alexander to T. G. Holmes, September 7, 1888, in Smythe Papers, South Carolina Historical Society; for 1908 U.S. Army Corps of Engineers dive to *Housatonic* wreck site and for subsequent newspaper story that failed to mention the *Hunley*, see Burton, *Charleston*, 238–39. For Alexander obituary, see *Mobile Register*, May 14, 1914. For Alexander's recollections, see list of his publications in Bibliography. Correct *Hunley* dimensions contained in e-mail from *Hunley* project archaeologist Maria Jacobsen to author, March 15, 2007.

14: Discovery, Recovery, Excavation

1. Background on John Augustus Walker mural and *Hunley* model drawn, respectively, from interviews with curators at Mobile and Charleston museums, where both works, as of this writing, remain on exhibit. For inclusion of Chapman's *Hunley* painting in Metropolitan Museum's 1939 World's Fair exhibit, see "Art Traps," *Time*, May 8, 1939. For Jackie

Cooper and *Great Adventure* episode recounting *Hunley's* story, see Internet Movie Database.

2. For "That's it" quote, see Hicks and Kropf, *Raising the Hunley*, 146. For caveat on wreck's position as evidence of final moments as working vessel, e-mail from *Hunley* project archaeologist James Hunter to author, June 18, 2007. Other background, interviews with Maria Jacobsen and Rich Wills, 2007.

3. Hicks and Kropf, *Raising the Hunley*, 146–61, 189–206. For finding of *Hunley*, disputes over rights to wreck, and plans for its recovery, see Murphy, *Hunley Site Assessment*, 6–13.

4. For Thurmond role in resolution, see Hicks and Kropf, *Raising the Hunley*, 160, 162–63. For sub tender USS *Hunley*, see *Dictionary of American Naval Fighting Ships*, online access. Other background on resolution of conflicts concerning *Hunley* wreck and plans for its recovery, interviews with Maria Jacobsen and Rich Wills, 2007. See also Oceaneering International, Inc., website.

5. Hicks and Kropf, *Raising the Hunley*, 164, 193–95, 196, 206–11, 213, 216. As of 2007, there are no plans to recover the badly decomposed and otherwise fractured and destroyed remains of the wooden ship *Housatonic*. Interviews with Maria Jacobsen and Rich Wills, 2007.

6. Interviews with Maria Jacobsen, 2006–2008.

7. Descriptions of research methods and crew background from interviews with Maria Jacobsen, 2006–2008.

8. Following more than a decade of searching, a team led by Charleston Civil War reenactor Randy Burbage in 1999 located the Seaman's Burial Ground and the remains of the first five men to die aboard the *Hunley*. The remains were found buried on the campus of the Citadel, Charleston's famed military college; for that and other background on crew funerals, see Hicks and Kropf, *Raising the Hunley*, 169–76, 234.

9. For sampling of past estimates of dimensions of *Hunley* and its two predecessor boats, see Wills, "*Hunley* in Historical Context," electronic access, n.p. For list of Alexander publications, see Bibliography. Actual *Hunley* specfications and descriptions of excavated items from interviews with Maria Jacobsen, 2006–2007. The 1999 film referred to is *The Hunley*, USA Television Network.

10. For gold coin story, see James Williams to Lizzie Williams, April 8, 1862, in Williams, *Terrible Field*, 53. For other references to Dixon by James Williams, see Williams, *Terrible Field*, 47, 54, 55, 64–65, 69, 72, 75, 79, 89, 90–91, 96, 100, 105–06, 110, 112, 114, 118, 123. For the Queenie Bennett story, see *Mobile Daily Herald*, April 26, 1910; Ragan, *The Hunley: Submarines, Sacrifice, & Success* (1995 ed.), 79–80, 164. For a partial refutation of the story, see Leader, "Dixon's Tintype," *Blue Light* 3 (win-

ter 2002): 6. For further refutation of the Bennett story, see unpublished report, December 2002, of Nicholas Herrmann, Department of Anthropology, University of Tennessee and interviews with *Hunley* archaeologist Maria Jacobsen, 2006–2007. "Isn't it pretty to think so?" from Hemingway, *Sun Also Rises*, 247.

15: The Signals Agreed Upon

1. For Flemming's testimony, see Proceedings U.S. Navy Court of Inquiry, Case 4345, RG 45, n.p., NA. For quoted baseball rule, Major League Baseball website, "Official Rules," Definition of Terms—"A Catch," rule 2.0. Cardozo, *Reminiscences of Charleston*, 124–25; Dantzler to John A. Wilson, February 19, 1864, in *ORN*, Series 1, vol. 15, 335; interviews with *Hunley* archaeologist Maria Jacobsen, 2007; and Jacobsen, "Did the *Hunley* Crew Signal?" *Blue Light* 9:6, 7. For Breach Inlet sandbar, see *General Map of Charleston Harbor*, 1865. Other background on sandbar and channel across it from interviews with Jacobsen and Richard W. Hatcher III, 2007.

2. For anoxia as a possible cause of death, see Hicks and Kropf, *Raising the Hunley*, 218, 247. Other possible causes were suggested in interviews with *Hunley* archaeologist Maria Jacobsen, 2006–2007.

3. For reconstruction of tides off Charleston on February 17, 1863, see K. G. Crosby, Tides and Currents Division, U.S. Coast and Geodetic Survey, to Louis J. Genella (a New Orleans–based *Hunley* researcher), March 13, 1958, in Barrow Family Papers, Tulane University.

4. Gray to Maury, April 29, 1864, in *ORN*, Series 1, vol. 16, 427. For article on Ockham's razor, see "William of Ockham," in *Encyclopedia of Philosophy* 8:307. For account of disturbances around *Housatonic* wreck site, see Conlin, *Housatonic*, 38–44.

5. "FOURTH CREW" from Friends of the *Hunley* website; quoted mission of Clemson's North Charleston campus from Clemson University website. For *Reader's Digest* allegations of *Hunley*-related wasteful government spending, see Sacha Zimmerman, "Your Money for This," *Reader's Digest*, February 2007, online edition. Crangle and Jackson quotes from "How Senator Steers Sub Under Radar," *The* [Columbia] *State*, May 14, 2006; for all three articles and various sidebars of *State* series by journalist John Monk on *Hunley*-related public expenditures, see *The State*, May 14–16, 2006; for McConnell's response to series, see McConnell, "Setting the Hunley Record Straight," *The State*, July 2, 2006. Percentage figure for African Americans in South Carolina from U.S. Census Bureau.

6. Speculation concerning Dixon's pocket watch from "Time Stands Still on the Hunley," *Blue Light* 9:8; author's interview with Daniel Nied, author

of National Association of Watch and Clock Collectors study of Dixon's watch, December 22, 2007; and "Hunley Commander's Watch No Smoking Gun," Associated Press, December 14, 2007. For speculation, respectively, concerning possibility of electrical battery as torpedo detonator and forward hatch lock, see Friends of the *Hunley* press releases, June 24, 2005, and July 14, 2005. All aforementioned matters also drawn from interviews with archaeologist Maria Jacobsen, 2006–2007. For McConnell quote on solving "the ultimate mystery," see *The Washington Post*, November 21, 2006. For Gide's injunction, see *Les Caves du Vatican*, 816.

Epilogue: Legacy

1. For quoted writings, see Maury to McClintock, April 3, 1871, in Records of October 1872 Interview by Royal Navy Officers with James McClintock, in Admiralty Records, National Archives of the United Kingdom; and *Harper's Weekly*, December 24, 1910, 22. For other described events and developments, see Roland, *Underwater Warfare*, 162; Perry, *Infernal Machines*, 4, 196; and Parrish, *Submarine*, 57. For Leonardo quote, see Leonardo, *Notebooks*, 96–97.

Appendix: The *Hunley*'s Three Crews and Deaths Aboard the USS *Housatonic*

1. The term *first crew*, though frequently used—and employed here—is actually a misnomer. When the *Fish Boat* was ordered transferred to Charleston in August 1863, it was originally crewed at its new port by a group brought over from Mobile, under the command of James McClintock. But shortly after it reached Charleston, the boat was confiscated by the Confederate Army, which subsequently placed a crew of Confederate Navy men aboard the craft—the so-called first crew, commanded by Lieutenant John A. Payne.

Bibliography

Manuscripts and Papers
Duke University: De Bow Papers.
Historic Mobile Preservation Society: Hunley Papers.
Historic New Orleans Collection: Henry Leovy Papers.
Huntington Library: Joseph E. Johnston Papers (particularly Dabney Maury correspondence therein).
Library of Congress: Matthew Fontaine Maury Papers.
Louisiana State Museum: Hunley Papers, Record Group 14.
Magnolia Cemetery, Charleston: *Lots Owners Book*.
Mobile County, Alabama, Probate Court: Records Division.
Mobile Public Library: Eustace Williams Collection and City of Mobile Death Certificates.
Museum of Mobile: Thomas M. McMillan Collection.
National Archives of the United Kingdom: Records of the Admiralty, Naval Forces, Royal Marines, Coastguard, and related bodies. Records of October 1872 Interview by Royal Navy Officers with James McClintock, and various other drawings and papers.
National Archives (U.S.): Various files and documents from Record Groups 45 and 109.
Naval Historical Center, Washington, D. C. Navy Department Library: Historical Manuscripts.
Peyton, Rev. James. Private Collection: handwritten entries for Hunley family, in "Family Record" section, Holy Bible.
St. Tammany Parish, Louisiana. Clerk of Court Office: Will of Horace Lawson Hunley, filed December 21, 1863.
South Carolina Historical Society: Henry Wemyss Feilden Papers, Middleton Family Papers, and Smythe Papers.

Tulane University: Barrow Family Papers and Louis J. Genella Papers.
University of North Carolina at Chapel Hill, Southern Historical Collections:
    Arnold and Screven Family Papers, Franklin Buchanan Letterbook,
    and George Washington Gift Letters.
University of South Carolina, South Caroliniana Library: Theodore Honour
    Papers.
Virginia Historical Society: Franklin Buchanan Letters.

Government Publications

*Charleston Harbor and Its Approaches, Showing the positions of the Rebel-
    Batteries.* U.S. Coast Survey, A. D. Bache, Superintendent, 1863.
Conlin, David, ed. *USS Housatonic Site Assessment.* Washington, D.C.: Na-
    tional Park Service et al., 2005.
Dictionary of American Naval Fighting Ships. 8 vols. Washington, D.C.: U.S.
    Superintendent of Documents, Naval History Division, 1959–81, and
    electronic access.
*General Map of Charleston Harbor, South Carolina Showing Rebel Defenses
    and Obstructions.* Prepared by direction of Rear Admiral J. A. Dahl-
    gren, U.S.N. by C. O. Boutelle, Asst. U.S. Coast Survey, 1865.
Murphy, Larry E., ed. *H. L. Hunley Site Assessment.* Washington, D.C.: Na-
    tional Park Service et al., 1998.
*Official Records of the Union and Confederate Navies in the War of the Re-
    bellion.* 31 vols. Washington, D.C.: Government Printing Office,
    1894–1922.
*Register of the Commissioned, Warrant, and Volunteer Officers of the Navy of
    the United States, including Officers of the Marine Corps and Others,
    to January 1, 1865.* Washington, D.C.: Government Printing Office,
    1865.
Report of the Commissioner of Patents. Richmond, Va.: Confederate States
    Patents Office, January 1863.
U.S. Census Records. 1850, 1860.
*War of the Rebellion: A Compilation of the Official Records of the Union and
    Confederate Armies.* 128 vols. Washington, D.C.: Government Print-
    ing Office, 1880–1901.

Published Records and Recollections

Alexander, William. "The Confederate Submarine Boat *Hunley.*" *Gulf States
    Historical Magazine* 1 (September 1902): 81–91.
———. "The Heroes of the *Hunley.*" *Munsey's Magazine* 29 (1903): 746–49.
———. "Thrilling Chapter in the History of the Confederate States Navy.

Work of Submarine Boats." *Southern Historical Society Papers* 30 (1902): 164–74.

———. "True Stories of the Confederate Submarine Boats." New Orleans *Picayune*, June 29, 1902.

Baird, G. W. "Submarine Torpedo Boats." *Journal of the American Society of Naval Engineers* 14 (1902): 845–55.

Barnes, J. S. *Submarine Warfare*. New York: Van Nostrand, 1869.

Barrow, Robert Ruffin. *A miscellaneous essay on the political parties of the country, rise of abolitionism and the impolicy of secession*. New Orleans: L. Marchand, 1861.

———. *Valuable and Worth Preserving! Pertinent Questions*. Broadside. New Orleans: privately published, 1861.

Beauregard, P.G.T. "Torpedo Service in the Harbor and Water Defense of Charleston." *Southern Historical Society Papers* 5 (April 1878): 145–61.

Bishop, Farnham. *The Story of the Submarine*. New York: Century, 1916.

Brady, Cyrus Townsend. *A Little Traitor to the South*. New York: Macmillan Company, 1904.

Callahan, Edward W., ed. *List of Officers of the Navy of the United States and of the Marine Corps from 1775 to 1900*. Compiled from the Official Records of the Navy Department. New York: L.R. Hamersley, 1901.

Cardozo, Jacob N. *Reminiscences of Charleston*. Charleston: J. Walker, 1866.

Champomier, P. A. *Statement of the Sugar Crop Made in Louisiana, 1859–60*. New Orleans: Cook, Young, 1860.

———. *Statement of the Sugar Crop Made in Louisiana, 1861 62* [*sic*]. New Orleans: Cook, Young, 1862.

Chesnut, Mary. *Mary Chesnut's Civil War*. Edited by C. Vann Woodward. New Haven, Conn.: Yale University Press, 1993.

Cohen, Leonard. *Stranger Music: Selected Poems and Songs*. New York: Pantheon, 1993.

Crowley, R. O. "The Confederate Torpedo Service." *Century* 56 (June 1898), 290–301.

Davis, Jefferson. *Rise and Fall of the Confederate Nation*. 2 vols. New York: Thomas Yoseloff, 1958 (originally published in 1881).

Fitzgerald, F. Scott. "The Swimmers" (originally published in *Saturday Evening Post*, October 19, 1929). In *The Short Stories of F. Scott Fitzgerald*. New York: Scribner, 1989.

Fort, W. B. "First Submarine in the Confederate Navy." *Confederate Veteran* 26 (1918): 459–60.

Freemantle, Arthur James Lyon. *Three Months in the Southern States, April–June, 1863*. New York: John Bradburn, 1864.

Gardner, C. *Gardner's New Orleans directory for 1861 . . . and a planter's directory*. New Orleans: C. Gardner, 1861.

Gide, André. *Les Caves du Vatican*. In *Romans, récits et sorties, oeuvres lyriques*. Paris: Gallimard, Bibliothèque de la Pléiade, 1958.

Grant, Ulysses S. *Personal Memoirs*. New York: Library of America, 1990 (*Memoirs* originally published in two vols., 1885–86).

Haskin, Brevet Major William L. *History of the First Regiment of Artillery*. Portland, Maine: Thurston, 1879.

Hemingway, Ernest. *The Sun Also Rises*. New York: Scribner, 1970 (originally published in 1926).

Hill, Horace C. "Texan Gave World First Successful Submarine Torpedo." *San Antonio Express*, July 30, 1916.

Holmes, Emma. *The Diary of Miss Emma Holmes, 1861–1866*. Edited by John F. Marszalek. Baton Rouge: Louisiana State University Press, 1979.

Jewell, Edwin Lewis, ed. *Jewell's Crescent City*. New Orleans: [E. L. Jewell], 1873. University of Michigan online edition.

Johnson, John. *The defense of Charleston harbor, including Fort Sumter and the adjacent islands, 1863–1865*. Charleston: Walker, Evans & Cogswell, 1890.

King, Edward. *The Great South*. Hartford, Conn.: American Publishing, 1875. University of North Carolina online edition.

Lake, Simon. *The Submarine in War and Peace*. Philadelphia: Lippincott, 1918.

Leonardo da Vinci. *The Notebooks of Leonardo da Vinci*. New York: Oxford University Press, 1998.

Maury, Dabney. "How the Confederacy Changed Naval Warfare." *Southern Historical Society Papers* 22 (1894): 75–81.

———. *Recollections of a Virginian*. New York: Charles Scribner's Sons, 1894.

McLaurin, D. W. "South Carolina Confederate Twins." Interview. *Confederate Veteran* 33 (September 1925): 328.

Mobile City Directory. Mobile: Farrow and Dennett, 1867; Mobile: Henry Farrow, 1869–75; Atlanta: Mutual Publishing, 1903; and Mobile: R.L. Polk, 1906–14.

Pacha, Hobart [Augustus Charles Hobart]. "Torpedo Scare." *Blackwood's Edinburgh Magazine* 137 (June 1885): 737–47.

Pierce, G. W. "Historical and Statistical Collections of Louisiana—Terrebonne." *De Bow's Review* 11 (December 1851): 601–11.

Pinkerton, Allan. *The Spy of the Rebellion*. Kansas City: Kansas City Publishing Co., 1883.

Porter, D. D. [David Dixon]. "Torpedo Warfare." *The North American Review* 127 (September–October 1878): 213–37.

Roman, Alfred. *The Military Operations of General Beauregard in the War Between the States, 1861 to 1865.* New York: Harper and Brothers, 1883.

Ruffin, Edmund. *The Diary of Edmund Ruffin.* Edited with introduction and notes by William K. Scarborough. 3 vols. Baton Rouge: Louisiana State University Press, 1972–89.

Russell, William Howard. *My Diary North and South* [orig. longer edition pub. 1863]. Ed. and preface by Eugene H. Berwanger. Philadelphia: Temple University Press, 1988.

Sherman, William Tecumseh. *Memoirs.* New York: Penguin, 2000 (originally published in 1875).

Stanton, C. L. "Submarines and Torpedo Boats." *Confederate Veteran* 22 (1914): 398–99.

Taylor, Thomas E. *Running the Blockade.* Annapolis: Naval Institute Press, 1995 (originally published in 1896).

Tomb, James H. "Submarine and Torpedo Boats." *Confederate Veteran* 22 (1914): 168–69.

Verne, Jules. "The Blockade Runners" (originally published in French in 1865). In *The Green Ray: including also The Blockade Runners.* Westport, Conn.: Associated Booksellers, 1965.

———. *Twenty Thousand Leagues Under the Sea.* Translated and annotated by Walter James Miller and Frederick Paul Walter. Annapolis: Naval Institute Press, 1993 (originally published in French in 1870).

Welles, Gideon. *Diary of Gideon Welles.* 3 vols. New York: Norton, 1960.

Williams, James M. *From That Terrible Field: The Civil War Letters of James M. Williams, 21st Alabama Infantry Volunteers.* Edited and annotated by John Kent Folmar. Tuscaloosa: University of Alabama Press, 1981.

Newspapers and Magazines

Augusta Daily Constitutionalist
Blackwood's Edinburgh Magazine
Blue Light
Charleston Mercury
Charleston *Post and Courier*
The [Columbia] *State*
De Bow's Review
Harper's Weekly
Mobile Advertiser and Register
Mobile Daily Herald
Mobile Daily Item
Mobile Register

Munsey's Magazine
New Orleans *Daily Crescent*
New Orleans *Daily Delta*
New Orleans *Picayune*
New Orleans *Times-Picayune*
The New York Herald
The New York Times
The North American Review
Philadelphia *Evening Bulletin*
Reader's Digest
San Antonio Express
San Francisco *Daily Evening Bulletin*
Scientific American
Time
The Washington Post

Secondary Sources

Adams, William H. *The Whig Party of Louisiana*. Lafayette: University of
    Southwestern Louisiana, 1973.
Albion, Robert Greenhalgh. *The Rise of New York Port*. New York: Scribner,
    1967 (originally published in 1939).
Arthur, Stanley C. "Early New Orleans Submarine Sired David." New Or-
    leans *Times-Picayune*, June 14, 1942.
———. *A History of the U.S. Custom House, New Orleans*. 2d ed. Baton
    Rouge: Survey of Federal Archives in Louisiana (Work Projects Ad-
    ministration of Louisiana), 1940.
Bak, Richard. *The CSS Hunley: The Greatest Undersea Adventure of the Civil
    War*. Dallas, Tex.: Taylor, 1999.
Bassham, Ben L. *Conrad Wise Chapman: Artist & Soldier of the Confeder-
    acy*. Kent, Ohio: Kent State University Press, 1998.
Becnel, Thomas A. *The Barrow Family and the Barataria and Lafourche
    Canal: The Transportation Revolution in Louisiana, 1829–1925*. Baton
    Rouge: Louisiana State University Press, 1989.
Bennett, Michael J. *Union Jacks: Yankee Sailors in the Civil War*. Chapel Hill:
    University of North Carolina Press, 2004.
Bolander, Louis H. "The *Alligator*, First Federal Submarine of the Civil War."
    Proceedings of the U.S. Naval Institute 64 (June 1938): 845–54.
Browning, Robert M. *Success Is All That Was Expected: The South Atlantic
    Blockading Squadron During the Civil War*. Washington, D.C.:
    Brassey's, 2002.
Bruce, Robert V. *Lincoln and the Tools of War*. Indianapolis, Ind.: Bobbs-
    Merrill, 1956.

Burgoyne, Alan. *Submarine Navigation, Past and Present*. New York: E. P. Dutton & Co., 1903.

Burton, E. Milby. *The Siege of Charleston, 1861–1865*. Columbia: University of South Carolina Press, 1970.

Butcher, William. *Jules Verne: The Definitive Biography*. New York: Thunder's Mouth, 2006.

Campbell, R. Thomas. *The CSS H. L. Hunley*. Shippensburg, Pa.: Bard Street Press, 2000.

Chaffin, Tom. *Fatal Glory: Narciso López and the First Clandestine U.S. War Against Cuba*. Baton Rouge: Louisiana State University Press, 2003 (originally published by University Press of Virginia, 1996).

———. *Pathfinder: John Charles Frémont and the Course of American Empire*. New York: Hill and Wang, 2002.

———. *Sea of Gray: The Around-the-World Odyssey of the Confederate Raider Shenandoah*. New York: Hill and Wang, 2006.

Coski, John M. *Capital Navy: The Men, Ships, and Operations of the James River Squadron*. Campbell, Calif.: Savas, 1996.

Davies, Roy. *Nautilus: The Story of Man Under the Sea*. Annapolis: Naval Institute Press, 1995.

Davis, William C. *Jefferson Davis: The Man and His Hour*. New York: HarperCollins, 1991.

Donald, David Herbert. *Lincoln*. New York: Simon & Schuster, 1995.

Duffy, James P. *Lincoln's Admiral: The Civil War Campaigns of David Farragut*. New York: Wiley, 1997.

Dufour, Charles. *The Night the War Was Lost*. New York: Doubleday, 1960.

Duncan, Ruth H. *The Captain and Submarine CSS H. L. Hunley*. Memphis: Toof, 1965. (Includes letters of Horace Hunley and family.)

Durkin, Joseph T. *Stephen R. Mallory: Confederate Navy Chief*. Chapel Hill: University of North Carolina Press, 1954.

Floyd, William Barrow. *The Barrow Family of Old Louisiana*. Lexington, Ky.: published by author, 1963.

Fowler, William M., Jr. *Under Two Flags: The American Navy in the Civil War*. New York: Norton, 1990.

Friend, Jack. *West Wind, Flood Tide: The Battle of Mobile Bay*. Annapolis: Naval Institute Press, 2004.

Gould, Elizabeth Barrett. *From Fort to Port: An architectural history of Mobile, Alabama, 1711–1918*. Tuscaloosa: University of Alabama Press, 1988.

Hagerman, Edward. *The American Civil War and the Origins of Modern Warfare*. Bloomington: Indiana University Press, 1988.

Hearn, Chester G. *Admiral David Glasgow Farragut: The Civil War Years*. Annapolis: Naval Institute Press, 1998.

————. *The Capture of New Orleans, 1862*. Baton Rouge: Louisiana State University Press, 1995.

————. *Mobile Bay and the Mobile Campaign: The Last Great Battles of the Civil War*. Jefferson, N.C.: McFarland, 1993.

Hicks, Brian, and Schuyler Kropf. *Raising the Hunley: The Remarkable History and Recovery of the Lost Confederate Submarine*. New York: Ballantine, 2002.

Hore, Peter. "A Secret Journey to Halifax." *Naval History* 16 (June 2002): 32–36.

Huntington, Tom. "The Hunley." *American Heritage of Invention and Technology Magazine* 20 (spring 2005): 38–46.

Hutcheon, Wallace, Jr. *Robert Fulton: Pioneer of Undersea Warfare*. Annapolis: Naval Institute Press, 1981.

Jacobsen, Maria. "Did the *Hunley* Signal?" *Blue Light* 19 (April 2006): 6–7.

Jones, Archer. *Civil War Command and Strategy*. New York: Free Press, 1992.

Kemp, Paul. *Underwater Warriors*. Annapolis: Naval Institute Press, 1996.

Kloeppel, James E. *Danger Beneath the Waves: A History of the Confederate Submarine H. L. Hunley*. Orangeburg, S.C.: Sandlapper, 1992.

Kolnitz, Lt. Harry Von. "The Confederate Submarine." *Proceedings of the U.S. Naval Institute* 63 (October 10, 1937): 1453–57.

Konstam, Angus. *Confederate Submarines and Torpedo Vessels: 1861–65*. Osceola, Wis.: Osprey, 2004.

Lambousy, Greg. *Monster of the Deep: The Louisiana State Museum's Civil War–Era Submarine*. Lafayette: Center for Louisiana Studies, 2006.

Lavery, Brian. *Ship*. Washington, D.C.: DK/Smithsonian Institution, 2004.

Leader, Jonathan M. "Lieutenant Dixon's Tintype." *Blue Light* 3 (winter 2002): 6.

Lewis, Charles Lee. *Admiral Franklin Buchanan: Fearless Man of Action*. Baltimore: Norman, Remington, 1929.

Lottman, Herbert R. *Jules Verne: An Exploratory Biography*. New York: St. Martin's, 1996.

Luraghi, Raimondo. *A History of the Confederate Navy*. Translated by Paolo E. Coletta. Annapolis: Naval Institute Press, 1996 (originally published in Italian in 1993).

Marx, Robert F. *The History of Underwater Exploration*. New York: Dover, 1990.

McPherson, James M. *Battle Cry of Freedom: The Civil War Era*. New York: Oxford University Press, 1988.

Menn, Joseph Karl. *The Large Slaveholders of Louisiana—1860*. New Orleans: Pelican, 1964.

Nepveux, Ethel Trenholm Seabrook. *George Alfred Trenholm*. Charleston, S.C.: Comprint, 1973.

Niven, John. *Gideon Welles: Lincoln's Secretary of the Navy.* New York: Oxford University Press, 1973.

O'Brien, Jack, Jr. "Where Was the *Hunley* Built?" *Gulf South Historical Review* 21 (fall 2005): 29–48.

Parrish, Thomas. *The Submarine: A History.* New York: Viking, 2004.

Parsons, William Barclay. *Robert Fulton and the Submarine.* New York: Columbia University Press, 1922.

Pecorelli, Harry, III. "The Equalization of Time." *Blue Light* 9 (August 2003): 8.

Perry, Milton F. *Infernal Machines: The Story of Confederate Submarine and Mine Warfare.* Baton Rouge: Louisiana State University Press, 1965.

Philip, Cynthia Owen. *Robert Fulton: A Biography.* New York: Franklin Watts, 1985.

Prichard, Walter. "The Effects of the Civil War on the Louisiana Sugar Industry." *Journal of Southern History* 5 (August 1939): 315–32.

Ragan, Mark K. *The Hunley.* Orangeburg, S.C.: Sandlapper, 2005.

———. *The Hunley: Submarines, Sacrifice, & Success in the Civil War.* Charleston, S.C.: Narwhal Press, 1995, and rev. ed., 1999.

———. *Submarine Warfare in the Civil War.* Cambridge, Mass.: Da Capo, 1999.

Robinson, William Morrison, Jr. *The Confederate Privateers.* New Haven: Yale University, 1928.

Roland, Alex. *Underwater Warfare in the Age of Sail.* Bloomington: Indiana University Press, 1978.

Scarborough, William Kauffman. *Masters of the Big House: Elite Slaveholders of the Mid-Nineteenth-Century South.* Baton Rouge: Louisiana State University Press, 2003.

Scharf, J. Thomas. *History of the Confederate States Navy.* New York: Rogers and Sherwood, 1887.

Schell, Sidney H. "Submarine Weapons Tested at Mobile During the Civil War." *Alabama Review* 45 (July 1992): 163–83.

Schneller, Robert J., Jr. *Farragut: America's First Admiral.* Washington: Brassey's, 2002.

———. *A Quest for Glory: A Biography of Rear Admiral John A. Dahlgren.* Annapolis: Naval Institute Press, 1996.

Stewart, Matthew. *Monturiol's Dream.* London: Profile Books, 2003.

Still, William N., ed. *The Confederate Navy: The Ships, Men and Organization, 1861–65.* Annapolis: Naval Institute Press, 1997.

Summers, Mark W. *The Plundering Generation: Corruption and the Crisis of the Union, 1849–1861.* New York: Oxford University Press, 1987.

Symonds, Craig L. *Confederate Admiral: The Life and Wars of Franklin Buchanan.* Annapolis: Naval Institute Press, 1999.

Vandiver, Frank. *Rebel Brass: The Confederate Command System.* Baton Rouge: Louisiana State University Press, 1956.

Walther, Eric H. *The Fire-Eaters.* Baton Rouge: Louisiana State University Press, 1992.

Wayland, John W. *Pathfinder of the Seas: The Life of Matthew Fontaine Maury.* Richmond, Va.: Garrett & Massie, 1930.

Wells, Tom Henderson. *The Confederate Navy: A Study in Organization.* University, Ala.: University of Alabama Press, 1971.

Williams, Frances Leigh. *Matthew Fontaine Maury: Scientist of the Sea.* New Brunswick, N.J.: Rutgers University Press, 1963.

Williams, T. Harry. *P. G. T. Beauregard: Napoleon in Gray.* Baton Rouge: Louisiana State University Press, 1954.

Wills, Rich. "The *H. L. Hunley* in Historical Context." Naval Historical Center website, May 2001.

Wise, Stephen R. *Gate of Hell: Campaign for Charleston Harbor, 1863.* Columbia: University of South Carolina, 1994.

———. *Lifeline of the Confederacy: Blockade Running During the Civil War.* Columbia: University of South Carolina Press, 1988.

Reference Works

Benét, William Rose. *The Reader's Encyclopedia.* New York: Harper and Row, 1965.

Biographical and Historical Memoirs of Louisiana. 2 vols. Chicago: Goodspeed, 1892.

Bowditch, Nathaniel. *American Practical Navigator.* Washington, D.C.: Government Printing Office, 1943 (originally published in 1802).

Cochran, Thomas C., and Wayne Andrews, eds. *Concise Dictionary of American History.* New York: Scribner, 1962.

Cross, Wilbur, and George W. Feise, Jr., et al., eds. *Encyclopedia of American Submarines.* New York: Facts on File, 2003.

Edwards, Paul, ed. *Encyclopedia of Philosophy,* eight vols. New York: Macmillan, 1972.

Garraty, John A., and Jerome L. Sternstein. *Encyclopedia of American Biography.* 2d ed. New York: HarperCollins, 1995.

Hewitt, Lawrence L., and Arthur W. Bergeron, Jr., eds. *Louisianans in the Civil War.* Columbia: University of Missouri, 2002.

Hutchinson, Robert. *Jane's Submarines: War Beneath the Waves, from 1776 to the Present Day.* London: HarperCollins, 2001.

Mitchell, B. R. *International Historical Statistics: Africa, Asia & Oceania, 1750–2000.* New York: Palgrave, Macmillan, 2003.

Morris, Richard B., ed. *Encyclopedia of American History.* rev. ed. New York: Harper & Row, 1961.

Peterson, Douglas. *United States Lighthouse Service Tenders, 1840–1939*. Annapolis: Eastwind Publishing, 2000.

Websites
Clemson University
Friends of the *Hunley*
Internet Movie Database
Major League Baseball
Mystic Seaport Museum and Library
Naval Historical Center
Oceaneering International, Inc.
U.S. Census Bureau
U.S. Coast Guard Historian's Office

Acknowledgments

The *H. L. Hunley* first cranked across my consciousness during my childhood in Atlanta, when I saw an episode about the craft on a short-lived CBS television series devoted to historical vignettes. It was 1966, the series was *The Great Adventure*, and the actor Jackie Cooper played Lieutenant George Dixon.

A submarine during the American Civil War? And a Confederate one at that?

Who would have known?

The next day, a friend and I huddled over a legal pad and sketched out a design for the submarine boat that we vowed to build. Our plan, à la Jules Verne, was to use this craft to explore the depths of Lake Sidney Lanier— a sprawling but distinctly un–Captain Nemo-ish reservoir created during the 1950s by the U.S. Army Corps of Engineers, north of landlocked Atlanta. It wasn't much, but that lake would be our Atlantic Ocean. Except for the fact that it involved some old oil drums and a welding torch, I don't recall much about our envisioned boat's design. But I am certain of this: given our shared lack of engineering skills, had our planned sub gotten beyond that legal pad, surely we would have been goners.

Closer in time, though I didn't know it then, the more immediate genesis of this book surfaced in spring 2006, during a walk along the beach near Fort Morgan, the brick citadel that guards the eastern shore of the mouth of Alabama's Mobile Bay. During the Civil War, Fort Morgan, along with Fort Gaines on the estuary's opposite side, lay at the heart of Confederate hopes of thwarting a Union naval attack upon the port of Mobile. Indeed, it was the "torpedoes," the stationary mines, floating off Fort Morgan, in August 1864, that Rear Admiral David Farragut, from his squadron's flagship, the USS *Hartford*, famously damned as he and his ships defiantly sailed past that redoubt.

On a splendid spring afternoon 144 years later, my wife, Meta Larsson, our dog, Zoie, and I were walking beside the wave-combed waters of that earlier confrontation. Joining us for the outing was Professor Jack O'Brien, of the University of South Alabama. I'd met Jack the day before, while I was doing a book signing at the Museum of Mobile. Having caught the *Hunley* bug, a common virus in Mobile, Jack recently had strayed from the focus of his day job—teaching and conducting research in marine biology—long enough to write and publish an illuminating scholarly article on Mobile's role in the construction of the *Hunley*.

On the subject of the *Hunley*, Jack speaks with an infectious enthusiasm. During our walk, he held forth eloquently on how, during 1862 and 1863, a business consortium whose numbers included Horace Hunley, a New Orleans lawyer and Confederate patriot, had successively tested two of its submarine boats—the *American Diver* and the *Fish Boat*, later renamed the *H. L. Hunley*—in this very bay whose waters were now lapping around our bare feet. That evening, after we'd had dinner with Jack at the town of Fort Morgan's wonderfully funky Tacky Jack's seafood joint, Meta said to me, "That's your next book."

I didn't see it at the time.

Two months later, I did.

Alas, however, as T. S. Eliot might have put it, between the conception and the creation fell the shadow. Weeks after contracting to write my book on the *Hunley*, a medical catastrophe ambushed me. While reaching for my morning coffee on an otherwise pleasant Saturday morning, I suffered an out-of-the-blue seizure. Rushed to the hospital, I was diagnosed with a brain tumor which, a week later, I underwent surgery to remove.

The tumor was benign, and I had a full-recovery diagnosis. But the surgery left the motor nerves on my body's right side impaired. Initially, I was unable to move my right-side limbs and fingers. Equally alarming—particularly for a writer—I suffered from expressive aphasia, a neurological disorder that renders it impossible for the patient to compose nuanced sentences. My internal thoughts remained fluid, but the vocabulary to give voice to them had disappeared into some cognitive Bermuda Triangle. Fortunately, following a month of hospitalization and three months of trying outpatient rehabilitation, I recovered all of my faculties.

I've written of these experiences in *The New York Times Magazine* and the *Oxford American*, and they need not be detailed here. Suffice it to say, however, that, following that ordeal, the writing of this book became, for me, an assertion of existential faith. And if I may invoke a point of personal privilege, I want to express my gratitude to all of the health care professionals associated with Emory University Hospital and Emory's Center for Rehabilitation Medicine who facilitated my recovery—particularly Ian Crocker, Rita

Lor, Christine Nawita, and Jeffrey Olsen. During the first weeks after my discharge from the hospital, two old and dear friends, Steve Johnson and Ernie Freeberg, in succession, came to Atlanta unbidden to stay with us and to keep me company—and by those acts of kindness I remain profoundly touched. My humble gratitude is due also to other friends whose acts of compassion sustained me during that period: Dan and Jane Carter, Bobby Lee and June Cook, Bernard and Teresa Cox, Terry and Andrée Daly, Steve and Lucy Enniss, Marie Hansen, Jack Haynes, John Inscoe, Gregg Johnson, Kirk Henderson and Jennifer Mullins, Chip Miller, Tim and Julie Ralston, Art and Cathy Vandenberg, and Katie Wood. I also thank my agent, Susan Rabiner, who during that period revealed herself to be as much caring friend as business associate. Gratitude is also due to my mother, Martha Burch Chaffin, and to my aunt Lydia Burch Stevens, for their love and support. For keeping me on task, thanks also to Walt Whitman for "Song of the Open Road," to Bob Dylan for "Tambourine Man," and to the Rolling Stones for "Start Me Up." Cumulatively, the kind deeds of and inspiration provided by all of these good souls eased my return to my life as a writer and thus made this book possible.

My father, James Thomas Chaffin, who died shortly before the onset of my medical adventures, also warrants mention. During World War II, he served as an officer in the U.S. Merchant Marine; and, on the evening of November 2, 1944, the oil tanker SS *Fort Lee*, on which he was serving, was sunk in the Indian Ocean by the German submarine *U-181*. My father managed to find his way into one of the four lifeboats launched that night from his ship. And he and his fellow mariners, after fourteen days, were rescued at sea. And while those events have no direct bearing on those depicted in this narrative, the stories that he related to me during my childhood, no doubt, on some level, haunt this work.

For assistance in the research and the writing of this narrative, I'm indebted to many talented professionals. The works of numerous historians of the Civil War and naval matters, as well as biographers of inventors and Civil War leaders, inform this book, among them John Coski, James P. Duffy, Charles Dufour, Jack Friend, Chester Hearn, Peter Hore, Robert Hutchinson, Thomas Parrish, William Barclay Parsons, Milton F. Perry, Cynthia Owen Philip, Alex Roland, Sidney H. Schell, Robert J. Schneller, Jr., Matthew Stewart, Craig L. Symonds, Eric H. Walther, and T. Harry Williams. Three other fine historians, Thomas Becnel, Bob Browning, and Bill Scarborough, assisted not only through their published works but also by patiently answering questions that I put to them.

Likewise, I thank Cliff Theriot, director of Special Collections at Nicholls State University in Thibodaux, Louisiana, for his help in, if not quite untying, then at least loosening the archival Gordian knot of Horace Hunley's Bayou Country sugar businesses. I also benefited from the works of Richard Bak,

R. Thomas Campbell, Ruth Duncan, William Barrow Floyd, James E. Kloeppel, and Mark K. Ragan, whose books, early in my research, acquainted me
with the essential contours of this story and alerted me to the existence of
many valuable primary-source documents. Thanks also to Brian Hicks and
Schuyler Kropf, whose writings proved helpful in the recounting of events associated with the *Hunley*'s final recovery.

Six gracious souls—all, in differing ways, experts on the *Hunley*—did me
the kind favor of reading various early drafts of the entire manuscript. Afterward, they offered astute comments, flagged errors, and otherwise tendered
constructive suggestions for improvements. And to those professionals, I'm
deeply grateful. They are Rick Hatcher, historian of the Fort Sumter National
Monument in Charleston; Maria Jacobsen, senior archaeologist of the *Hunley*
project at Clemson University's Warren Lasch Conservation Center in North
Charleston; Greg Lambousy, director of collections at the Louisiana State
Museum in New Orleans; Jack O'Brien of the biology department at the University of South Alabama in Mobile; Rich Wills, diver, archaeologist, and
physical anthropologist, now at the U.S. Defense Department's POW/MIA
Central Identification Laboratory in Honolulu, Hawaii, who participated in
the U.S. Navy's survey of the *Hunley* wreck site and served as a consultant for
the recovery plan for the boat; and Steve Wise, Civil War historian and director of the U.S. Marine Corps' Parris Island Museum, at Parris Island, South
Carolina.

Heartfelt gratitude is due also to individual archivists and other profes-
sionals, among them Jane Aldrich of the South Carolina Historical Society;
Lia Apodaca of the Library of Congress; Silva Blake of the Historic New Orleans Collection; John Coski of the Museum of the Confederacy in Richmond, Virginia; Christine Cramer of the Historic Mobile Preservation
Society; Elizabeth B. Dunn of Duke University; Kevin Foster of the National
Park Service's National Maritime Heritage Program in Washington, D.C.;
Linda Gupton of the Athenaeum Rectory in Columbia, Tennessee; Guy Hall
and Maureen Hill of the Southeast Region of the National Archives in At-
lanta; Ed Hampshire of the National Archives of the United Kingdom in Kew,
England; Collette King of the Mobile County, Alabama, Probate Court; Tom
Lanham of the Louisiana State Museum in New Orleans; Robin Leckbee and
Katy Munson of the St. Tammany Parish, Louisiana, Clerk of Court's office;
Sheila Lee, coordinator of the Louisiana Newspaper Project at Louisiana
State University in Baton Rouge; Elyse Marley and Shea McLean of the Mu-
seum of Mobile, in Mobile, Alabama; Nelson Morgan of the Hargrett Rare
Book and Manuscript Library at the University of Georgia; Jill Palmer of the
Huntington Library in San Marino, California; Trevor Plante of the National
Archives in Washington, D.C.; Suzanne Savery of the Valentine Richmond
History Center, in Richmond, Virginia; Melissa Smith, Lee Miller, and Bill
Meneray of Special Collections, Tulane University; Sheryl Somathilake of the

Mobile Public Library; Michael Thomason and Scotty E. Kirkland of the University of South Alabama; and Irene Wainwright of the New Orleans Public Library's City Archives and Special Collections. For research assistance in Washington, D.C., thanks to Carolyn S. Billups. For coordinating assistance from the Friends of the *Hunley* organization in Charleston, I thank Kellen Correia; and for his lovely painting of the American Revolution–era submarine the *Turtle*, I thank the artist John Batchelor, of Wimbourne, England. And for various other help, I thank my neighbor Matt Taylor; *Hunley* aficionado Kim Johnson; and my friend in Charleston, the historian Jack Bass.

Appreciation is likewise due other archivists and curators at the Gilder Lehrman Institute of American History in New York; Magnolia Cemetery in Charleston; the National Archives in Washington, D.C., and Atlanta; the Naval Historical Center in Washington, D.C.; the University of North Carolina at Chapel Hill's Southern Historical Collection; the University of South Carolina, in Columbia; and the Virginia Historical Society in Richmond. For their sharing of materials related to their ancestor Horace Hunley, I thank the Rev. James Peyton, and Wilson and Wanda Gaidry. And for help in quote wrangling, I thank a trio of André Gide scholars—John Lambeth, Todd Sanders, and Jocelyn Van Tuyl.

At Emory University, in whose history department I held an appointment as visiting scholar during my work on this book, I thank Jana Lonberger, the resourceful American history librarian in the Robert W. Woodruff Library. Thanks also to Margaret Ellingson, Marie Hansen, Anne Nicolson, and Sarah Ward of that institution's ever capable interlibrary loan office, as well as the staff of Woodruff's Manuscript, Archives, and Rare Book Library. And for their diligent work in preserving the *Hunley* and extracting its long-held secrets, I'm indebted to the conservator Paul Mardikian and the archaeologists Robert Neyland and the previously mentioned Maria Jacobsen, and all of their talented colleagues at, or otherwise affiliated with, the Warren Lasch Conservation Center. But as I thank all of the aforementioned historians, scientists, and other *Hunley* experts who helped me with this work, I also wish to emphasize that all of the expressed opinions herein, unless otherwise attributed, are mine, not theirs.

At the Hill and Wang imprint of Farrar, Straus and Giroux, I thank publisher and editor Thomas LeBien and ever gracious and astute assistant editor Elizabeth Maples. At Farrar, Straus and Giroux, gratitude is due also to production editor Lisa Silverman; to Aaron Artessa, who designed the book's jacket; to Jonathan D. Lippincott, who produced the book's overall design; and to publicist Steve Weil. I also thank Walter Havighurst for his expert copyediting; Jeffrey Ward, who created the book's maps; and Michael Crisafulli, who produced the drawings of the *Hunley* that adorn this work's endpapers.

Finally, for their companionship and good cheer, I thank my wife and best friend, Meta, and our lovely dog, Zoie, recently departed but not forgotten. Throughout a season of woe and challenges, in an infinity of ways, Meta graced my works and days with the sort of unstinting love, strength, and fierce integrity that the Bard of Avon likened to "an ever-fixed mark / That looks on tempests and is never shaken / It is the star to every wand'ring bark."

Index

H. L. Hunley, as mystery (*cont.*)
190–91, 209–11, 225–26, 239,
240–44, 247; public interest in,
215–16; unexpected location of,
239, 248–51; unreliable memories
in, 211–13, 230–32, 233; *see also*
blue-light signaling, alleged
H. L. Hunley, wreck of, xxv, 216–37,
239–55; archaeological excavation
of, 222, 223, 224–29; *see also*
Warren Lasch Conservation Center; ballast tank areas in, 217,
224–25, 240; bull's-eye lantern
found in, 234, 241–43; cast iron
caps in, 232–33; clothing fragments in, 225; condition of, 217,
224, 239; conning towers in, 217,
224, 240, 243; correct design revealed by, 230–34; crew chamber
of, 224–26, 247–48; damage observed on, 217, 239–40; differential gearbox in, 233, 234; Dixon's
gold pocket watch found in, 234,
254–55; expected location of,
208–209, 239; federal-state legal
battle over, 218–20; hand-crank
screw propeller in, 233–34; in situ
videotaping of, 218, 219; iron
plates in, 224–25, 232–33, 239;
location of, 216, 219–20, 222,
239, 248–51; marine concretions
on, 217, 232, 239; misconceptions
corrected by, 230–37; 1995 discovery of, 216–18, 219–20, 224;
organizations interested in, 218,
221; personal objects in, 225,
234–35; position of, 217, 222; potential looters of, 219–20; public
interest in, 223, 251–53; recovery
of, xvi, xxv, 221–24; rivets in, 224,
232–33; South Carolina's possession of, 220, 251–53; spar in, 221,

233; U.S. Navy divers' search for,
208–209; view ports in, 217, 233,
240, 243
H. L. Hunley, wreck of, crew's remains in, 225–30, 263–64; burial
of, 229–30; facial imaging of, 251;
forensic identification of, 226–29;
location of, 247–48; slow death
scenarios for, 190, 247–48,
249–50
Holland, USS, 59
Holmes, Emma, 122–23
Housatonic, USS, 176–78, 179–85,
213, 216, 245, 248, 251; commander of, 183, 184, 185, 190,
206–207; Dahlgren's fleet defense
orders to, 182–83; deaths aboard,
185, 198, 264; explosion in, 184,
250; *Hunley's* approach observed
by, 183–84, 241; salvageable vestiges of, 189, 208–209; sinking of,
xxiv, 184–85, 187–93, 198, 200,
259; size of, 179; small-arms fire
from, 184, 190, 239, 240, 250;
survivors of, 185, 249; timeline of
attack on, 184–85, 254–55; U.S.
Navy court of inquiry investigation
of, xxiv, 206, 240–43; weaponry
of, 179–80
Hunley, Horace Lawson, vii, xviii,
xxiv, 8–9, 15–24, 38–40, 56, 62,
63–64, 65, 67–69, 73, 75, 76, 114,
143–46, 147–51, 197–99, 263;
Adela commanded by, 15–17, 83,
105; anti-Confederacy attitude of,
18, 82–83; appearance of, 20;
background of, 17, 18–19;
Barrow's investments handled by,
27–28; burial of, 150–60, 161,
229–30; business and financial
ambitions of, 17–18, 30, 40, 43–
44, 69; "Captain" as honorific of,

mines, 36, 50–51, 100–101, 203, 258
Minnesota, USS, 61–62
Mississippi River, 5, 14, 39–40, 63, 66, 74, 85, 104, 133, 148
mitochondrial DNA, 227
Mobile, Ala., xxv, 7, 9, 60, 76, 79–117, 121, 125, 131, 135, 145, 148, 155, 159, 174, 175, 181, 212, 219, 235–36; army vs. navy authority in, 87, 126; character of, 80–81; defenses of, 79–80; history of, 80; Hunley and Park crew imported from, 143, 145–46, 147, 148–49; Park and Lyons Machine Shop in, 87–89, 107, 147, 149, 155–56; population of, 80; Seamen's Bethel Church in, 107; Union naval blockade of, 81, 86, 94, 96; Union naval invasion feared in, 85–86; Walker's *Hunley* mural in, 215
Mobile (Alabama) *Advertiser and Register*, 33–34
Mobile Bay, 80, 81, 90, 94, 95, 96–97, 207; *Fish Boat* trials in, 111–14, 181; Singer torpedoes in, 101
Mobile Bay, Battle of, 204–205
Monitor, USS, 94, 115
Monturiol i Estarriol, Narcís, 54–56, 70
Morris Island, 128–29, 133
"M.T.," 50
Museo Universal, El, 55
Mustang, 60
Mute, 52

Napoleon Bonaparte, 35, 52, 130
Napoleonic Wars, 36
National Park Service, 218
National Underwater and Marine Agency, 218

Nautilus: Fulton's, 51–52, 71, 130; Verne's, 48, 51
Nautilus pompilius (chambered nautilus), 51
Navy, U.S., 34, 70, 93, 94, 95, 103, 111, 123, 127, 135–37, 163–64, 166–67, 211, 223, 225, 228; Confederate ship torpedoed by, 36, 258; court of inquiry convened by, xxiv, 206, 240–43; crews recruited from, 137–43, 168–69, 174–76; divers of, 208–209; Franklin Buchanan honored by, 204; Fulton as consultant of, 52; intelligence operations of, 61, 62, 68, 107, 123, 135–36, 142, 172, 181; ironclads of, 94, 115, 127, 129, 135, 136, 138, 163–64, 165, 166, 181; New Orleans invasion planned by, 63–64; number of ships possessed by, 37; *Pioneer* drawing archived by, xxv, 207; submarine boats of, 56–59, 60, 102–103, 116; Thurmond's threat to, 220; torpedoed ships of, 36–37, 163–64, 258; *see also Housatonic*, USS; underwater warfare division of, 35
Navy, U.S., Southern ports blockaded by, 13–17, 32, 34, 37, 61, 91; in Anaconda plan, 13–15, 125; Charleston, 115–16, 125, 126, 127, 131, 135–36, 162, 179–85, 187–89; Mobile, 81, 86, 94, 96; New Orleans, 30, 65–66, 68, 69; privateering for destruction of, 42, 43
Neafle & Levy shipbuilding firm, 58
Nemo, Captain (char.), 48, 51
New Ironsides, USS, 127, 163–64, 165, 166, 181
New London, USS, 74